WHAT I DON'T

KNOW ABOUT

ANIMALS

WHAT I DON'T KNOW ABOUT ANIMALS

JENNY DISKI

Yale UNIVERSITY PRESS

NEW HAVEN AND LONDON

Library of Congress Control Number: 2011928606
ISBN 978-0-300-17684-1 (hardcover: alk. paper)

A catalogue record for this book is available from the British Library.

This paper meets the requirements of ANSI/NISO Z39.48-1992
(Permanence of Paper).

10 9 8 7 6 5 4 3 2 1

To Chloe and Oliver with love

CONTENTS

PART ONE

IN THE BEGINNING

Here is Edward Bear, coming downstairs now, bump, bump, bump, bump, on the back of his head, behind Christopher Robin. It is, as far as he knows, the only way of coming downstairs, but sometimes he feels that there really is another way, if only he could stop bumping for a moment and think of it. And then he feels that perhaps there isn't. Anyhow, here he is at the bottom, and ready to be introduced to you. Winnie-the-Pooh.

When I first heard his name, I said, just as you are going to say, 'But I thought he was a boy?'

'So did I,' said Christopher Robin.

'Then you can't call him Winnie?'

'I don't.'

'But you said—'

'He's Winnie-*ther*-Pooh. Don't you know what "ther" means?'

Winnie-the-Pooh, A. A. Milne

1

THE REAL AND THE STUFFED

I was born in the mid-twentieth century in the dead centre of a great city. I am what one historian calls *post-domestic*.* My grandparents came to England from the shtetl: they had been traders, furriers, tailors, not animal husbandmen, but at some point they must have ridden horses, or used them to pull carts. They would have kept chickens and killed them under the watchful eye of the rabbi. My mother, although born in London in 1912, knew how to singe and dress chickens that came, head and feet on, all the insides inside, from the kosher butcher behind Warren Street underground station. Even so, like many children of immigrants my parents put the shtetl behind them as much as possible. Their broken-accented old people were old-world embarrassments, for all that they had made the bold journey from a hostile middle Europe to unknown and faraway city centres.

Neat, clean clothes confirmed how far we had come from the old

*'"Domesticity" refers to the social, economic, and intellectual characteristics of communities in which most members consider daily contact with domestic animals (other than pets) a normal condition of life.' Richard W. Bulliet, Hunters, Herders and Hamburgers, 2005, Columbia University Press.

country. My mother did not mess with dirtying nature, except in the kitchen to prepare it to look other than what it had been by chopping and cooking. My mother and father both fled from the ghost of the shtetl into the urbane. When I was young we lived in a centrally heated block of flats. A man way down in the basement stoked the boiler; another man came every week and took the dirty sheets and brought them back washed and ironed. My mother spent her days dusting and polishing and cleaning, but our flat was so small, I can't imagine how it occupied her for more than half an hour a day. She washed herself and me as if we spent our lives excavating dark and grimy tunnels. Especially *down there*, in the animal – the natural – the private – parts. She flung a handful of washing-soda crystals into my bath to get rid of any 'germs' that lurked on my body. Not that it had much opportunity to get dirty – clean knickers every morning and careful lessons in how to wipe yourself after urinating or defecating. My mother was prepared to confront the dirty animal, but only to ensure that it never, ever got a hold on our existence. My father shaved with a strap-sharpened razor, left a manicured garden of moustache on his upper lip, forced his wavy hair flat on his head with a hair cream and vigorous brushing and splashed more scented stuff on him to keep the smell of body at bay. But according to my mother, he was not as fastidious as she was in the matter of washing or in matters of other people's natural parts. My mother abhorred his washing and sexual behaviours as 'filthy'. Good things were 'nice', bad things were 'not nice'. Clean was 'nice and clean'. Good was not making a mess of the clothes that were specifically chosen to show how much we were not people of the countryside. When I wailed miserably about my woollen vests, which I insisted were scratchy, she told me they couldn't possibly be, they were made of the finest wool to be bought in 'Brussels'. Shops in cities, not sheep in fields, ensured their goodness and quality. *Post-domestic*.

Any dogs, cats or birds I encountered on the streets were always to be ignored and avoided. But there were exceptions. The great masses of starlings in central London at that time were a sight to see, worth stopping and looking up at, swarming in their tens of thousands on the roof of the National Gallery in the late afternoons, and taking off simultaneously in a fluttering, shrieking cloud that swooped and rose all of a piece across the London sky. And in Trafalgar Square, I regularly fed the pigeons that stood ravenously on my hands, shoulders and head to get at the corn on my open palm. A strange anomaly of urban animal wariness. Now pigeons are flying rats, filthy and disease-ridden. They have been exiled from Trafalgar Square, and are shot in the dead of night to discourage their presence on public buildings and under bridges. The millions of starlings have disappeared too. But I have a photograph of my mother and me, standing at the foot of Nelson's Column, with pigeons perched on our heads and shoulders, and my mother smiling quite benignly.

I went with her to the butcher and sat in my pushchair, close to the pale sawdust, looking at slabs of meat on the counter, tidied with string into unfleshy shapes that bore no relation to anything that had ever lived. It was the shop where they neatened death into food. And it was a kosher butcher, which meant, additionally, that the meat had been drained of its life blood and prayed over as it was killed. By the time it got to the front of the shop, it had been processed as far away from the once-living creature it had been as it was possible. And the processing continued back home in the kitchen. Salt beef was an oval cylinder bound with string; fish was filleted and covered in matzo-meal batter or moulded with carrots and simmered into wet, doughy balls; liver was chopped and mixed with egg and onion into a pâté. Only chickens remained somewhat lifelike. At the butcher, they were whole, though dead and featherless, hanging by the neck from hooks in the window. A little bit of bucolic reality. They even retained their shape and features in the cooking, after my mother had burned away the last bits of feather. Chicken soup – essential Jewish food – was made with the whole unjointed chicken, minus the head, but including the giblets (gizzard, liver, heart, neck), any unlaid eggs (a special treat, little hard-boiled yolklets), and the amputated feet. Actually it was as much Chinese as Jewish, but gnawing on a chicken's claw, all succulent and chewy gristle and bone, and being presented with the rubbery gizzard, was a weekly childhood happiness. So all my experience of the non-human animal was the smell in the butcher's shop, various mediated parts of a cooked chicken, close encounters with disease-ridden flying pests and an appreciation of starlings.

Yet not quite all, because in the far reaches of my memory is a farm. I can't verify this at all because no one remains who would know, but I have certain pictures in my head of being very young and on a farm. A holiday farm is my first thought. I stayed there more than once. I remember the kitchen table and sitting round it with elderly grown-ups and quite a lot of other children, as I only very rarely sat round a tableful of people at home, and certainly not one in a kitchen, but at a dining-room table, for special occasions and separated from the manufacture of food. My parents weren't with me on the farm, but I have an image of them arriving (both, I think, together) to visit me at least once, nor was there anyone that I knew or can identify. There were pigs, and I adored them. I can see myself in their pen making friends with them. I can't specifically remember any other animals though there is a generic feel of farm animals around. I also have the manure smell of the farm in my memory, and the recollection of feeding, even possibly of me trying to milk a cow. I think I liked being on that farm. There is a young woman with trousers tucked into wellington boots showing me how to look after the pigs and not be afraid of them. I must have been very young indeed, the recollections are so fleeting, set tableaux without much context, but I remember people smiling, being kindly. I don't doubt that this happened once or more than once, but I'm surprised. There are two possibilities: either it was a holiday place that took children, and my parents thought I should have the experience of farm living, or it was a foster home during some time or times of trouble – which were plentiful enough for me to have been fostered on various later occasions, which I do remember clearly. It is possible that the local council sent me there during some crisis. It makes sense of the powerful memory of kindness. This strikes me as more likely because I can't imagine my mother or father sending me off alone anywhere at that age, and surely not back to the countryside of their old people's past. It was dangerous and embarrassing. We were among those, in the 1950s, who drove to the outskirts of London, picnicked by the side of an A road and considered it a day out in the country. At quite a young age, I roamed around London quite freely, often alone, but streets were considered safe once I got the hang of crossing the road. A farm was so strangely *away* and remote from anything I remember about my parents. Or perhaps the children's farm is a figment of my imagination. I don't think so, but I really can't be sure. For whatever reason, I think there was just a little muck and domesticated animal life in my childhood. I still love pigs.

There were a few flesh-and-blood non-humans in my urban childhood. A budgie called Georgie. Blue. He said 'Who's a pretty boy?' a lot, and sometimes answered 'Georgie' when asked his name. He lived in a cage on the sideboard, and once a week flew around the small living room when his cage was being cleaned by my mother. He perched on my finger with his sharp, grasping claws, and stood on my head when he came to rest. There was something a little alarming about him flying free in the living room, and I was always quite relieved when he was put back in his cage. I can't say that I had a sense of Georgie's individual existence: he was an entertainment enclosed in a cage within a room, not unlike some of my wind-up toys, a simulacrum of Tweetie Pie. If asked, I would have said I loved Georgie, but then I said all sorts of things I knew I was supposed to say, often enough about love. One day when his cage was being cleaned Georgie flew out of a window my mother had forgotten to close. I may have cried, but I didn't really care.

There was also one or several goldfish, which I won at Battersea or Hampstead Fun Fair. There was always only one at a time, and it repeatedly jumped out of its small circular bowl and was to be found dead on the carpet, or I'd wake in the morning to find it floating on its side on top of the water. All goldfish were one. They swam around for a while and then they died. I don't think anyone asked me if I loved the goldfish.

And once I found a baby bird at the base of a tree in Regent's Park, fallen from its nest. I scooped it up carefully and took it home, cupped in my hands, to the flat. My mother, confronted with the poor, helpless, squealing thing, overcame her distaste and got a saucer of bread soaked in milk. We tried to feed it with tweezers, but it wouldn't or couldn't eat, and writhing in our nervous, urban hands, wriggled away and fled to the darkness and warmth behind the radiator, where it got stuck. It was a grim nature lesson. My mother, panicking, as I would now in the same circumstances, tried to tease and then poke it out with a prod of some sort – a wooden spoon, a fish slice? The wretched little creature screamed for its own kind, and shrank from the probe, and we wailed and flailed around trying to get at the trapped bird, making it retreat even further into stuckness, and us all the more appalled. It was doubly in the wrong place. Not at the foot of a tree under its nest, and wedged in the domestic human space between a far-too-hot metal radiator and the living-room wall. Eventually, the cheeping stopped. My mother flapped on the phone to the porters down in the entrance hall and one of them arrived to dig out and dispose of the corpse.

It was an experience that was much more distressing than watching my mother prepare a dead chicken for the pot. Baby birds, like baby anything else, are fearsomely attractive, with those same big eyes and rounded head that evolution happened upon to make hearts melt. It was helpless and I rescued it, as I thought, and then it all went terribly wrong. This was the danger, and always has been with befriended animals, even the ones we call pets. It would not behave as a rescued creature was supposed to behave. It didn't understand enough. It couldn't be told or reassured. It wouldn't eat, it didn't love us or trust us, it tried to get away from us, and turned from a sweet baby creature into a trapped and dying animal. A disappointment. A let-down. A regret. Unlike my three stuffed bears who were completely reliable. Once the baby bird was behind the radiator, I didn't want it any more. I only wanted it not to be there, never to have seen it, not to have picked it up. I knew it wouldn't survive, and that I hadn't saved it. It was a baby thing that I had brought home to die a much worse death than if I had left it alone. At any rate, a death in my presence. The first and, until I was in my forties and my cat was put down, the only one. My fault, but its fault, too, for not behaving properly. For not complying with the rules about humans saving animals; but having a life – a nature – of its own. I was disgusted by its horrible end in my flat. As soon as it was stuck behind the radiator, actually, as soon as it refused to eat, I wished it would shut up and die immediately.

The memory of the baby bird I rescued must be in the shadows of the story I wrote at primary school about ducklings. It was a school composition the class had been set when I was about nine, perhaps a couple of years after the bird died in the flat. *Write a story.* A vague command frequently asked of children, but something most editors would hesitate to demand of professional writers. My story became a literary scandal, which, I like to think, suggests I was always a natural writer. I wrote about a country-living girl of my own age who, walking along the river one day, sees a family of ducklings cheeping helplessly around the dead body of their mother. The girl goes home, gets a cardboard box and collects the baby birds, the whole squawk of them. She takes them back and keeps them in a barn (a proper rural story, this – not a pavement in sight). She nurtures them with bread soaked in milk. They thrive. Little by little, they grow. They rush to greet her when they hear her footsteps coming home from school and follow her everywhere. She lets them swim about in the bath and collects worms and other slimy creatures for them. She is their mother. Other children envy her and she allows them to visit her ducklings sometimes. No adults interfered in this story. I must have supposed, probably rightly, that country children had much more freedom from them than we city kids had. Eventually, the ducklings are fully grown, and their saviour wisely decides that they must live natural lives. She leads them crocodile-fashion down to the river, with tears in her eyes but knowing she is doing the right thing. At the water's edge she stops and even as they cluster around her legs for comfort in an alien environment, she hardens her heart and shoos them in. One by one they flop into the water, flap about in panic and then each of them gets the point of their webbed feet. They set off immediately, quacking, ducking and diving, and swimming off down (or up, what did I know about which way ducks swam?) the river. The girl – let's call her Jenny – though I'm sure I wouldn't have then, stands and watches them disappear into the distance. Not one of the ducks looks back, not one of them offers a sentimental farewell, they go off and get on with their lives without the slightest indication of gratitude or even memory of their nurturer and saviour. Jenny watches them go, and understands that they are different; she had no right to expect anything from them. She goes back some time later and her ducks are there, she recognises them. She throws them some bread, and as they pluck it from the ground she calls out their names. The ducks take no notice. She reaches out her empty hand. The boldest duck runs forward and pecks at her outstretched fingers with an angry quack. As soon as they finish up the bread, they waddle away back to the water and swim off without a sign that they ever knew her.

I left it at that and let the moral draw itself. It was a tough little tale for a small girl to write, cynical even: the knowing structure set up to be sentimental and sweet and then pulling all that sickly stuff away from the reader at the end without flinching. I'm interested that I knew about gratitude and the lack of need for it between humans and animals, and that Jenny, the character in the story, had such a resigned acceptance of it. I can imagine writing something very like it even now.

The story was sent in to a competition for all London primary schools and it got second prize. I was and still am a little galled by only getting second prize, but I was called up in assembly and given a certificate and a book token. Everyone clapped. Then the scandal began. Three or four weeks before, *Bunty*, a comic for pre-adolescent girls, had a strip cartoon about a girl who saved a duckling and how it became her devoted friend, following her to school and sleeping in her bed. The whispers grew that I had stolen my story from *Bunty* and that I was a copycat. I explained when confronted in the playground that I hadn't copied it. It was my story. The duck in the comic had stayed with the girl, loved her, been her constant companion; my ducklings swam off into the sunset and couldn't care less about their rescuer. That's just the end, they said. That's a completely different story, I said. And I was right. Of course I'd read the *Bunty* strip, and of course, that was where I'd got the idea from (where do you get your ideas from, people always ask), but I'd written my story. I had no doubt about that. What made the plagiarised duck story my story – a story I had made up myself – was not just my grasp of the difference between the toy and story animals I knew and the real animals I hardly knew at all, but that, unlike the comic story, I knew the difference between animals and humans was where the real story lay.

❦

All the animals I knew in the early years of my life were stuffed: Georgie and the baby bird in one way, the nursery creatures in another. Of the home menagerie, only the Three Bears remain brilliant in my memory. Small, bigger, biggest. Baby, mother, father. Just like us. Except that I never thought of Baby Bear as having a gender, and it surprises me to think of it even now. Father Bear was huge; it was some years before I could carry him anywhere and see where I was going. Of Mother Bear on her own I don't have such a strong recollection, either because she was middle-ish, or for some other more personal reason. Though Baby Bear was the one I took to comfort me when it was dark, they were all my confidants; one or other in particular, or the three together in a huddle. As far as I know, I never didn't have them, and I kept them until I was about seventeen, in the various places I lived, sent on or brought by a visiting parent from where I had been to where I presently was. Eventually, an adult suggested I was too old for them and that I should give them to a little girl we knew. I regret that I did, though it seemed easy enough to do at the time. Not that I want them now. I'm just sorry I agreed.

Utterly stuffed was the manky old brown bear reared up to an enormous height, his mouth gaping wide full of sharp conical teeth, his front paws raised, vicious claws extended, ready to strike. But he held no fears for me. He was a native of my territory, standing, forever on the verge of pouncing, guarding the entrance to a shop (furniture, I think) on the corner of Tottenham Court Road and Goode Street when it was closed. He towered over me, but I never passed him without climbing on his plinth, putting myself under his vast protection, giving him a hug and doing a small dance between his stubby legs. His hair was wiry and spiky to the touch, not soft and silky and smelling inert like my three beloved bears. He smelled of stale sawdust and something else. There were two black circles on his chest, the size of threepenny bits. That was where he was shot, my father or mother told me.

My three bears were not bears like the stuffed bear in Tottenham Court Road. The same noun was used for both, but it meant quite different things. In my bossier moments, I told them off as I had been, or soothed them when they fell over – or I'd flung them on the floor in order to practise my comforting skills. However, I remember most clearly that they were my allies. I told them my woes and my fears, and they listened with all the quiet solemnity of a psychoanalyst. They were not just my children, nor were they surrogate adults – they were comrades, whom I trusted to understand as adult humans did not. I don't remember them arriving in my life, so it was at a time when neither they nor I could speak. I left them behind in terms of language. I surpassed them and became a chattering human. I wasn't at all daunted by their silence. Their silence was essential. I didn't think at them, or just cuddle them, I spoke to them about what I thought, feared and hoped, and their wordlessness did not prevent conversation. I didn't speak on their behalf. Their silent attention contained replies that I understood perfectly. The imbalance between

13

us didn't require that I give up speech, or that they were worthless as non-communicators once I learned to talk and they remained dumb. I knew the difference as difference, but difference wasn't a barrier.

If the Three Bears were magical beings it was only in relation to adults that they were so. I knew perfectly well that they weren't flesh and blood. It was of their essence that they weren't. I couldn't hurt them, even when I twisted their eyes out. I knew cloth and stuffing when I saw it, and I knew that bears came in other forms. I'd seen them at the cinema and often in the zoo. I knew that the bear in the shop doorway in Tottenham Court Road had once been a real bear and only pretended to be a giant version of my own. The two dark circles made all the difference. The difference being that the Three Bears had never lived. My bears had no relationship to those other bears, those huge brown killers, filmed by Disney, that scooped up fish in rivers and tore their heads off, or the mad, captive bears that paced crazily to and fro on their fake mountain in Regent's Park. There were the *Three Bears* and there were *bears*. As I say, differently stuffed.

While I was still young there were also assorted small, glass creatures, bought with pocket money or persuasion: most memorably, a giraffe, with spindly neck and legs, that always looked too frail not to have been broken already, and doubtless eventually was. The glass animals were clear outside with swirls of colour inside, like a stick of see-through rock. There were china creatures, too – a cat, for sure. Black, now I come to think of it, tall and shiny, also with an elongated neck, sitting neatly like an Egyptian statue (or like a cat), and (less like a cat) with a pink organza bow round its neck. And in the British Museum, which was a regular and local playground in my life, there were, not actual living cats, but Egyptian cat figurines and statues, tiny ones and more imposing ones in glass boxes sitting in just the same manner as my china gewgaw, which came, I'm beginning to believe, from a fun fair like the ever-dying goldfish – a prize for throwing hoops or rolling pennies or aiming darts. I clearly recall an entire farmyard of Britain's model farm animals: pink plastic pigs and piglets and the odd saddleback, black-and-white cows, ducks and grey sheep, as well as the farmer with a hat on and a shepherd holding his crook, all of which I arranged on a moulded plastic layout of humpy hills and fields, printed with grass, pens, folds and ponds.

There were also confectionery pigs for special occasions and entrancing treats. I can easily conjure the sweet intense smell of the pink sugar stuff, and the slight unnameable frisson, which was almost certainly pleasure but wouldn't exactly reveal itself as such, of spoiling something, by undoing the pretty bow (blue this time) and deciding which bit to nibble on or suck out of shape first. Chocolate bunnies, lined up in a box with a see-through cellophane top were eaten one ear at a time, then down to the feet. I don't think I've ever eaten a bunny from the bottom up. Edible creatures required the decision of how to deform them. I dare say it's inevitable that soft furry creatures were caricatured in pastel shades on objects I used for eating, drinking, on clothes for sleeping, printed on my cot and my playpen. I pushed along a dog on wheels, white and brown, a sort of terrier, I think, as I started to walk in the corridors of the flats and out on the pavement. A huge rocking horse, too, just like the one the Little Prince had, I was told. Dapple Grey, I called him, with no 'd'. In my memory, I confuse my pleasure riding him back and forth with the D. H. Lawrence story 'The Rocking Horse Winner' but I was probably not frantically rocking for the recuperation of what was wrong with my family. I knew about the comfort contrived animals could bring but didn't, I think, confuse it with magic. Oh yes, and little circular boxes covered in paper printed with the relevant creature made animal sounds when you turned them upside down. Baa, moo, neigh, tweet, woof, miaow. Those were the words for the sounds the boxes and animals I'd never encountered made that I learned in the third-floor flat in Tottenham Court Road, London, WC1.

Most Sunday mornings my father took me to museums. Sometimes the British Museum, but often the ones in South Kensington. Science, Geology, but best of all was the Natural History Museum. Certainly, the Natural History Museum had the most grandeur. It was a massive, airy, echoing palace of petrified life forms. The snap of my footsteps on the stone floor of the towering entrance hall, when I finally stopped going round in the revolving door, signalled the transformation from ordinary London street to the theatrical stillness of the long-dead creatures contained in the Victorian red-brick arches and the glassed dome far above. The entrance hall housed at its centre, facing the door, the great dinosaur. Enormous and skeletal. Ribcage, skull, but mostly vertebrae practically from one end of the hall to the other, its anciently dead (or reconstituted) snout reaching forward to greet visitors. He (dinosaurs, like rocking horses and stuffed bears, but unlike baby bears, were inevitably male) was all neck and gradually diminishing tail; a gigantic balancing toy, like those magical ducks that bobbed down towards a glass of water. He seemed always on the point of taking off, crashing through the doors and heading into London's grey, rainy streets. At the very least, I expected him to sway a little from his perfect point of balance. This reconstructed monster who stood guard over the wonders of nature was actually, I learned soon enough, a diplodocus. But even now, just for an instant, the word dinosaur always conjures up the great, bony beast of Exhibition Road.

Upstairs in a special gallery, another monster, a blue whale, was suspended by wires from the ceiling. This was, I suppose, a model, pale blue with parallel ridges running the length of its lower body, starting just below its button-bright, tiny eyes. The blue whale was even bigger than the dinosaur, and dangerously hanging in mid-air. I never could understand why a sea creature was displayed in that way. Flying and swimming are, apparently, exactly the same in terms of movement and muscle, but it seemed to me that flying was over and swimming was under and I was never convinced into believing that I was in a simulated ocean environment where air represented water. Perhaps I had no imagination and had too great a respect for categories, as children do. The great beast only ate minute shrimpy things, my father explained. Millions of them, it was true, but that such a vast thing should manage on the tiniest of animals amazed me every time. Ah, well, you see, it left enough room for Jonah to sit in its (whales: no gender) belly and have his tea, my father said. On the first floor above the open-plan main hall, a minstrels' gallery was lined with display cases of that Victorian favourite, the taxidermist's craft. Animals I would never see alive in their natural surroundings (the English countryside, the African veldt, the Indian and Asian jungle) posed artfully in death, doing just what they were expected to do. Raptors swooped down on stuffed rabbits, hyenas snarled, a tiger pounced on a doe-eyed deer. All dead, still as death, arrested in mid-action, and all, somehow in my memory, grubby, moth-eaten and dusty. There was an awful dreariness about them. No tygers burned bright here. Only relics crammed in multiple tableaux, without, I think, much care for ecological likelihood, inside the dark wood and glass cases, for us to gaze on with wonder at the wonders of the world. But even the dreariness was part of the pleasure of my visits. The whole museum was, in those days at least, incredibly cluttered, like some storybook dusty old uncle's dusty attic. I suppose that the building in the 1950s had hardly changed since 1881 when it was built.

2

DREAM ANIMALS

On Sunday afternoons, after the museums, my father and I moved on from Exhibition Road to view a different kind of animal. News cinemas were dotted all over the place. We went from one to the other, on a really good day hitting four, even going as far as the one in Victoria to finish off before getting the 24 bus home. They showed fifteen or twenty minutes of Pathé or Movietone newsreels (the deaths of old Queen Mary, George VI and Stalin, the coronation, the Korean War, the four-minute mile, Suez) in which I had no interest, and then for the rest of the hour, before the whole programme repeated, the cartoons we were really there to see. Tom and Jerry, of course; Goofy, Donald Duck, Pluto, Mickey and Minnie Mouse, Bugs Bunny, Sylvester and Tweetie Pie, Woody Woodpecker, Daffy Duck, Porky Pig, Road Runner. There were different stables: Warner Brothers' Looney Tunes announced themselves with the big bull's-eye with Bugs Bunny in the centre, biting down viciously on a carrot, eyeing the audience dangerously and demanding 'What's up, Folks?', and Disney with Mickey Mouse's beaming face bursting on to the screen – also at the centre of a bull's-eye, or am I misremembering?

These were neither real nor stuffed animals. They often wore trousers and sweaters, and most of them talked. None of them were inexpressive: on the contrary they were excessively expressive, though some were nevertheless inscrutable. Though they hardly looked anything like the real animals they pretended to be, some of the housebound creatures, like Tom and Jerry or Tweetie Pie and Sylvester, led essentially domesticated animal lives, under the control of human beings who chastised and petted them. In secret, when out of human sight, they had wilder, more 'natural' lives. The cat chased the mouse or the canary, the dog chased the cat, but with the unreal twist that the mouse and canary (and sometimes the cat) always got the better of the predator. They were naughty children, making a nuisance of themselves with what Hollywood understood to be their innate child/animal ways in the domestic world of the typical middle-class American family and their servants, who were generally only shown as legs, or a hand holding a broom. But they weren't merely naughty, and in that sense were not just an adult view of the 'natural' reality of their children: they were lethally violent, no-holds-barred wilful. No walls or grown-ups (people) were allowed to get in the way of their passionate pursuits. Read Bataille or de Sade or Genet (cutting out the overt sex) and you get something very like those cartoon rebuttals of civilisation. They burst through brick, broke windows, fell from unimaginably high cliffs, got beaten flat by heavy objects, and nothing stopped them, they reshaped and continued the chase. Not only wilful but vicious: they grinned with delight at whatever awfulness befell their enemies, no pain too great for their joyous, uncensored pleasure. 'Uhhh, what's up, Doc?' asks Bugs Bunny of Elmer Fudd, whose head has been replaced by black curling smoke from the gun with which he has shot himself, instead of Bugs. 'Beep-beep' hoots Road Runner as he leaves Wile E. Coyote smashed, a smear on the tarmac, though I always heard it as 'meep-meep', which I prefer. The boundaries were all there, just as they were in real life, but the cartoon creatures ignored them (as children daren't and can't) – for all the world as if they were mere lines on paper. Though the stuffed animals in the Natural History Museum were obliged to exist within their human makers' vision of nature until they crumbled to dust, the drawn ones seemed to get away from the human hands that created them and ran riot over all natural or domestic constraints. In one cartoon, Mickey Mouse actually appropriated the pencil and drew himself back on to the page, as a human hand tried, fruitlessly, to rub him out. Nevertheless, for the ultimate security of the adults and their children, the cartoon animals were stuffed, too, in their way. Their chaos was always contained on the flat, rectangular screen. What was broken always repaired itself.

The picture books began early. Oddly, I have no recollection of Beatrix Potter. I don't think I read them until my daughter was born. Perhaps my parents, children of immigrants, didn't know about the necessity of Beatrix Potter for every proper English child, or perhaps for some reason Peter Rabbit and Benjamin Bunny just didn't stick with me in the way that my 1950s reprint of the 1916 *The Real Mother Goose* did. Inside for my endless delight were ducks with neat, spotted headscarves, cradling a wicker shopping basket on one elegant white wing, not so dissimilar to Jemima Puddle-Duck, but there was more and different. A leaping cow danced a jig right over an outraged crescent moon, while a cat on hind legs played on the fiddle like a furious demon. A snuggle of naughty kittens in their basket pretended not to have lost their mittens. Little pigs went to market, some returned home crying 'wee, wee, wee' all the way, each as pink as my sugar pigs and Mr Britain's plastic pigs, walking on tiptoe, their tails tight-curled and springy. A sky full of cobwebs was being swept away along with their makers, the angry space-spiders, by the witchy old woman in a basket. And on the cover, inside the black-and-white chequered border, Mother Goose herself, a jovial old crone, held the reins of the huge snowy bird she rode side-saddle through orange clouds, also with a basket on her arm (so many baskets for a small child to take in), this one with a cheery baby inside, arms and eyes wide with delight at the high-flying adventure. When I wanted a change, there were Kate Greenaway's untameable rats, nestling inside men's Sunday hats and biting the babies in their cradles, before being drawn eerily by the sound of the Piper, scampering around him, with his drooping nightcap, himself as thin and long as his pipe, in his burnt-orange robe, leading them to their doom at the edge of the River Weser. And then the procession of children, just like the rats, scampering happily, dancing tragically, excitingly, away from the town.

There was a waywardness about the nursery rhymes, and a rejection of the adult world that's as clear as it is in the cartoons. Perhaps more so: the senselessness was more senseless since the narrative didn't bother itself with coherent story if it didn't feel like it, as the cartoons did, having to echo the necessity of chase and follow, of consequence, even if the consequences were reversible. I suppose it is, in part, that nursery rhymes come from everywhere, political scandal as well as baby-babble. Satire and nonsense, as wild as you like, not only having to tie itself down to domestic mirroring. The animals fluted and flaunted, danced and went about the world, or off it to the moon or the spidery sky, slightly off-centre or madly off-centre from the life of animals as created by humans. Like the fantasy of the teddy bears and other toys coming to life when everyone was asleep, it seemed perfectly possible to a small child that there was a space in existence, a sideways invisible space, where the real animals behaved as crazily and mockingly as they did in the nursery rhymes. They were as undercover as children were, with our, as I learned, secret thoughts and strange interior games that the grown-ups could never know about. At least we could imagine them so. And along with their faux cuddliness, there was another human use for animals, discovered early in life.

I know how important and how gratifying animals were, but it's impossible to recall the actual understanding I gained at the time from reading about Pooh and Piglet trying so hard to be in the world, the smug know-all disappearing Cheshire Cat, the hilariously dangerous ticking Crocodile, Moley listening with immense concentration to Mr Badger and Mr Toad not paying attention at all. What I am sure I learned was that animals were available to humans for representing thoughts, ideas, fears and wishes. At any rate, I learned to use them in that way, as we all did, each culture and period in its own way.

Urban, post-domestic child that I was, I may have had very few real animals in my life, and mostly been responsible for the death of any naturally occurring ones (the baby bird, and bees that stung me, ants I stepped on, beetles and snails I matchboxed), but the stories I was told and then read for myself were massively populated by non-human creatures. The protagonists weren't all animals – some were supernatural beings, like fairies and ogres – but what they had in common was that they were not human. Human children and adults do inhabit the pages of books, but rarely at the earliest stage, and as a rule they are dangerous to the animal heroes. Well, *of course* they are; stories about non-human creatures are the way we tell children about the ways of humanity. It's paradoxical because although the children are to identify with them finally, at first the *humans* in their book must show what not to do. They are usually to be feared for their killing, habitat-destroying, unnatural ways. Animals are good versions of us, humans are bad versions of *them,* meaning the adults, who are not exactly us – just for the time being.

Analogy and allegory come before social realism. We presume that it's easier for children to grasp the nature of the species they belong to through the medium of other species, as if indirection works better on young minds. Children, knowing first nothing and then little about being cultural humans, are more amenable to smaller, softer, rounded, furry-animal forms than tall, clothed, angular human forms. I doubt very much (trying hard to look back) whether young children really think of themselves as the same species as adults. Indeed, they are so different, so lacking in cultural understanding, as well as physical adeptness, that in a real sense they aren't human like adults are until they become so – a good many years after their birth. It may also be that adults see their babies and toddlers as beings more akin to the animal world. The task is to bring them slowly into the human fold. Certainly, we give them teddy bears and bunny rabbits before we give them dolls.

Beyond the sensory or observational grasp we begin to attain as babies, by osmosis, about our own species, most of our early instruction on how to be human comes from the animal world. Nevertheless, one of the things we learn, even while we are identifying with the animals, is that it is better, in the sense of most potent, to be human. Peter Rabbit fears Mr McGregor, whom we may not like, but he does have the shotgun and the power to control the life and death of our gentle hero. And all those transformation tales we are read confirm our suspicions. Not being human is invariably a form of punishment. People can be alienated from their real form and their true selves by wicked magic, from which they can only be rescued and redeemed by love. The Frog Prince returns to his upper-class manly form, and the Beast is brought back to unswinish humanity by Female Beauty. Love looks human (and female); animals are beastly, ugly in form and spirit, terrifyingly other, unless they can be saved. The transformation is from the good to the bad to the good (they are usually innocent of any very terrible crime, the young men who suffer the magic). Six princes are turned to swans by their evil stepmother, but are saved by their devoted sister who spends years sewing enchanted shirts against a deadline, to bring them back to themselves. She succeeds but doesn't manage to finish one sleeve of one shirt in the time allowed, and the last brother lives with a swan's wing instead of an arm to remind us all of something quite important that need not and should not be said. Bottom becomes an ass. Ulysses' men are turned to pigs by Circe.

The stories suggest that the border between human and animal is by no means fixed and impermeable. It's perfectly clear that only certain civilising influences (love, domesticity, inner struggle) can hold us in place – above the animals – or bring us back from occasional forays into animality. Love, domesticity and inner struggle become qualities distinctly human and humanising. The Beast grasps civilisation as a tragic lack and tries to hold Beauty to him, but only when Beauty responds to the Beast as if he were a human, with love *even as he is*, can he cross the barrier and return to himself. It does seem to be specifically the human male who is in danger and closest to the animals. They have to be known for their animality but domesticated back into civilised being by their womenfolk. But I remember a certain regret when the enchanted creatures returned to their regular princely, human selves. And regret too that the redeeming princesses never had the opportunity to become Frog-girls or Beast-women, and who wouldn't want to be a swan by night and fly around the world? But then, do I remember? When did I start to regret the animals turning back into humans? Now I would give anything to have the chance to inhabit the being of a non-human animal. That is, to be and experience self and the world as something utterly other, which is how, as an adult, I choose to see animals, rather than as wild versions of humans. But children, perhaps, only want to hear stories about otherness, and be reassured that they can be rescued from their wild state. Or do they? I just can't remember.

Narrative is infinitely pliable. Allegory and parable turn inside out, or take another route, as their creators and users wish. Fables, which aren't necessarily stories for children, offer us animals as qualities which humans need to practice. We are already beyond and above animals by the time we perceive the moral of the Hare and the Tortoise. The animals don't get it, the stories tell us, but we can. In any case, the creatures in Aesop's fables don't live lives of their own, but exist only to represent human vices and virtues. As teaching materials in Western and Eastern traditions, animals are borrowed for their perceived human qualities, slow-and-fast become hasty-and-cautious for our edification, or represent sticking points to spiritual progress – the scorpion can't help stinging the frog who has carried him across the river. In other forms, animals are blank canvases on which to paint human characters. They are put in trousers, and stand for order and chaos, becoming indistinguishable (aside from their fur and paws) from human actors dressed up, which they later become in pantomime. The riverside and woodland creatures in *The Wind in the Willows* and Beatrix Potter's small farm animals all wear the human clothes and characteristics of the peasantry and gentry of nineteenth-century England. Mr Badger, Moley, Ratty, Toad and the Weasels all translate directly to classes and types that middle-class children in the early twentieth century would have been familiar with. For a while, the incorrigible Mr Toad is transformed into a human female by the kindly gaoler's daughter (beauty and the beast again) – an opportunity to become the very force that saves creatures from their coarse animality – but he only uses it to escape from prison and can't sustain ordinary decency. He returns to his wilful, thoughtless ways, just like any bumptious landed gent. Like the Beast, he lives in a fine house and lacks nothing but manners and refinement. The only creatures Mr Toad fears are the unruly Weasels from the Wild Wood who, Ratty says, are 'all right in a way . . . but . . . well, you can't really trust them'. These low-class riotous villains (early versions of the crazy cartoon animals) mirror Toad's upper-class chaos, and destroy Toad Hall to teach Mr Toad (and any wayward children) a lesson about the virtue of the middle way. E. H. Shepard's illustrations keep the animals well covered in human clothing. It's very hard, even if you've spent hours of your life reading and rereading *The Wind in the Willows* to see an actual toad and think of Kenneth Grahame's creation, while the human world is full of rich boors who, even in these differently-classed days, fit the bill perfectly.

If the characters in *The Wind in the Willows* are ciphers for adult human types, Winnie-the-Pooh and his friends are much closer to the child who is reading about them. For one thing, they are soft toys and a very miscegenated bunch of creatures from the woodland, the outback, the farm and the jungle. They come together in the nursery in the charge of Christopher Robin, and they are always in need of his advice and assistance. They are less clever, less knowing than him or the readers and have no desire to rebel. They simply get things wrong. They are children to children, and the human children laugh as adults would at how their intellectual and social inferiors' lack of understanding gets them into trouble. Even the wise Owl – wise for Hundred Acre Wood, that is – spells his name wrong on his house. A small child who sees this and knows that owl is spelled *Owl* and not *Wol* is for a change in a position of superiority. Friendship, even love is possible between Christopher Robin and the soft-toy characters, but it's always an unequal friendship. The love, the friendship depends on this inequality. It doesn't transform either party. The names of the animals are, of course, the names that

Christopher Robin, adamically, has given them, misspellings and all. Pooh, who is 'a bear of very little brain' gets stuck in Rabbit's front door having greedily eaten too much honey while visiting; Piglet goes round and round a spinney following his own footsteps in search of a mythic Woozle; and Tigger bounces about annoying everyone just as younger brothers and sisters do. Eeyore is a special case. He might be a lost adult, not part of any community, or perhaps he is one of those strange children who are born grown-up. He lives in a no-man's land. He doesn't know more (he's a stuffed toy, after all) but he is cursed with knowing that he doesn't and that his fellow nursery toys know even less:

'Eeyore, what are you doing there?' said Rabbit.

'I'll give you three guesses, Rabbit. Digging holes in the ground? Wrong. Leaping from branch to branch of a young oak tree? Wrong. Waiting for somebody to help me out of the river? Right. Give Rabbit time, and he'll always get the answer.'

'But, Eeyore,' said Pooh in distress, 'what can we – I mean, how shall we – do you think if we—'

'Yes,' said Eeyore. 'One of those would be just the thing. Thank you, Pooh.'[1]

I've got to admit, I had very little interest in stories about animals as animals rather than animals as surrogate or allegorical humans. I always liked the idea that stories could be about something other than what they appeared to be about. I couldn't be bothered with *Black Beauty*, Anna Sewell's novel narrated by a mistreated horse. Dogs like Lassie or Old Yeller and horses like Flicka showed – albeit uncanny – devotion and intelligence while instructing children on how to behave decently to animals, as well as teaching them the obligations of human love. But they didn't excite me. I don't remember wanting a dog or a horse to love and be loved by, but perhaps the impossibility of getting one had something to do with that. Or maybe my baby-bird experience had made me wary.

There is an obvious educational and civilising value in children being told via stories and films to behave well to other creatures and to treat them kindly, but it also alerts them to their special position as separate and superior animals. Only the fact of our dominion over them enables us to consider treating them with kindness. It is a form of noblesse oblige that teaches children the value of animals as sentient creatures, but also establishes the child's own place in the world, owned and managed by humans, inhabited also by animals who live on human sufferance or because they give humans pleasure in some way, or because humans haven't yet figured out how to eradicate the very annoying and dangerous ones like mosquitoes. Animals even serve humans, in extremis, by loving us (in our terms), at any rate accepting us, more than other people do. The homeless often have dogs, and it's not hard to see the use value, but also the emotional value, even if they have to be fed. Jack London tells another kind of story in *Call of the Wild*, in which Buck, a wolf-like domestic dog, after experiencing both mistreatment and kindness (which he loses through human-on-human violence), gives up the domesticated world and chooses to live in a state of nature with a pack of wolves, becoming, as it were, his real self. But this is not a book for the nursery – it tells a supplementary tale to older children who have already found their place in the scheme of things.

Most of the devoted-animal stories have translated iconically to the screen. Highly trained animals acted out their roles: dog after dog, male and female, played Lassie in the movies and on TV over the years, saving their humans, usually at the risk, fictionally, of their own lives (though two real horses died in the 2006 remake of *Flicka*). I'm not at all clear what the relationship of an animal movie star is to a human movie star, but I imagine, which is the best I can do, that a trained animal actor benefits less from either the pride or the perks of movie stardom, and suffers as least as much if differently as its human equivalents. The dogs who play Lassie, and the other animal actors, live out, as well as act out their subservience to human wishes. We can't know, though some animal trainers have opinions. In the early 1990s Vicki Hearne, an animal trainer, poet and writer, visited the Las Vegas show of Bobby Berosini and his trained orangutans. He had been sued by PETA (People for the Ethical Treatment of Animals) for cruelty in his training methods, and Berosini sued back, insisting that no cruelty was involved in his act. Hearne, who we will come to again later, was astounded by the performance, which is largely an extended joke about the animal subverting the authority of the trainer. Berosini tells the audience how he trains them:

'You have to show them who is boss.' He brings Rusty out to show him who is boss, and Rusty not only refuses to jump onto the stool provided for the purpose but tricks his trainer into doing so by pretending incomprehension until Berosini finally demonstrates, jumping onto the stool himself. Once Berosini has dutifully jumped, Rusty invites the audience to applaud. Berosini goes on to mock much scientific and popular wisdom about operant conditioning training that relies more on the carrot than on the stick by demonstrating how he doesn't need to train the orangutans at all because 'I have magic orang cookies'. A fast and lively slapstick round results from his failed attempts to get Bo to eat a cookie, the cookie is juggled, spit into the audience, hidden, fed to Berosini, but never eaten by the orang-utan.

Hearne, talking to Berosini after witnessing the show, made a judgement about how the trainer got his orangs to perform in the act:

> The radical claim . . . is that the animals are 'referring to', or at least imitating, these gestures deliberately, with some sense – if not precisely our sense – of the meaning of what they are doing. Berosini says that Bo is in on the joke, or at least on some joke, and that it is her interest and pleasure in such monkeying around that makes it possible for him to work with her as he does. This is speculative, of course, but it could be argued that Berosini's is a more parsimonious explanation than an explanation based on conditioning would be. Indeed, it's questionable whether any model of conditioning, however elaborate, can explain behaviour this complex, particularly since every performance the act changes, with both Berosini and the orangs offering improvisations. Talk of conditioned responses may be helpful in understanding part of a trained animal's development (or, for that matter, a dancer's or a poet's or an actor's or a philosopher's), but animal performances at this level make more sense when viewed as rudimentary expressions of at least one primeval artistic impulse – the impulse to play with meaning.[2]

Hearne is careful in her speculation about the motives of animal performers – how can we know what the animals themselves think? Does thinking as we use the word bear any relation to what it is they do – might it be perfectly possible to have 'consciousness' yet not 'think' in any way we can understand? In 2008 Fourth Estate published *Me, Cheetah*, the autobiography of the chimpanzee who starred in the Tarzan movies with Johnny Weissmuller. Cheetah, aged seventy-six and in retirement in Palm Springs, tells his own story – his childhood in the jungle, the accident that killed his mother and left him alone, the rescue and his wilderness time in Manhattan where at last he met King Kong and understood the centrality of Hollywood in the collective unconscious – plus all the gossip that libel laws allow about his long-dead fellow Hollywood actors. Veronica Horwell reviewed the book in the *Guardian*, and praised Cheetah's polemical brilliance as he argues against the contemporary use of animated simulacra rather than real animal actors, as they did in his day, though the rot, of course, started back with Disney and Looney Tunes: 'an animated Pixar pixel hasn't suffered for its art, hasn't eluded death, there's no soul there even if every hair is exactly replicated'. No ghostwriter is named in the book; this is all Cheetah's own work. The use of the animal voice in sophisticated satire and adult fiction is not uncommon – from Kafka's *Report to the Academy* given by an ape to Sam Savage's 2008 novel *Firmin*[3] narrated by a book-consuming rat – but clearly, Cheetah's autobiography also represents a collective unconscious – the powerful wish we all have to communicate with animals, to find out what they really 'think' or how they really think. Deep down *Me, Cheetah* must disappoint; we can only go along so far with the conceit. We know we don't really know and we know that Cheetah isn't really telling. But even the most grown-up of us wishes that he was.

The cartoons that delighted me as a child had caricatured animals as wild children behaving the way no one was allowed to. They followed the logic of the impossible escalating the violent and the uncivilised into extreme and absurd consequence. But Disney, one of those dealers in pandemonium, also made full-length narrative cartoons, and the early versions are quite different from the short evocations of chaos that were churned out for the news cinemas by the cartoon studios. *Bambi* (1942) is allegory, plain and simple. A picture of the social world as it should be, even including a little tragedy to be overcome. *Bambi* is a story only in the sense that it narrates the desired patterns of human life. Even Disney couldn't present deer life precisely in terms of the upper-middle-class American nuclear social unit, although the distant antler-phallic stag somewhat mirrors the remote paterfamilias of the wealthy family, even if his world was on the very cusp of changing. Deer reality is glossed into suburban family values in this version of nature-as-allegory. These deer are drawn to be as reminiscent of humans as possible – their huge eyes are human eyes, not blank, but meaningful windows on the soul. Their faces express emotion – happiness, sadness, fear – in a way that no deer could manage even if it felt such things in the way that humans do.

Dumbo, made the year before, shows another way with animals. It's just as sentimental but much more vibrant. These animals don't live in nature, but at the circus, the least natural existence a wild animal can have. They are all female, apart from Dumbo himself, and wear little caps and bonnets, gossiping and whispering among themselves at the slightest sign of nonconformity, exactly like the stereotype of suburban matrons during their coffee mornings. *Dumbo* is certainly allegory, too. The baby born with gigantic ears is immediately a pariah, and the elephant matrons turn their very large buttocks on him. His only supporters are his fiercely loving mother (that is what mothers should do and animals show: love fiercely), who is eventually locked up and labelled 'mad' for her defensive anger, and Timothy, a feisty mouse. It is a glorious cartoon as the rather dully animated *Bambi* isn't, which includes the wild and thrilling improvisation of the drunk scene in which Dumbo and Timothy hallucinate pink elephants that dance and morph into pure colour and form. Not surprising that in the late 1960s, *Dumbo* was sought out (along with Kubrick's *2001*– remember those apelike hominids?) as a perfect accompaniment to an acid trip. After getting drunk and waking in a tree the morning after, Dumbo's preposterous ears enable him to fly.

He's what we would call 'differently abled'. Up in the tree, the crows doubt Dumbo's spectacular talent, and get to sing and dance the jazzy, snazzy, sinuous 'When I See An Elephant Fly'. This is another joy of the film. It is also a real problem. The crows are black, as crows are, but in the cartoon, they are cool black dudes, who talk jive and whose leader is called in the credits 'Jim Crow'. The freaky Dumbo triumphs as a flying elephant entertainer with flapping ears, and the black crows perform their well-known dancing and singing skills. Neither elephants nor crows (nor deer) can be depicted as elephants and crows simply, but must be caricatured into their nearest equivalent in human society. Big, fleshy, smug matrons; hip, musical, oppositional black men; isolated children who come right in the end. Dumbo triumphs over his persecutors and flies to a kind of achievement, but it's not a flight to freedom. His happiness is that he becomes a star of the circus. There is no suggestion, no thought that he belongs elsewhere. He will fly for the pleasure of the human audience. In return he will garner admiration and the best conditions (his mother is seen at the end relaxing on the veranda of the finest coach of the circus train). The film ends there, but Dumbo will certainly end up like Cheetah, in luxurious retirement in Palm Springs, relaxing by his swimming pool, writing his memoirs.[*]

There was another kind of Disney film, not animated: the Disney wildlife movies that sometimes accompanied the film you actually had gone to see, and sometimes were the main event. I remember them mostly as second features, something I had to sit through, along with the interval and the advertisements, until, at very long last (time is so protracted for a small child) the cinema darkened again and the real film started.

---

[*]Though we shouldn't forget Nelly the Elephant who packed her trunk and said goodbye to the circus, setting off on the road to Mandalay.

They were in full colour with full-throated soaring music and had titles like *White Wilderness*, *The Living Desert*, *The Vanishing Prairie*, *The African Lion* and *Beaver Valley*. Their stated aim was to show the wonders of nature, but if nature didn't oblige for the camera, they fixed it so it was wonderful. Most famously, in *White Wilderness*, Disney actually created the myth that we all now 'know' to be true, that every seven to ten years, lemmings commit mass suicide by running off the edge of a cliff to drown in the sea. The wildlife crew filmed in Alberta, Canada, which is not the habitat of lemmings, who live in Alaska. To remedy this annoyance, the Disney filmmakers bought lemmings from Inuit children in Manitoba and set up the sequence in the way they thought best for their movie. I remember the voice of Winston Hibler, smooth and authoritative and so confidently American. His script and his vocal cords made complete, indubitable sense of what we saw, sitting in the cinema in London, a million and more miles as it might have been from Alaska, Alberta or the moon. The lemmings massed to fill the huge screen, and then ran, as if following the Piper, for the nearest cliff top and, like a waterfall, dropped off the edge and fell to their deaths in the broiling sea. Hibler narrated the lemmings' thoughts and motivation: 'A kind of compulsion seizes each tiny rodent, and, carried along by an unreasoning hysteria, each falls into step for a march that will take them to a strange destiny . . .They've become victims of an obsession – a one-track thought: Move on! Move on!'

But, according to a 1983 investigation by Canadian Broadcasting Corporation producer Brian Vallée, the lemming scenes were faked. Those lemmings tumbling into the sea, apparently leaping voluntarily to their death, which I watched with my own eyes, were in fact thrown off a cliff by the Disney filmmakers. The great migration we saw and marvelled at in the cinema was actually a few dozen

Manitoba lemmings running on snow-covered turntables, shot with tight camera angles and edited to within an inch of its life. It seemed OK to stage an event for the benefit of educating and entertaining people about the natural world. But actually, the event itself was invented. Lemmings don't commit hara-kiri, they simply do what most animals do, they move on when their feeding grounds become depleted. They can swim, and they cross rivers in search of good places to feed. 'Sometimes they drown,' explains zoologist Gordon Jarrell of the University of Alaska.[4]

Much of what I 'learned' as a child came from Disney wildlife films. Prairies were beyond my experience, but I know about them from Westerns and from Disney. Nature, for Disney, was to be manipulated for our entertainment. That's what film did. If the reality didn't make a great sequence, the magic of film would fix it. A good deal of what we were told when I was a child turns out not to be the truth, and, after all, manipulating stories of what animals do and are is what people have done since they acquired art and language. Creation myths, cave art, fables, allegory, all take animals and shape them to our own ends as if they were made of plasticine or dreams. In some sense they are: the natural world and everything in it that isn't us, are aspects of our mind. They are taken in by our senses and become our understanding of what is outside ourselves. But nothing we observe and think about is entirely outside ourselves.

Occasionally, we have moments when we wonder if the world outside us has a life of its own – but how could we ever know, since all we have are our own minds with which to think and apprehend the world? 'Why do we treat animals like animals?' the film version of Dr Dolittle asks the judge who wants to send him to an insane asylum. And earlier, before his parrot starts to tutor him, he sings his dream:

If we could talk to the animals, learn their languages
Think of all the things we could discuss
If we could walk with the animals, talk with the animals,
Grunt and squeak and squawk with the animals,
And they could squeak and squawk and speak and talk to us.

PART TWO

US AND THEM

Chuang Tzu and Hui Tzu were strolling along the dam of the Hao River when Chuang Tzu said, 'See how the minnows come out and dart around where they please! That's what fish really enjoy!' Hui Tzu said, 'You're not a fish – how do you know what fish enjoy?' Chuang Tzu said, 'You're not I, so how do you know I don't know what fish enjoy?' Hui Tzu said, 'I'm not you, so I certainly don't know what you know. On the other hand, you're certainly not a fish – so that still proves you don't know what fish enjoy!' Chuang Tzu said, 'Let's go back to your original question, please. You asked me how I know what fish enjoy – so you already knew I knew it when you asked the question. I know it by standing here beside the Hao.'

The Complete Works of Chuang Tzu,
trans., Burton Watson

3

DIVISIONS

The Judaeo-Christian version of the beginning of the world is not the only creation story. All origin tales account for the arrival, close in time, of humans and animals on the earth. Sometimes they exist already although in separate spheres. The Iroquois believed that there was a Water World, where the animals lived, and a Sky World inhabited by people. A woman fell from the Sky World and was saved by the birds. They made her some land to live on and she gave birth to a daughter who populated the Water World with human beings. In the Chippewa beginnings, a single cave-dwelling woman lived in a world of animals. She was impregnated by a dog and became the mother of the Chippewa people. A Chinese myth has the world created from a hen's egg. And sometimes, as in Egypt, human and animal existed within the same creatures. It's clear to all peoples of the earth that human and animal are dependent on, as well as battle with, each other. They always have a vital relationship, because creation myths explain the world that is already known. For all societies, until quite recent history, we inhabit a world where animals and humans coexist, where animals are magical, powerful and cunning, where animals can help humans, where, even if animals are hunted, they are party to the necessity. Animals, whatever their origin, are the friends and companions of humans on earth.

Even in Genesis, God hoped to find a friend for Adam among the animals. But here the companionship was undermined by the gift of dominion. The animals came first, in the first creation story of Genesis, before the man-and-woman. Though not before the light and darkness on the first day, the firmament dividing the above from below on the second day, the dry land and the seas, and on the earth the grass, the herb-yielding seed and the fruit tree yielding fruit after its kind, whose seed is within itself on the third day (it was a busy day), the sun and the moon and the stars on the fourth day. Only then was everything in place for sentient life. On the fifth day:

> And God said, Let the waters bring forth abundantly the moving creature that hath life, and fowl that may fly above the earth in the open firmament of heaven. And God created great whales, and every living creature that moveth, which the waters brought forth abundantly, after their kind, and every winged fowl after his kind: and God saw that it was good.

The sixth day was a rush to get everything done before the sabbath day of rest. The

> living creature after his kind, cattle, and creeping thing, and beast of the earth after his kind.

And when all of them were in place

> . . . God said, Let us make man in our image, after our likeness.

In this first version of the beginning, man was man-and-woman, a duality called *them*. He blessed them and told them to replenish the earth and subdue it. He gave them

> . . . dominion over the fish of the sea, and over the fowl of the air, and over every living thing that moveth upon the earth.

But he didn't tell the man-and-woman they could eat the animals. He introduced the herbs bearing seeds and the fruit of the trees yielding seeds and told the man-and-woman

> . . . to you it shall be for meat.

And to the animals he gave

> . . . every green herb for meat.
> And then he saw everything and it was very good.

A vegetarian world, then; no hunting by humans, no predation by animals. But unequivocally the man-and-woman had dominion over the beasts.

The second chapter of Genesis has a different version of creation. First the Lord God created the earth and the heavens, and the plants and the herbs, everything in the earth waiting to grow because it hadn't rained yet. The Lord God made it rain and then from the wet earth he moulded man – just a *him* all on his own. He made a garden eastward in Eden with trees and a river and minerals. He told the man to tend the garden and that he was to eat the fruit of the trees, all except for one. Then the Lord God decided the man needed help:

And out of the ground the Lord God formed every beast of the field, and every fowl of the air; and brought them unto Adam to see what he would call them: and whatsoever Adam called every living creature, that was the name thereof. And Adam gave names to all cattle, and to the fowl of the air, and to every beast of the field; but for Adam there was not found an help meet for him.

In this version, friendship is required and animals might have been the answer, but it turned out that animals were not able to provide it. So Eve was made out of Adam's rib. She was a help meet, a human being like and of Adam, not an animal being who was separately made.

In both versions the early writers are keen to distinguish the human from the animal. The second story is not so absolutist about the original distinction. God thought that animals might be satisfactory companions, they and Adam were all moulded from the same wet earth; but he was not like them, it turned out, and needed another of his own kind – although Eve was made differently from either Adam or the animals. In the second story, there is no mention of dominion. Adam is made a gardener, a cultivator of trees and herbs. There is no indication of how he is supposed to relate to the animals, except that he does that most human of things: gives them names. Adam has language, which gives him a naming edge over animals. Nevertheless, aside from naming, it sounds as if the humans and animals led separate but equal existences in the garden. Eve talks and listens to a serpent. Only when she takes its advice, and chooses to believe its word (so the animals had language, too) over the Lord God, and then blames it for the whole disobedient mess, does a distinction come. The Lord God told the serpent:

And I will put enmity between thee and the woman, and between thy seed and her seed; it shall bruise thy head, and thou shalt bruise his heel.

Yet even though the man and woman are exiled from the garden, and the ground is cursed so that from then on making a living from it will only happen by the sweat of Adam's face, there is still no mention of animals as food.

In chapter two of Genesis, Cain and Abel are already adult, and we learn that Abel is a keeper of sheep, while his brother is a tiller of the soil. Domestication and farming have arrived, as has a ritual life where the brothers make sacrifices of their products to the Lord. The Lord is pleased with Abel's burned fatty lamb offering, but isn't impressed at all with Cain's vegetable produce:

And Abel, he also brought of the firstlings of his flock and of the fat thereof. And the Lord had respect unto Abel and his offering: But unto Cain and to his offering he had not respect.

Only now, and without explanation, man controls animals and meat has become so desirable that the Lord himself prefers it to salad. Meat causes the first human killing, though it seems that killing animals has been happening for some time.

After that, animals are entirely in the control of man, so that when God plans to wipe out all life from the earth, he instructs Noah to bring in reproductive pairs of animals in order to repopulate the planet. In our Western ancient justification of the world, man herds the animals, man kills the animals and man saves the animals.

Adam may have named the animals, but we have no idea what he called them or on what basis he called them what he did. This is aggravating because nomenclature is very important to human beings. Luckily, we have Linnaeus, the man who gave us taxonomy, the Adam of the Enlightenment. There are many ways to name animals: you can see them as individuals, as we see our cats, dogs and goldfish, and call them Gerald, Isabel and Archimedes. This was how I imagined the naming of the animals when I was small. When we name animals like this, it's because we recognise them and can easily tell one from another – so Gerald the tabby who lives in your house is perfectly distinguished from Isabel the tabby and Archimedes the tabby who both also live in your house because, well, you know them, like you know your kids. But you still need a name for the group of animals that are dogs, and another for the group that are cats – at the very least so that their bowls don't get muddled up.

Unless you don't. Suppose that in some societies people do not classify types with names, but simply know them. How then would they refer to them to other people when the animals aren't present? 'Fancy a haunch of deer?' 'That monkey is really annoying me in the mornings with its howling, I'm off to deal with it.' The howler monkey is distinguishable from another kind of monkey by its howling, but if you don't need to refer to monkeys in the abstract ('Monkeys are a very interesting and particular group of animals and I want to write a book about them.') you could call everything Isabel and use individual descriptions according to need – howling creature/Isabel in the tree, slithering creature/Isabel bit me on my leg. As for lunch, you can work the other way round: meat is meat, whether it comes from a deer or a mammoth. *Meat*, rather than roots and fruit for lunch today. It could be all rather contingent and unproblematical. Choice is for supermarkets, not the forest or steppe. No need to bother with verbal categories. But even if you don't have to distinguish between animals on the grounds that you take what you can get, still, they look different, one from the other, and you take that into account when you draw them on the wall of the cave. You might even have feelings about them beyond their food value: their size, availability, tameness, usefulness, speed, beauty. Those feelings, along with the quality of their taste, become how you know them and mark them off from other living creatures, whether you name them or not.

In wealthy groups with plenty of resources, meat needs categorisation. After all, it can be good-tasting, so-so-tasting, or bad-luck-to-it-feed-it-to-the-dogs-tasting meat. Choosing which genus of meat to have for lunch would be a luxury no subsistence-hunting community could afford. But once everything has got more complicated and you are writing and sending what you write to strangers, inviting them to supper to show off, you need to clarify. When you achieve a surplus rather than living hand-to-mouth, and you can exchange things, you do find one kind of meat more desirable, for taste or status, than another. Choice requires names for things. And if my lunch (a hard-to-get and delicious kind of meat, or more likely a hard-to-get and *therefore* delicious kind of meat) can indicate that I am of a higher status than you, then we had better distinguish it from what the peasants eat if they're lucky. It's very hard to do without names for types of things that come in many and varied forms, as everything on this planet happens to. We humans may have language, but evolutionary multiplicity comes first, and requires that we use the logos to make categories. Gerald and Isabel don't know that they are 'cats', since they don't have our language. They know something, though. They seem to know that they are like each other in a way that they are not like birds or dogs, however they might conceive of 'birds' and 'dogs'. Human language does much the same thing: it tries to pin down the differences. You may not have to have a name for your dog, but even if you try and avoid it and call it 'dog', it still acquires a capital D and the specifics of your particular whippet.

We learned to classify, to separate and universalise. Some groups of people in the past classified their animals by the way they moved. They fly, crawl, walk on all fours, swing through the branches. Not all that helpful, really, in a post-domestic society, but there are no end of systems to be discovered once human beings start. Unless you're a believer, the classificatory nature of the early books of the Bible looks like proof positive that they were written by us. Only a human being could conceive of a God so obsessed with separation and hierarchy. Linnaeus performed intellectually as God did with his world-making. Separation and hierarchy. Organisation. Kingdoms are divided into phyla, phyla into classes, classes into orders, families, genera and species, and species into subspecies. He used structural similarities to make his scheme. From Wikipedia, we learn that

> Mammals (formally Mammalia) are a class of vertebrate animals whose females are characterised by the possession of mammary glands while both males and females are characterised by sweat glands, hair, three middle ear bones used in hearing, and a neo-cortex region in the brain.
>
> Except for the five species of monotremes (which lay eggs), all mammal species give birth to live young. Most mammals also possess specialised teeth, and the largest group of mammals, the placentals, use a placenta during gestation. The mammalian brain regulates endothermic and circulatory systems, including a four-chambered heart.
>
> There are approximately 5,400 species of mammals, distributed

in about 1,200 genera, 153 families and 29 orders (though this varies by classification scheme) . . . Mammals are divided into two subclasses, the prototheria, which includes the egg-laying monotremes, and the theria, which includes the live-bearing marsupials and placentals. Most mammals, including the six largest orders, belong to the placental group. The three largest orders, in descending order, are Rodentia (mice, rats and other small, gnawing mammals), Chiroptera (bats), and Soricomorpha (shrews, moles and solenodons). The next three largest orders include the Carnivora (dogs, cats, weasels, bears, seals and their relatives), the Cetartiodactyla (including the even-toed hoofed mammals and the whales) and the Primates to which the human species belongs. The relative size of these latter three orders differs according to the classification scheme and definitions used by various authors.

In order to create these categories someone must go to wherever the animals are and collect samples, but after that, you can stay indoors, first in the anatomy theatre, and then in the study with plenty of candles and quills, and you think out the reality into abstraction. Once that is done, and done in a universally agreed language, everyone can discuss and refer to all the creatures on the planet without either the animals or the people having to be anywhere nearby. This is a tremendous step forward for learning, and it's the point at which the mythic beasts on those old maps of uncharted waters are known to be impossible figments of the imagination. We can tell the truth from fiction without having to have the creatures to hand. And look, we've even made that separation of real and fantasy animals. These days, taxonomy has changed as we've learned more from biochemistry, but the scheme itself survives (although infinitely more complex) to allow us to tell one living thing from another with finer and finer distinction.

Above all, hierarchy ensures that some animals are more advanced than others. From the unicellular amoeba to the bipedal primate *Homo sapiens*, everything has a place in the scheme. Complexity is at the top, simplicity at the bottom, in the middle are what we easily recognise as 'animals'. And it is us, *Homo*, us at the top, who have produced this laddered arrangement of life. Human animals have decided what 'advanced' and 'primitive' mean, what 'complexity' and 'simplicity' mean, and made that our way of judging where everything in the world is to be on the scale that goes from us downward. We even have the privilege of doubting our former certainties. In 1780, Brissot de Warville wondered

> What import do the divisions of the species have . . . they are nothing but definitions, 'chimerical divisions' that have no existence in nature. All bodies belong to the same nature. Within this space, there has been established the capacity of some beings to dispose of others, a capacity that Brissot dubs 'the right of property'.[1]

How can we do it any other way, since it is us doing it?

Scientific classification isn't the only way to do it, and although it has been the most recent and most popular way these past three hundred years in the Western hemisphere, perhaps other ways are at least as interesting. Freud thought so, and so did Native Americans when they assigned particular animals to their tribe as their spiritual representatives. Totemism takes animals and classifies them in order to make useful ways of thinking about human groupings. For Lévi-Strauss it didn't matter at all which animal was chosen; the totemic animal was arbitrary, the whole point was precisely to classify, not to make perceived animal qualities representative of the human group, but simply to make differences in the world, and in that, he said, the

Indian tribes of North America were as scientific as we are. The older anthropological functionalists, like Firth and Fortes, had believed that the animals were specifically chosen to represent particular physical or psychological aspects that the tribe found desirable. The strength of the ox, the ferocity of a jaguar, the hunting skills of an eagle. By using the idea of the animal, it became their spiritual creature and would confer those desirable qualities on the tribe. Malinowski, even earlier, thought that the totemic animals were simply those which were designated good to eat, or were useful – for clothing, or for arrow-making. And Freud, interested in a quite different story, made the totems the tool of the unconscious, enabling tribes to blame or justify guilt by externalising it as the will of their totemic spirits, and using them as emblems to ensure that tribes inter-married rather than contravening the innate law against incest.

All of which are examples of Lévi-Strauss's description of our relation to animals: that they are 'good to think with'. We can and do use animals to think about anything and everything. All the various ways we have contrived to cook them – roast, boil, fricassee, grill, stew, sauté, make soup of, put with herbs, spices, fruit, nuts, vegetables, mix with other kinds of meat, dry, sauced, liquidised – parallel the multitudinous ways we have contrived to think about them as props to increase our own understanding of ourselves and the world. The animals, very often, are incidental. Perhaps 'animals', that category of non-human life which we have lumped into a single noun, exist more in our thoughts than in reality. When we worry, as we increasingly do, about the possible extinction of the northern white rhino (those last thirty-five northern white rhinos living their actual lives in Central Africa at the time of writing), are we really concerned for the creatures themselves, as anxious as we might be about the possible extinction of our aunt or our neighbour's mother, or is the northern white rhino – rarely seen by most people in the world – in fact a thought we have that, like Native American tribes, we use to describe the world? The idea of the white rhino wandering in the bush is what we want. We abhor its absence, though for all we know, right now, at this moment, there are none left. The loss of the last northern white rhino on the planet might make you cry – it's almost making me cry now – but we can't be crying about Noname, who died last of all in Central Africa and doubtless, until it was inevitable, resisted her death as all living creatures do up to a point. If someone told us the white rhinos were out of danger, we'd be relieved; if they go extinct, we'll be distressed. But like the tree falling in the forest, who knows what extinct or not extinct means to us, or, far more mysteriously and perhaps importantly than that, what it could possibly mean to the white rhinos?

Human beings can do more than one thing at a time. We can do several apparently contradictory things at a time. We can think with and about animals, worry about the loss of a species, and also breed animals far from their original phenotype and genotype for our eating or aesthetic pleasure and benefit. We can worry about an invisible white rhino and the loss of diversity in 'nature', and we can farm virtually monocultured domesticated cattle and sheep, keep chickens, race horses, breed dogs that we have manipulated over many generations to produce the qualities of growth, taste, speed, looks and obedience that we best desire for profit, pleasure and usefulness. We can see a herd of cows or a flock of sheep as we drive along the motorway. They're not mythic beasts, not even far away in 'Africa', but right here and now, manufactured creatures. This is another result of the original naming and dividing. We remake and redivide our categories, creating them just like God moulding Adam and Eve from the dust after the rain had made it malleable. Cattle divide now into the limited breeds we have created that best provide our varied requirements: milk, meat, clothing, strength, good reproductive qualities. There are, as a result, rare-breed farms that keep some of the older stock, antiques (though these were already selectively bred), some butchers who sell, and wealthier individuals who are prepared to pay a premium for their meat on the grounds of improved (meaning unimproved) taste. The rare breeds are only as rare and endangered as white rhinos because of the creation and marketing of the ubiquitous breeds; millions of animals which we think about, if we think about them at all, in terms of taste or commerce, that are, apart from those moments when we pass them on the motorway, most known from their parts on butchers' counters or on plastic-covered trays in the supermarket chill cabinet.

The last white rhino falling in the forest, and the millions of Aberdeen Angus steers born to be meat, the puppy in the pet shop, the working sheepdog, the dream camel interpreted by your shrink, the horse you put money on in the Derby, the glass giraffe on your shelf, the bird singing right now in the tree outside, next door's cat crapping in your garden, the book you're reading published by Penguin, my lunch, the squishy bear your toddler is clutching, the *Just So* stories you read her at bedtime, the fish you pull from a river, the simile you last used to describe speed, or grace or cold-eyed calculation – all these and so much more are our animals. What animals are to themselves is a question mostly left to philosophers to fail to come to a conclusion about.

4

OTHERNESS

I've had cats in my life since I was fostered at the age of fifteen. When I arrived at the house in London, the woman who was fostering me greeted me at the door, holding a small grey kitten under her arm.

'This is Grey Cat,' she said. 'I only got her yesterday.'

Grey Cat and I were co-fosterlings. She was supposed to be my cat to help me settle in and she behaved impeccably. She slept in my bed, had her first kittens in the cupboard in my room. Then she became a mature, independent cat. Perfectly friendly, but being an intelligent animal she chose to belong, in the sense that cats belong at all, to our mutual foster-mother: the one who always remembered to feed her and was available (as a teenage girl was not) for petting and stroking according to Grey Cat's timetable.

Since then there have been other cats, with very few periods without one or more. Black Cat (I had the impression that all cats were to be given names for their colour), Sniff (for his wayward sinuses), who adopted me and sat outside my back door for days with immense patience but sneezing a lot, I can only say doggedly, because I thought I didn't want another cat, until I understood that I did and let him in. There was Mungo, Phoebe, Flora (named, my small daughter told her friend, 'because she had short legs so she was close to the floor'), and over the past twenty years the three most recent, who have overlapped. Oscar came first, then Darcy a couple of years later, and finally Bunty arrived, the smallest and youngest, fourteen years ago. Bunty is the last remaining cat. Until 2001 they lived with me in London, then the four of us moved, with robust complaints (vocal and faecal) from the cats in the back of the car, to Cambridge. They settled in well enough, although Bunty always hated Darcy who tried to play with her and got mercilessly screamed at as if every approach were a life-threatening attack. Bunty is a bit of a drama queen. After a couple of years I threw caution to the wind and moved into the house directly opposite to live with The Poet, the reason for the shift to Cambridge in the first place, and I had to explain to the cats that they lived here now, too.

Something happened to Darcy. Although he'd been crossing the road back and forth as comfortably as I had for two years, spending evenings at The Poet's house, returning to feeding base in the morning with me, once I finally left the house across the road he refused to move in with us. New people moved into the old house and Darcy disappeared for several days. Then he started coming into our house at night, sleeping in the newspaper basket in the kitchen, but every morning, as soon as we got up, he shot out of the cat door. Sometimes he came into the garden and when I saw him, I went out and tried to talk to him, to offer him food, but he behaved as if he were terrified. He stood off at a distance, frozen, and stared at me while I spoke, put down a bowl of food and extended a hand to him. I would say he looked as if he were in desperate conflict, but cats don't really have expressions on their faces, they don't have the musculature and it's not how they communicate – so I can't say what he was thinking. He'd approach a few steps and then turn and run off as if he'd hit a wall and something had terrified him. He came less and less, although he always looked well fed and healthy. I spoke to the vet and described his behaviour.

'There's new evidence that cats can get a form of Alzheimer's disease. The stress of another move might have triggered it, or maybe it was just a coincidence.'

It made peculiar sense. Darcy had always been a gentle, friendly soul, whatever Bunty thought, who only wanted to spend his time sharing a chair with me or anyone willing to give him a stroke. Now he seemed angry and confused. A transformed, unhappy creature. Something sudden and catastrophic had happened either to him or with him. The vet was doubtful about catching Darcy and bringing him in for an examination. The stress would make things worse. Eventually, Darcy stopped coming to the house altogether. At around the same time, I noticed that some people a dozen or so houses down the road had moved away. I'd seen Darcy sitting outside their door, and knocked several times to see if he was being fed by them, but I never got an answer. I think that Darcy had adopted them, or they him, as Sniff had adopted me, and when they left, they took him with them, thinking him a stray who was now their cat. At least, I hope so.

Oscar was given a killing injection when he was seventeen and his kidneys failed. I held him for the injection, as I had Mungo, years before, who had cancer. As with Mungo, the vet had to say that Oscar was dead now, I could stop holding him. I knew of course. When you hold a live animal in your arms and he is given an injection that stops his heart, there is an instantaneous transformation, and you can feel the creature you are holding to be lifeless. Not to be losing life, but abruptly to be no more than a body, without any muscle tension. The limpness of a dead cat, which a moment ago had been alive, is very disturbing. The weight in your arms increases, but there is no resisting, responding life in it. It is absolute. Even so, I held them both until told to stop, and murmured close to their ears comforting words I had spoken often to them: that it was all right, all right, that they were so beautiful, such clever cats. How strange it is to say such things to a live purring cat, let alone to the dead creature in your arms. The feeling of their toneless weight stayed on my arms for weeks. You realise that all our contacts with other people, from the children we cuddle to the hands of strangers we shake, depend on the meeting of tensions, muscle against muscle. Response. Being post-domestic as I am, I have only held cats in my arms, not people, while they made an instant transition from life to death. It would be a less extraordinary experience for anyone born a few decades before me for whom death was a more common and closer event. But the limp body I held on both occasions were animals that I had lived with for years. So now only Bunty remains, a transformed cat herself, now that she's on her own, much more contented without Darcy and Oscar sharing the house and the available cat-affection: less nervy, curled asleep in her habitual place, her head resting on her haunch or on the edge of my warm laptop, pressed close against my leg on the sofa as I type.

I'd say in a casual sort of way that I've known all my cats, in much the same way that I've known other people; better, really, because the cats each lived with me for much longer than any human beings except my daughter and now The Poet. But, of course, thinking about it more carefully, I haven't known them at all. I could even doubt how well I really know my daughter and The Poet, on the level at which I mean, but my best guesses – what we call empathy – help with them. I make the same best guesses with cats, but if I empathise with cats to try and discover who they are and what they experience, I'm likely to fail on the grounds, very simply, that they are cats and I am not.

The common ground they and I have is where we live. Cats have not actually been domesticated, as dogs were, bred from packs of wild wolves that accompanied groups of early humans to benefit from their leavings. The more friendly ones were kept around and bred with each other. People and dogs have more in common than people and cats. Dogs, if bred for their juvenile characteristics (the friendly, learning ones) easily become dependent on human society. Cats turned up in human settlements and benefited from the rats that benefited from the stored grain. The people benefited from the cats killing the rats – look, we're back to the Pied Piper – but until very late in our symbiosis they didn't try to breed cats into the useful or decorative and crippled creatures that dogs became. Those flat-nosed snuffling Persian horrors, bred only for show, are a very recent development. So cats learned to live with people, enjoyed the warmth and comfort the humans provided, ate the food which kept them around and on the prowl when rats and mice were scarce, and didn't mind at all being petted, somewhat. And so they are now. A cat turns feral very easily, and lives quite successfully outside human habitation. If you draw one of those diagrams of two circles with a shaded section of each overlapping – a Venn diagram – the intersection area is the space where humans and cats live together. Our houses actually. The rest of the two circles, by far the largest area of both, are humans and cats quite uninvolved with each other. But if there were a way to draw a Venn diagram so that one circle overlapped the other circle more than the other circle overlapped it, then this would better describe the situation. Dogs would overlap humans more – thinking themselves more part of the human world than they are (because they have been bred to think and be so), while humans would overlap the cat circle more, humans thinking we are more part of the cat world than we are. But that, of course, is still just a fantasy I have, rather than anything I really know about cats. It seems impossible to find a less anthropocentric way to think about the creatures with whom we share our daily space.

We have returned to that awful film of *Dr Dolittle* and his longing:

> *If we could talk to the animals, learn their languages*
> *Think of all the things we could discuss.*

Dolittle has to prove himself sane in court (and fails) on account of his desire to communicate with non-human animals, and though he is rescued from the madhouse, he is never more than that typical, harmless and faintly ambiguous eccentric with which literature and showbiz like affectionately or sentimentally to toy. I take Dolittle's fancy perfectly seriously, as a proper and not at all mad longing. I recognise the longing in myself and I think it represents a general ache that we popularise and render quaint because we know it to be unachievable. Dolittle's desire is an expression of our own. *If we could talk to the animals, if they could talk to us.* The massive black hole in our understanding of the creatures with whom we share the planet, as vast and compelling a mystery as the universe, is intolerable, not just because we can't talk to the animals, but because it reminds us of how we can't really know any other consciousness, not even those of our own species. Not even those we are closest to: our parents, our lovers, our children, our rivals. Best guess is best we can do, and it won't do. It doesn't scratch the itch. It reminds us that each of us is inescapably alone inside our heads. Make yourself think about that fact, force yourself, even as your mind swerves away from what it can't deal with, insist on thinking it, and a quiet terror descends. Whoever you are, whatever you do, you are alone, not known, not knowing. It's impossible to hold that thought for long. So the otherness of animals matters to us enormously, even if we are not whimsical professors or metaphysical philosophers.

But, being adaptable creatures, we behave most of the time as if we were convinced and content simply to think of ourselves as masters of the universe and to consider the space between us and 'animals' unbridgeable for perfectly knowable reasons that have, admittedly, changed and been argued about for millennia. The single category 'animals' covers a multiplicity of species as the category 'human' doesn't. That animals are different from us goes without saying; indeed 'animal' essentially means 'not human', even if we do the modern liberal thing and call ourselves 'human animals'. Our unquenched thirst for knowledge coexists (though not comfortably) with our assumption that the world is essentially at our command, to think and do with what we want. Even when we get excited about having overused the planet's resources, and some clamour to use it less or differently, the fate of the planet is still believed to be in our control, to save if not destroy. Exploit it or conserve it, we're in charge of it. Those who want to use it well want to keep it going, to preserve it, as we want to preserve rare species, and to feel that it will be there, and bountiful for our great-grandchildren. Yet planets come and go for all sorts of reasons, and if rampant, self-serving *Homo sapiens* are what evolved here to consume everything and therefore succeed spectacularly as indeed we have as a species, then our consumption of the earth may be just another way planets live and die. I am not, let me say hurriedly, allying myself with anti-ecology movements, only suggesting that we always assume (doubtless rightly and wrongly) that we are and should be in charge of the planet's salvation. Even if we allow ourselves the possibility of going beyond species-survival behaviour as a further cultural evolutionary development, we remain the supreme beings on little earth, in charge of whether it becomes a garden or a wasteland.

There's no way out of anthropocentrism for us. The only world we can live in is the world in which we evolved to live in; the only way we can see our world is through our own planet-earth-evolved eyes and consciousness. It is a trap consciousness lays, a game of everlasting mirrors, which we can't escape – though some people don't want to, or see no reason why we should. If it's a problem at all it's a metaphysical one, and probably a waste of time. But me, I'm hooked on unanswerable questions. The matter of Them and Us intrigues and teases me.

It has been perfectly clear to some people for thousands of years that they are them and we are us, and why that is so. Ever ambivalent about animals, we have nevertheless used them to define what we most fear in ourselves. 'Consider your origin; you were not born to live like brutes, but to follow virtue and knowledge', writes Dante in the *Divine Comedy*.[1] The brute, the beast in us, always lurks, always needs suppressing and is the main target of religions and governments everywhere. It is the animal in us that threatens to destroy the very planet on which we live. Therefore, the great distinction must be made between the savage and the civilised inside and outside our own being. We choose animals to represent our savagery (although they bear little resemblance to it) so they can't be us or our whole project is in trouble. They become a categorical 'not-us', a thought so familiar that it hardly needs saying. Individuals or groups who transgress civic norms are animals, beasts and brutes (sometimes monsters) and we wonder, amazed, that they have no 'humanity'. Animals/savages are instinctual, while humans are thoughtful; animals/savages act without exercising control over themselves, where exercising control is quintessentially what it means to be human. We have the old animal brain, low down, and above it the new frontal lobes that particularly define the human. We have consciousness, self-reflection and all sorts of useful ways of making a clear distinction between ourselves and the brutes. But still we remain troubled because, even though our knowing is how we differentiate ourselves from animals, we cannot know *them*.

Jacques Derrida suggests a very particular distinction between man and animals (although note how he qualifies 'generally thought' with 'though none of the philosophers I am about to examine actually mentions it'), but he also helpfully lists most of the other differences that have been noted over time:

> It is generally thought, though none of the philosophers I am about to examine actually mentions it, that the property unique to animals, what in the last instance distinguishes them from man, is their being naked without knowing it. Not being naked, therefore, not having knowledge of their nudity, in short, without consciousness of good and evil . . . In principle, with the exception of man, no animal has ever thought to dress itself. Clothing would be proper to man, one of the 'properties' of man. 'Dressing oneself' would be inseparable from all the other figures of what is 'proper to man', even if one talks about it less than speech or reason, the logos, history, laughing, mourning, burial, the gift, etc.[2]

Most of those more spoken-of aspects of humanity that are said to distinguish us from brutes have by now been acknowledged to exist in some form or other in animals. Even if you argue about the use of the word 'language' to describe the way animals employ sound and gesture to communicate with each other, the once absolute barriers are now much fuzzier than they have ever been. Mourning, concern for the dead, tool use, playfulness, symbolism, generational learning, non-reproductive sex and even mirror self-recognition has been witnessed in one or several species of 'animal'. But what of the nakedness Derrida speaks about – the 'last instance' that distinguishes them and us, which nonetheless is not mentioned by those thinkers he wishes to talk about?

He is referring, in this late lecture, to a very particular confrontation between animal and human, and a very particular nakedness. Specifically, the fact that his pet cat has a habit of following him every morning from the bedroom into the bathroom and staring at Derrida without his clothes on. Derrida stands naked in his bathroom. The cat stares at his genitals. Derrida, the man, is naked as animals apparently can't be, which is consciously naked, self-consciously naked, knowing good and evil and therefore finding himself filled with a difficult-to-define sense of guilt.

But the matter is more interesting than Derrida's unease at having his genitals exposed to the gaze of an animal. He is not, he insists, talking about 'an animal', a generality: he is talking about a real, here and now, pussy cat:

> I must immediately make it clear, the cat I am talking about is a real cat, truly, believe me, a little cat. It isn't the figure of a cat. It doesn't silently enter the bedroom as an allegory for all the cats on the earth, the felines that traverse our myths and religions, literature and fables.

It is his own cat that sees him naked. 'If I say "it is a real cat" that sees me naked, this is in order to mark its unsubstitutable singularity.' And it comes to me as this irreplaceable living being that one day enters my space, into this place where it can encounter me, see me, even see me naked. Nothing can ever rob me of the certainty that what we have here is an existence that refuses to be conceptualised [*rebelle à tout concept*]. And a mortal existence, for from the moment that it has a name, its name survives it. It signs its potential disappearance. Mine also, and that disappearance, from this moment to that, fort/da, is announced each time that, with or without nakedness, one of us leaves the room.[3]

This moment between Derrida and his pussy is both disturbing and perfectly familiar – which makes it what Freud defines as 'uncanny'. At the start of every day the cat follows Derrida into the bathroom; it is morning, she wants her breakfast, but as soon as she's in there, the door having been closed, and Derrida is naked, on the lavatory, showering, towelling himself dry, brushing his teeth, or spraying deodorant at his armpits, all the business of getting ready for his day, she demands to leave the bathroom. Derrida wishes to get on with his morning routine. The cat looks at him, and waits.

This is pretty much how the day starts for you and me and our cats. Every cat in the world hates having a door shut behind them as they enter a room. I've given up shutting the door to my study. Bunty (my named, irreplaceable living cat being) follows me into my study, after we've done the bathroom thing and I'm ready to start work, and settles herself comfortably on the sofa, but if I then shut the door, she gets up and sits at attention by the door, looking back at me where I've settled myself on the sofa with my laptop. So I get up and open the door for her. Bunty leaves the room for a moment and then comes back in, returns to the sofa and gets comfortable. I close the door and sit down. Bunty gets up and sits by the door . . . We could repeat this sequence all day and it wouldn't change. If, in an attempt to circumvent the routine, I close the door when Bunty isn't in the room, she will scratch outside, claw up the carpet by the door trying to get in. I get up and let her in, and if I close the door I have to open it to let her out again. So in the name of getting work done, and getting comfortable on the sofa myself, I no longer close the door, although I like to work in a room with the door closed.*

Derrida's cat seems to be looking at him with a purpose. Let me out. She seems to be looking and waiting, just like Bunty does. Derrida's nakedness, his vulnerable genitals and his feeling about being seen unclothed by his cat are entirely his own concern. The cat has other things on her mind. Looking, waiting, in order to get the door opened. Looking-waiting is the method cats use to demand that people do what they want. Or so I suppose. Derrida supposes the cat looks at his genitals; I suppose the cat looks to have the door opened. Neither of us can be sure what the cat supposes. We can't even be sure that while she looks, she is waiting. Waiting is what we would be doing if we were a cat sitting, looking at a person, in front of a closed door that we will go out of when it is opened. But the cat is opaque to our human interpretation of her behaviour.

There is no doubt that cats look at you, that much is certain. Among other times, when they want you to open the door they look at you long and hard. Does the look mean 'Open the door'? Does it mean 'What to make of that creature who feeds me and opens the door, strips off its outer skin and underneath has a dangly thing just there, not quite within reach, almost like a half-dead mouse, and it moves a little, quite unpredictably'? Does it mean 'Here is another form, different from the one which I followed from the bedroom. I wonder how it got here and if it's well-trained enough to know that when I look at it, it must open the door'? Or is it a look that doesn't

*See Epilogue, p. 298.

63

mean any words we impose on it, because cats don't have words and therefore, although we might sometimes be able to translate their conceptual world into wishes we can fulfil, most of the time we have no idea what goes on inside their heads? I've been trying to avoid mentioning Wittgenstein, but I can't hold out any longer: if lions could talk, we wouldn't understand them. He means surely: even if they could talk in our own language, we still wouldn't understand them because they are lions and we are not.

What about the look that cats give you when (it would seem) they don't want anything at all? Sometimes Bunty is beside me on the sofa and when I glance at her she is sitting, or lying there, looking directly at me, staring hard and purposefully at me; it seems, at any rate, her eyes are fixed unblinking on my face. It happens in the bathroom, in the study, while I'm watching TV with her on my lap or on the arm of the sofa, on the stairs. She looks at me, long, hard and quite often. And for extended periods. Eventually, if I look back at her for long enough, she will look away, but it is as if I've interrupted her stare with my own, not that something else has caught her attention. Sometimes I talk to her. 'What? What do you want?' but she never answers, just carries on looking, often, it seems to me, even more intensely. Why does she look at me? The expression on her face is the only expression her cat face can have. But her eyes seem intently, intentionally staring, meaningfully, I'd say, but I can't say why or what they mean. It looks as if she has something urgent to tell me, if she could only find the words, or if I could only find the comprehension of her glance.

It can be perfectly clear. If I go into the kitchen and she wants me to put more food in her bowl, she will follow me, look up at me and miaow.

'Hungry?' I say.

'Miaow,' she'll say, while I get the food and put it in her bowl.

She goes to the bowl and eats, and our transaction is over.

She has a cup of water in the study. When she wants more, she sits on the chest above it, beside the bathroom door where the water comes from and miaows. Again, I do what she wants, she jumps down and drinks the fresh water. Mission accomplished. This is communication with a purpose. Or at any rate something I can assume has a purpose (can I be sure that Bunty doesn't miaow and eat because she believes that is what I would like her to do, and she's merely being kind? Or that she hates drinking from the glass cup in the study, but goes along with it, to keep me happy or because she can't find a way to explain that she'd rather have a pottery bowl?). Does she have a purpose when she seems just to be looking at me with no particular want, one that I can't fathom? Or is she just looking, her eyes open and gazing in the direction her face is pointed? Sometimes, in exactly the same way, she sits with her back to the room and stares just as hard at the blank wall. Nothing is crawling on it, that I can see – it is a wall, uneventful and a shade of white. She sits alert and just looks at it. What could just looking possibly mean? *Meaning*, a word, a concept, that as far as I know only humans have. She looks at me, and I don't know what she means by it, and if she doesn't mean anything at all by it, she's just sitting there, what is she doing, why, what could that possibly mean? Are you looking at me? It drives me crazy. It has always driven me crazy. It's partly the reason for writing this book.

Derrida qualifies the 'irreplaceable living being' of his cat by declaring that her name gives her a relation to him and to time (another human invention that cats might have no truck with). The name that survives her, that makes her not there (but somewhere) when she walks out of the room. 'Bunty isn't here' therefore she *is*. This is again a Derridian world view, not at all necessarily a cat world view. T. S. Eliot understood that cats might also have their own ineffable and secret name.

The name, whether it's 'cat' or 'Tootles', is given to her by the human name-giver: Adam-Derrida-Diski. We name animals, as we name everything, because it allows us to relate to them and to bring them into our world of time. Though sometimes some animals respond to the sound we make when we call them by name, we have no way of knowing what it means to them. Certainly, it doesn't survive them from their point of view. Neither Oscar nor Bunty (as far as I can possibly know) have a concept of 'Oscar' who is dead. Only I do – and now you. And it's true that this gives them a place in our world, but tells us nothing about how *they* understand their place in our world, or possibly our place in their world.

What Derrida and I agree on is that we believe something is going on in the staring creature's mind, even if we can't grasp it. What we acknowledge, with or without specifying it, is that the creature has a mind. But, of course, that's just another name we give to what we still do not really comprehend. Descartes had no trouble with this. Mind meant soul, inner being, and animals did not have one. The greatest divider after God, Descartes codified the distinction between man and beast. They are automata, which function without self-reflection. They do not deliberately do anything or feel anything, because they can only respond to stimuli. Hungry, they seek out food; tired, they sleep; while human beings, us soul-owners, can deliberate and decline on occasion, for a reason, to follow our instincts. Reason. We have it, they do not. I am because I think, they are not because they don't. Or so Descartes thought. And no animal contradicted him because they did not have his language and he didn't look at them in such a way as to possibly guess that they might have something like mind themselves, because he had already worked out from first principles (human reason, the only sort we know) that they did not.

So, why do Derrida and I accept that animals have minds, consciousnesses? It just seems to be the case from our observation of the animals who live with us – neither of us being zoologists, ethologists or behaviourists, we have no evidence that science would approve of one way or the other. It seems to be the case that Bunty is a cat and that she has an individuality, I would dare to say consciousness. She is certainly different from me. Derrida would call it an abyssal difference. I don't understand her sometimes when she stares at me, and although I don't understand people sometimes when they stare at me, they usually have a way, if they want to, to tell me what it is they are thinking. A man stared at me the other day in a chemist shop. I looked back at him. 'I'm not drunk, I'm mental,' he said, explaining exactly what he wanted me to know. But there are some who don't or can't explain. There are people who don't have the speech, or social skills, or the capacity for cultural learning that we think of as precisely human. We have always given those people born without what we think of as essential human capacities the benefit of being human because they are our species. In much the same way, but in spite of differences of species, Derrida, I and every other cat owner in the world, give their feline the benefit of consciousness, and since we don't know what their consciousness is like, we impose on them a watered-down version of our own. What else can we do unless we are to live entirely separated, parallel lives under the same roof?

In 1677 Spinoza explained that it was the degree of otherness that made us the masters of the animal world:

It is plain that the law against the slaughtering of animals is founded rather on vain superstition and womanish pity than on sound reason. The rational quest of what is useful to us further teaches us the necessity of associating ourselves with our fellow-men, but not with beasts, or things, whose nature is different from our own; we have the same rights in respect of them as they have in respect of us. Nay, as everyone's right is defined by his virtue, or power, men have far greater rights over beasts than beasts have over men. Still, I do not deny that beasts feel; what I do deny is, that we may not consult our own advantage and use them as we please, treating them in the way which best suits us; for their nature is not like ours, and their emotions are naturally different from human emotions.[4]

By 1870 Thomas Huxley (referred to then and now as 'Darwin's Bulldog') had written a paper asking 'Has the Frog a Soul?' responding to the ubiquitous use of frogs as experimental animals. They were, it was commonly accepted, mere machines, whose main use in the world was to be dissected in the laboratory to uncover the workings of muscle reflexes. Claude Bernard referred to them as 'the Job of physiology'. Paul S. White describes their trials in his essay on 'The Experimental Animal in Victorian Britain':

> The frog was clearly a creature driven from below. Its ability to perform without limbs, without its head, or indeed to be practically decomposable into parts was a central feature in physiological experiments throughout the nineteenth century and long before.[5]

But were the twitching muscles in the amputated leg or the decapitated body evidence of purposive behaviour? Was the leg thinking when it tried (is that the right word?) to wipe an irritant off its back, while its head was somewhere entirely else? If separated into its component parts, where, exactly, did the soul of the remorselessly active bits of the frog reside? The experimenters discovered the autonomic nervous system, and although they debated the possibility of the froggy bits having a soul, or at least a purpose, that didn't mean that the experiments should stop. A frog's soul, even if it had one, was not a matter for consideration in the way that a human soul was.

There were those who held views in advance of their time and show what looks like a basis for the contemporary concern for animal welfare, nevertheless they do not question the otherness of animals as many modern radical animal-rights proponents would. Jeremy Bentham, perhaps the founding father of the animal rights movement, wrote about the need to treat animals with consideration, whether or not they possessed soul or mind:

> The day may come, when the rest of the animal creation may acquire those rights which never could have been withholden from them but by the hand of tyranny. The French have already discovered that the blackness of skin is no reason why a human being should be abandoned without redress to the caprice of a tormentor. It may come one day to be recognised, that the number of legs, the villosity of the skin, or the termination of the os sacru, are reasons equally insufficient for abandoning a sensitive being to the same fate. What else is it that should trace the insuperable line? Is it the faculty of reason, or perhaps, the faculty for discourse? . . . The question is not, Can they reason? Nor, Can they talk? But, Can they suffer?[6]

There are ethical reasons for respecting the lives of animals. Blake howls: 'A robin redbreast in a cage, puts all heaven in a rage.' Kant says of Leibnitz that he 'used a tiny worm for purposes of observation, and then carefully replaced it with its leaf on the tree, so that it should not come to harm through any act of his. He would have been sorry – a natural feeling for a humane man – to destroy such a creature for no reason.'[7]

We do not wish to hurt animals when there is no reason to because we are humane, but that is because we are human and they are ineluctably other and under our control. They are other as plants are; the question is, can plants feel, can they suffer? We are sure they can't. They don't move, they don't remind us of us in any way. Animals are other, but even before Darwin, everyone knew that there was something about them that was like us. Descartes said they were automata, but nevertheless he felt the need to make that distinction between us and them; the question didn't arise about the nature of plants. Thomas Huxley, discussing Edward Tyson, who in 1699 suggested the closeness of man and ape, is not over-impressed with his precocity:

> Tyson, in other words, did not place his chimp on the rung just below ourselves because he had freed his mind from the cultural habit of interpreting animals in human terms, but for quite the opposite reason – because he longed to affirm a conventional view of human superiority.[8]

And once Darwin had shown what many people were already aware of without the actual theory, that there was a physiological continuum between them and us, it became all the more essential to mark the differences. Even those who didn't resist the idea of evolutionary theory retained the laddered view of the Elizabethan chain of being. In the twentieth century, most philosophers have been certain about the differences between humankind and the animals. Heidegger has a chain of being of his own: 'the stone is worldless, the animal is poor in world, man is world-forming'.[9] Derrida describes Heidegger's version of the cat in the house:

> What is 'living with the animal'? What is 'cohabiting' with the animal? That is the question of *mitgehen* and *mitexistieren*. The

animal can *mitgehen* with us in the house; a cat, for example, which is often said to be a narcissistic animal, can inhabit the same place as us, it can 'go with us', 'walk with us', it can be 'with us' in the house, live 'with us' but 'it doesn't exist with us' in the house.[10]

This is all about language, of course, and the way in which it structures consciousness for us. Heidegger explains: 'When we say that the lizard is lying on the rock, we ought to cross out the word "rock" in order to indicate that whatever the lizard is lying on is certainly given in some way for the lizard, and yet it is not known to the lizard as a rock. If we cross the word out . . . we imply that whatever it is is not accessible to it as a being. The blade of grass that the beetle crawls up, for example, is not a blade of grass for it at all.'[11] Then again, neither is it 'lying' or being 'on' the thing which is not a rock to the lizard. It doesn't seem to me to get us very much further than saying that lizards don't speak our language. In fact, Heidegger doesn't actually quarrel with the word 'rock'; he speaks in German, of *'felsplatte'*. So when I'm lying on a *felsplatte*, like the lizard, I'm not lying on a *felsplatte*, which Heidegger, should I be lucky enough to have him lying beside me, is lying on, but a *rock*. It says no more than that we cannot know exactly how the world is to another who does not have our language. It doesn't make them poor in world, even if they don't have a word at all for what they are lying on. Yet, so poor in world are animals, indeed, to Heidegger that he doesn't consider that they can die. Not as we can. They, having none of the knowledge of death that language brings, merely 'croak' (*crève*) as the translation of Derrida from the French to English puts it.[12]

According to Levinas, animals don't even have a face.

I cannot say at what moment you have the right to be called 'face'. The human face is completely different and only afterwards do we discover the face of an animal. I don't know if a snake has a face . . . You ask me at what moment one becomes a face. I do not know at what moment the human appears, but what I want to emphasise is that the human breaks with pure being, which is always a persistence in being . . . A being is something that is attached to being, to its own being. That is Darwin's idea. The being of animals is a struggle for life. A struggle for life without ethics. It is a question of might.[13]

A face, which according to Levinas, dogs might have and snakes probably don't, is what is required to address the other, and the address says, basically, 'Don't kill me.' Without a face, there is no plea, no ethical requirement beyond our own benevolence, so humans should not mistreat animals because they suffer pain, not because they are to be considered as we would consider ourselves. They are increasingly *them*, alien and at our mercy or otherwise, according to their owning of a face: the capacity to allow us to think they are thinking as we do. Animals don't require us to be thoughtful towards them because they don't merit the attention that our own kind do, having a sense of our own being, who struggle with life but have ethics. Levinas is suggesting that there is not all that much to know about animals, not that much to think about. They deserve our consideration because we are ethical beings, not because of what they are.

This is not the same as saying that we can't know them. Being unable to know animals allows for the possibility of animals being different, but not lesser, beings. It says nothing about a scale. When Thomas Nagel sets out to show that we can't possibly know what it is like to be a bat,[14] he isn't making any claim about what bats are, or what we are. Only what we aren't, and therefore can't know. We don't do sonar. How can we imagine being a creature whose being in the world is based on possessing such an unfamiliar mechanism to apprehend their environment? We can analogise about the sonar we use for finding what we can't see, but those are machines that compensate for the senses we rely on. The world of the bat is not our world, not even accessible to our imagination, nor even our language. We can, he says, only imagine what it would be like *for us* to be a bat, not what it is like for a bat to be a bat. Perhaps it is only possible for me to imagine what it would be like for me to be you, not for you to be you. This isn't an ethical distinction between bats and me, or you and me, but an abyss of knowledge that we simply can't cross. It is not, in itself, a quality distinction.

Animals do things we know in ourselves. They run, walk, sleep. But what is it like for them? What is their running world like? Bunty dreams – I see her sleeping and she twitches and mews. Sometimes she bursts awake, actually leaps to her feet and stares around her, as if transported from somewhere where things were quite else and she was doing something different. It takes her a moment to settle down, and recollect where she is. All this I recognise from my own dreaming and waking. But if she dreams, what is it like being a cat dreaming? We turn our firing synapses into narrative either when we are sleeping or when we recollect the images when we wake. Cats? I don't know, though I am clear that there is a waking state and a sleeping state and sometimes an indication that something is going on in the cat's brain in her sleeping state. Still, when she jolts into wakefulness, I stroke her, calm her down with whispers, remind her which world she has suddenly arrived in, as if I knew what she was going through, and she settles down, as if she were reassured. Even less than what I know about her, is what I think she knows about me. I have language to imagine her world. I don't know if cats imagine anything at all. What I don't know, and what I don't know about what she knows, is almost everything. Nevertheless, we get along well enough together, sharing the house and the world, however differently. As far as I can tell.

Jacques Derrida, convinced of the singularity and consciousness of his little cat, also knows that not only are they not like us, and that the differences are not about this or that faculty. He considers there to be an absolute rupture. 'I have . . . thus never believed in some homogeneous continuity between what calls itself man and what he calls the animal.'[15] There is an abyssal difference between us and them, he insists: between the ones who give names, and the ones who are named. The very fact that we see them from our point of view, our very interaction with them creates the differences: 'The relations are at once intertwined and abyssal, and they can never be totally objectified.' We can't really know animals, though we can make educated guesses by watching them in various ways – we know that animals are beyond us because we are doing the looking. We 'cannot look around our own corner: it is hopeless curiosity that wants to know what other kinds of intellects and perspectives there might be' says Nietzsche.[16]

But it is irresistible to wonder nevertheless. When Bunty looks at me, and I look at her, we are perhaps each gazing into the abyss and by acknowledging it – through the looking, the staring, the mutual muteness – we are also acknowledging the fact of the other. Derrida says that there are some

texts signed by people who have no doubt seen, observed, analysed, reflected on the animals, but who have never been seen by the animal. Their gaze has never intersected with that of an animal directed at them (forget about their being naked). If, indeed, they did happen to be seen seen furtively by the animal one day, they took no (thematic, theoretical, or philosophical) account of it. They neither wanted nor had the capacity to draw any systematic consequence from the fact that the animal could, facing them, look at them, clothed or naked, and in a word, without a word, address them. They have taken no account of the fact that what they call 'animal' could look at them, and address them from down there, from a wholly other origin.[17]

This text, the one you are currently reading, is signed by someone who even admits that it is an intermittent but continuing surprise to her that other people actually exist within their own consciousness. I confess that I have sometimes to remind myself that everyone I come across, those I am close to, those I pass by on the street, has an inner life of their own. I suppose it without thinking about it, but when I do actually think about it, I am brought up short, quite taken aback by the fact of all that inner reality, so many inner realities going on around me. So too with Bunty. When I catch her looking at me, I am sharply reminded of her innerness, though I know I can't really grasp it. What she is thinking I will never apprehend, and yet I look back into her eyes for as long as she will allow me to and wish, hopelessly, as Nietzsche quite rightly says, I could get a clue.

'What, what, what?' I say to her, pleading. But, like Alice's Cheshire Cat, she just looks at me from inside her head, and, even as I look back at her, disappears from view.

PART THREE

WATCHING

When I asked Zahavi about experimentation, he told me, 'Of course we do experiments with babblers. We ask them to come, and we tell them what we want them to do and the question we are dealing with. And they do it.' I will never be sure Zahavi wasn't serious.

Vinciane Despret, *Ethology between Empathy, Standpoint and Perspectivism: the Case of the Arabian Babblers*

5

GETTING NEARER NATURE

At the Zoo

The various stuffed, retrieved, story-fied and cartooned animals in my young life were supplemented by all the beasts of the forest, jungle and desert. Every day, beginning in my pram, when it wasn't pouring with rain, my mother took me to the nearby London Zoo in Regent's Park to pass the time for me and her. On Sunday mornings I went there with my father when the zoo was closed, except to members, and the keepers were on hand to take us round to the back of the cages and wrap a snake around my neck. The zoo, that particular zoo, its animals and its topography, was embedded in my brain the way that language is, growing in me as I grew with it. And it remains there vividly. It is a particularly tangled language because what I learned at the zoo was a language that was not of the animals (how could it be?), but a version of my own human kind, one structured by reminiscence of colonialism and fantasy, and the fact that they, the creatures, were all in the wrong place, often in the wrong way, purely, it seemed, for my entertainment and interest. It's not without relevance that the alternative to the zoo on rainy days was often Selfridges, the department store: another place we could spend most of the day, wander around, look, imagine and wonder at objects from all over the world. Both were city spectacles for a mother with a small child. Alternate days out.

The zoo back then was a terrible place for the animals, especially the wilderness ones. The lions and tigers were housed in Victorian iron cages with thick black bars which bulged pregnantly at the front, giving the viewer the thrilling sense that the beast inside was getting closer as it prowled the perimeter of its world. Inside the Lion House, at the back, the cages, which the animals entered through a lockable door at feeding time, at night and if it was wet, were plain, flat-fronted and separated each from the other by institutional brick. As if to enhance both the reality of post-war austerity and the sense of passive spectacle, there was a sign on a wall between the cages that said not 'Beware of the Dangerous Lions', but 'Beware of Pickpockets'. The indoor lion and tiger cages were a series of proscenium stages, enclosed in a long, drab theatre with a high arched roof. Directly opposite the bars of the cages were rows of raked wooden benches where people sat and stared at the pacing beasts, as both waited expectantly for feeding time. I sat there being passed sandwiches by my mother and watched great hunks of red meat being poked through the bars by the keepers of the lions and tigers. The animals were let into the indoor enclosure beforehand and knew that they were about to be fed. They roamed up and down purposefully, not at their usual languid rate of creatures that knew they were getting nowhere, nor did they sprawl drearily on the concrete floor as they did outside. With feeding time on them, they moved faster, restlessly (what's keeping lunch?), so you could see the muscles in their thighs working. They rumbled in their throats, a sound that threatened to become a roar, and which rose and echoed around the high-beamed ceiling before drifting down over the audience for them to make of the echo whatever threat and excitement they could. When the bloody chunk of beef was finally pushed through the bars at the end of huge toasting forks (a little teasing went on by keepers who knew that they were showmen as much as caretakers, and knew, too, that even lions want their lunch to be interesting), the great cats, each in their own cage, hunkered down to it, their necks sunk between their shoulder blades, high and sharp, their teeth tearing at the flesh, almost making love to it, immobilised with their outspread claws.

Parents made jokes to their children about table manners, or encouraged the imagination with tales of faraway human beings torn apart in the jungle (lions and tigers always stalked in jungles rather than roamed over grasslands) by these mangy man-eaters. And there was always the story to be recited or remembered from home of the terrible fate of Albert Ramsbottom, told in a broad Lancashire accent on scratchy 78 records by Stanley Holloway. Albert met his end at Blackpool, but I could only envisage the sorry tale happening in front of me in the lion house at London Zoo.

Jungles, cautionary tales, lessons in table manners and broad comedy were the essential ingredients of a visit to the lion house, along with the smell of animal that lingered on the damp cold concrete. I remember most powerfully, not the cats themselves, but that smell and the glossy black bars of their cages. These days the big cats are housed in what is called a 'Pavilion'; there is a moat, landscaping and open air, and round the other side, at the back, thick glass, but those cages and bars they replaced, ornately coming together into a dome at the top, serried and regular at the front, are my real recollection of the lions and tigers of the London Zoo. They were sinister, and teased the observer with the threat of what lay behind such solid, wrought protection. If they were to get out . . . they said very clearly, offering a little secure mayhem. The spaces between each bar were glimpses of the wild: an alternation of captivity and freedom, of safe watching and imminent danger. Possibly, a small child might have slipped through the bars and certainly the front leg of a lion could easily get through and swipe you to death with those deadly claws. That was why there were additional railings in front of the cages. Even the black bars were not quite enough security against the lords of the jungle. I think the actual lions and tigers were poor, slow, captive creatures, without expectation or curiosity, demented with boredom, lack of proper company and range, but the bars were fierce and deadly and made whatever paced behind them into monstrous threats to life and limb, as least for the spectators.

The lion cages became the shame of London Zoo when public opinion finally got round to empathising with the miserable lot of captive animals rather than simply laughing at their amusing (though often, in reality, psychotic) antics. In those days elephants danced in skirts, dogs jumped through hoops of fire and lions sat up and begged at the crack of a whip in circuses all over the country, and hardly anyone blinked an eye, or mentioned dignity or cruelty. In the zoos, polar bears and other wild creatures developed obsessive-compulsive behaviours, biting at their fur and feathers, walking to and fro in mad bursts and nodding their heads repetitively, and for all most people knew that was just how animals behaved. Eventually, the concrete and black iron lion cages came to represent suffering rather than a lingering imperialist show of the power to incarcerate creatures from all parts of the world for the entertainment of those who waited at home for the benefits. The 1950s, when I was growing up, was a last gasp of insouciance, before consciences slowly began to prick, until gradually, over the next two or three decades, different values were at least embedded in the statute books and in how people were allowed to treat and be amused by non-human animals. There must have been pity and anger from some people, but no one mentioned it to me, and I wasn't so sensitive a child as to see it for myself rather than take my pleasure in watching the exotic. At any rate, the zoos and the circuses slid into a crisis, and by the turn of the twenty-first century were obliged to change their ways and pay lip-service to a consideration of animal welfare beyond the provision of food and a roof. Undoubtedly the keepers held their charges in great affection, knew their needs and tried to enhance their lives as much as they could. But the concrete zoo remained small and concrete and remote from the lives that many of the animals would have led when they were captured, or the only kind of existence those born in it could or would ever know. And there were very few constraints about the kind of entertainment and use we thought we were entitled to get out of animals.

Back then, in my childhood, I watched the chimpanzees' tea party – held on a small grassy patch every day, if it wasn't raining, at 3 p.m. A table and chairs, tea, sandwiches and the collusion of the keepers to enchant us children at the chaos which ensued as the chimps grappled with implements like teapots, teacups and napkins, for which they had no use or need, and made an unholy mess, spilling milk, taking the insides out of the sandwiches, diving face first into the sugar bowl and being told off in pantomime finger-wags by their straight men, the keepers. It was carnival, a delicious topsy-turvy of civilised manners. The children shrieked with pleasure at the naughtiness that they themselves had to keep in check. Then it was time for an elephant or a camel ride. The elephant would be led from its house to the strip of tarmac it was to pace up and down for an hour or so, carrying adults and children on its back in a contraption that held us seated on either side of its back, though I think you faced front on the camel. Watching the elephant and camel being led along the paths humans walked was the most exciting thing, that and the fact that you had to climb the wooden steps to get on to the animal. Elephant and camel waited with immense patience while they were loaded up and then, led on a leash by a keeper, they walked, swaying (each in a different way), along the path, turned around and walked back to the wooden steps where we got off. Uneventful, but somewhat dream-inducing. The rides were an even clearer imperial moment than the caged lions provided, a brief taste of a glorious past when white men learned the ways of those they colonised and used them for leisure purposes: hunting tigers or entertaining the children back home. Perhaps the elephant and the camel were pleased enough at this break in the monotony of their day. I can't say. As far as I know they never reared up or bolted or threatened the squealing humans who rode on their backs. But then animals are almost certainly nicer than people.

It didn't feel political either, to me, or to my mother or father, neither of whom, being just a first generation away from the shtetl, had fantasies of empire. It was simply uncomplicated, enjoyable fun. I was deliriously happy at the zoo and watching the animals was among my most treasured pastimes. I counted Guy the Gorilla a friend. I stood in front of his cage every day and looked into his eyes which looked back at me when I managed to catch his attention. And because Guy looked back, I imagined that we knew each other well. In reality, the eyes were pretty blank, looking but not taking an interest in the sameness he was offered day after day. Perhaps this is how Bunty looks at me, not looking at all, but just gazing in a quite different way. Guy had arrived at the zoo four months after I was born, having been captured in the French Cameroon as an infant – his mother presumably having been killed. He went first to Paris Zoo and was then traded to the London Zoo for a tiger. He lived alone in his barred quarters for twenty-five years, until a female, Lomi, was found for him, though they never mated. The current website for the zoo tells how Guy would 'gently' scoop up sparrows that landed in his cage and peer at them before letting them go. He was a gentle creature, but then gorillas are. He was also grossly under-stimulated. Mostly he sat with his legs splayed and his arms by his side or masturbating in a desultory fashion, and stared out through the bars at the people who stared back at him. He seemed to me old and wise, although in fact he was incarcerated and most likely depressed. That stare I most recognise as despair, which I've seen in the eyes of humans, but I suppose I'm being anthropomorphic. I thought we were friends. I loved him, and told him things.

The zoo, as I remember it, before it was reconstructed as a more acceptable breeding and educational environment rather than pure spectacle, was at one with Britain of the 1950s. It's difficult to reconstitute it as I felt it then, so many layers of thought and knowledge having been added, but the sense that it was the colour of concrete, dank and drab is impossible to shake off. I loved the animals and felt completely familiar and at home in the zoo, but looking back it was a cheerless place, for all that it was built in the pretty green space of Regent's Park. So was London cheerless, still dotted with bombsites and almost palpably convalescent from the recent war we heard so much about from our families. The zoo was uniformly grey. You walked around a network of tarmacked paths, through the tunnel under a canal bridge, and stopped at cages made of concrete and iron and indoor animal houses of brick with concrete floors. It was practical for keeping the animals clean, but no colour was permitted; nothing, as I recall, was painted. There was straw and rubber tyres for the monkeys and apes to play with, and a concrete pool for the seals to splash in, some areas of grass here and there, a concrete trench around the elephants and rhinoceros to keep them in and us out, and some fake wall paintings of mammoths and bison in the tunnel under the canal. But everything, in my recollection, was as grey as the rest of the world I inhabited. Even the brilliantly coloured parrots and cockatoos were kept in a sort of shed that seemed to do its utmost to damp down their glory. Actually, there were contemporary architectural masterpieces in the zoo: the circular, white-painted concrete and black bars of the gorilla house and the reinforced concrete, grade-one listed, swirling walkways of the penguin pool were both designed by Berthold Lubetkin in the 1930s and are still considered modernist masterpieces. The director of the London Zoo in the 1950s, George Cansdale, resisted the moves to have both buildings listed as National Trust treasures because, fine design though they were, he didn't think they paid enough attention to the needs of the animals they housed. He was overridden: human aesthetics trumped their functional failings. In fairness, the penguin house, at least, does look as if it is a stylised attempt to consider the natural environment of the penguins, who have to struggle up and down its walkways just as they have to on Antarctic glaciers. The snow would be softer, but perhaps the concrete is less cold on their feet. Who knows if the penguins consider this a good exchange?

On the Telly

In addition to all the caged and captive animals I delighted in gazing at, in what was my real life if not theirs, there were, increasingly, animals on television. In fact, I only specifically remember one animal from my childhood TV watching – I'm not counting Silver, Lassie, Rin Tin Tin and Tonto who were, after all, actors. What I actually recall with the special soft-focus clarity reserved for the distant past are the human beings who presented the animals. Some of these were zoo-keepers. Cansdale, the same man who disapproved of listing the beautiful but functionally dubious penguin pool, often brought small or baby animals from the zoo into the studio on various programmes to show to us 'boys and girls' who turned on the black-and-white TV at teatime. He was moustached, neatly rounded and avuncular, a kindly, smiling sort of man who spoke in received pronunciation directly to us and to the animals he introduced while holding them in his arms. He even chuckled. People sometimes did then. It appears he was exactly as he seemed: married for fifty-two years to the same woman, a regular at his local parish church and a man of quiet but insistent principle, who took the children of his village to accompany him to the studio, two by two, but in strict turn.

He was not popular at the zoo, the administration of which has often been seen as a microcosm of the times[*] – and at that time it represented the harsh, needy period that people were suffering through after the war. The humans at the zoo employed some of the same solutions the rest of the country had found to alleviate the effects of wartime and post-war austerity. When Cansdale took over as director he discovered that the ticket collectors were pocketing about 10 per cent of the entry fees, and keepers regarded it as their right to take home the best cuts of meat and quality fruit and vegetables to their families rather than feed them to the animals. Turning a blind eye was endemic and institutional. Cansdale was deeply resented when he put a stop to it. One night, working late, he went into the reptile house and when he turned on the light, discovered that the floor was crawling with cockroaches. He was very surprised when the keepers strongly resisted his order to have the place de-infested. It turned out that they were actually selling cockroaches for sixpence each. Biddy Baxter, who wrote his obituary in 1993 for the *Independent*, doesn't say who was buying them

[*]For example, *The Ark*, an extraordinary 1993 BBC TV documentary directed by Molly Dineen.

or for what purpose: collectors, schoolboys, mad scientists, beetle aficionados, food manufacturers? Cansdale was got rid of in 1953 – the trustees abolished his post rather than risk the scandal of an outright sacking. Not only was he unpopular at the zoo but he was disapproved of by academic zoologists who thought that showing children animals on television in his amiable sort of way was too populist.

Cansdale stood behind a table and held on to his wriggling charges as best he could, speaking to camera about them and why they looked and behaved as they did, how they differed according to their needs and niches, at least conveying to us that all of the creatures came from and were adapted to somewhere other than a zoo, that they were representatives of real lives lived away from cages. We learned ways of looking and thinking about animals we never would have from walking around the tarmacked paths. And he laughed when they bit him. But there was no suggestion that the animals he showed us shouldn't be in a zoo. How else could we see them and become educated and enthusiastic about them? If you didn't live in the country and spend your time peering into ponds and collecting beetles, George Cansdale offered a knowledgeable and affectionate glimpse of the Other, even if it was painted by the exoticism and incarceration of the zoo.

In the late 1950s, Desmond Morris, a zoologist employed at Regent's Park, who was to turn up later in another guise, continued Cansdale's elementary introduction to animal anatomy and behaviour with *Zoo Time*, which was broadcast from the grounds of the zoo itself. He had that one particular animal I remember from those days on television, as most of us who watched it must: Congo, the chimpanzee, appeared as Morris's sidekick and was given artist's materials to paint abstract pictures that were admired, so it was said, by Picasso, or proof to those who abhorred 'modern' art, that any chimp could paint as well as Picasso. Congo was employed to give us a close-up view of an animal that was profoundly connected to us human children. It was an early, gentle lesson in basic evolutionary theory. Morris treated him like a child-friend, told him off when he was naughty but laughed, too, and showed us how similar Congo was to us, as well as his limitations in human terms. The question of how much like us Congo was, and why that should be, was always hovering over the jocularity. They were educational and they were cosy, those programmes, but they nevertheless featured captive animals for our human edification. Though we were reminded that there was also a 'natural' habitat for these creatures, we saw animals in the charge of humans and, again, there was no suggestion that there was any problem with that, any more than that we were in the charge of adults. It's very difficult to shift that idea of evolution as analogous to a child growing to adulthood – as in less to more, progress, better and better. It was clear, however, that while they were in charge of the animals, both Cansdale and Morris had respect and affection for them, and that was an important impression to give to developing minds.

I was, even at the time, not as comfortable with a programme that started in 1960 called *Animal Magic*. It probably thought of itself as educational, but disguised it with a fictional narrative that starred Johnny Morris, well known as a children's storyteller on the radio. Morris played a downtrodden fictional zoo-keeper who was filmed talking and play-acting at the animals in the cages who were given funny and 'appropriate' voices to respond with by Morris when he was back editing in the studio. The animals became comic people, talking in stereotyped posh or cockney accents, with human, not animal concerns. They were like the cartoon creatures who were given animal features while behaving not like themselves but like us – trapped, as it were, inside their inadequate bodies (as, of course, we children were). I didn't like the programme; it wasn't interesting.

There was something quite wrong about it, though I couldn't have properly defined it. I wanted real animals, and someone authoritative telling me about them. Of course, I was probably too old in 1960 at thirteen, to be much amused, but I can't say that I was morally or scientifically outraged so much as feeling in some way cheated. Johnny Morris is quoted later as having similar thoughts about the programme: 'Some hated it because it was anthropomorphic. And anthropomorphism is one of the deadly sins. To make animals appear as though they were talking was totally and absolutely unscientific. Not only that, but it was a cheap and facile way to entertain boys and girls. To indulge in such worthless underhand tricks week after week was a disgrace.'

In the mid-1950s a new kind of programme about animals appeared on television. The words 'wild' and 'wildlife' began to be used, where they couldn't have been before in the zoo-bound, studio-bound programmes. The new words came with investigations using portable cameras to find, track and observe animals where they actually lived. It was a substantial intellectual shift in the idea of educational entertainment. Previously, field studies were for professionals: people went to where the animals were, either as hunters to shoot them or scientists to observe them, after which they mounted heads on their walls or wrote their findings up for professional journals, but no one had thought to include the general public in the dissemination of the knowledge gained, let alone the investigations themselves. New film technology, lightweight cameras and sound equipment were certainly initially responsible – we can do it so let's do it – but once it was possible and actually happening on television screens, a real change of consciousness gradually began to take place.

In the cinema there were the Disney wildlife films, but they were not so very far from Johnny Morris's human impositions on the natural world. They were called *True Life Adventures*, and although they were neither true, nor even sometimes depictions of life, they *were* adventures in the sense that the film-makers were adventurous with reality. The Disney movies felt ersatz even while watching them: that over-scripted voice-over and what we saw on the screen always meshed so neatly, not a moment's hesitation, no search, no doubt. At least there was a sense with Cansdale and Desmond Morris that the animals might do something unexpected *because* they were animals. In the Disney films, everything happened exactly as it was supposed to – according to the human script. No chance, as happened on TV sometimes (if you were lucky) of anyone being bitten or a baby elephant taking a pee in the wrong place. Even when the films weren't downright invention, the animals were as captive in the lens of the camera as the lions pacing in their cages at the zoo. The new television programmes were different partly, and strangely, because they weren't in the glorious, glossy Technicolor of Disney, and because we watched them at home, eating supper. They were domestic and although they were, of course, edited, the rough edges and accidents were often left in, unlike Disney's remote, superior productions. Jungles and grasslands may have entered our understanding as being entirely in shades of grey, but oddly, now that everything we see on the television is in enhanced colour, they never felt less real for it.

To begin with, they were husband-and-wife affairs, a strange fact that greatly enhanced the programmes for the suburban, domestic audience, making the adventure a little less remote, if a husband and wife could do it together. Hans and Lotte Hass were uncannily similar to Armand and Michaela Denis: a stolid, serious and knowledgeable, though besotted, middle-aged man was accompanied by a glamorous, brave, adventurous and younger blond wife who 'humanised' the jungle or the sea, and the zoology. The difference between the two couples was that Hans and Lotte were underwater, while Armand and Michaela tramped over the earth. This gave Lotte the advantage of being beautiful in a wetsuit, but Michaela was dedicated to elegance and renewed her lipstick (clearly bright red even in black and white) frequently when preparing to meet the last white rhino in existence or capture an orphaned baby elephant. The women were followers, always, but kept up, while the men admired the gumption of their women, and so did we. The idea was that they could have sat at home and waited for their man to return from his investigations of the grubby and dangerous world, but they followed him gamely, learning the necessary skills while at the same time providing a ladylike or womanly take on what they were seeing. Apart from the undoubted gender stereotyping, it was a format that allowed a conversation to go on between husband and wife, which enhanced the sense that we were looking in on someone's passion. They were excited at coming across an unknown fish or a member of a vanishing species, to each other, not to us. The voice-over (of Hans and Armand, with interpolations by the wives) was accompanied by the gesticulations and excited glances on screen (the film was usually silent with jungle sounds edited in) between the stalking land-based couple, and the breathless eye contact under-water. It was intimate and gave a sense of real time, of being there and of being astonished. But it was also domestic. The couples would sometimes gently disagree or make mild fun of each other as if they were discussing the morning's news or each other's little ways, rather than some exotic creature far away or deep down. It kept the wild and the tame in a balanced relationship. And from time to time, they spoke to us directly from the studio, all dressed up for the telly. A clip on the BBC Wildlife website from 1954 shows Armand and Michaela at the beginning of their second series. He is in a suit, with slicked-back but slightly wayward hair and round owlish glasses – a scientist scrubbed up, plump, almost comically dowdy – while Michaela sits beside him wearing an unequivocal evening dress (perhaps of her own design, as she'd been a dress designer before her marriage to Armand), possibly silk shantung, low-cut and standing a little proud at the shoulders with a tight bodice, dangly earrings and fiercely coiffed blond hair. They both sit with their hands neatly in their laps and Michaela looks at Armand, smiling toothily (it was her only physical flaw – no orthodontistry back in 1954) while he speaks in a strong, continental accent:

> This is wonderful, to be back here in the television studios of the BBC . . . It has been a pleasant surprise, pleasant beyond any expectation to find how many friends we've made . . . We've been flooded with many letters of welcome and displays of affection. I want to thank you all for it, but Michaela can do it much more prettily than I can.

The camera pans to Michaela, who shows even more teeth. 'Thank you from the bottom of our hearts. I'm trying to answer all the letters, and I'm doing it a little each day.'[1]

There isn't the slightest whiff of insincerity, even watching now; they are moistly grateful and genuinely delighted, it seems, to have been taken to the hearts of the British television public. It looks naive and so unpolished compared to the shiny professional gushing with which twenty-first-century presenters thank their audiences for watching and keeping their viewing figures and salaries up. Seeing Armand and Michaela in 'real' clothes, dolled up, is a kind of present to their audience. We were so used to seeing them in khaki safari suits, though hers fitted very much better than his, and she wore her shorts to considerably more effect. But they are awkward here in proper outfits for television, in a formal setting, like the visual oddness of someone who suddenly takes off the spectacles they ordinarily wear, and are all the more vulnerable and trustworthy for that. The clothes are very different, but their niceness and mutuality is just the same as when we see them creeping through the bush or signalling to each other.

Of course, they do interfere in the wild and capture the baby elephant, remarking, as a makeshift cage is put together to contain it, on the wonderful ability of their native assistants to find whatever materials are needed from what is available in the bush. They were white, Western, middle-class, of their time. And so were the children who watched – I can't recall minding about or questioning the senior, educational role of the men of each couple, and inasmuch as I daydreamed of being part of the safari, I imagined taking his role rather than hers, without any sense of incongruity. The animal world was still unquestionably to be managed by humans, but aside from sentimental captures, these humans at least tried to keep their presence to a minimum, not only to get their pictures, but because the pictures they wanted required the animals to be wild and in the wild. There was an implicit and growing understanding that animals could only really be seen for what they were in their natural habitat.

It was going to become increasingly clear that observation of 'the wild' or anything else is a tricky thing (the physicists had already discovered this), and that what we see is never natural, by the very fact of our seeing it. This is also the question of what we see being always conditioned by what we think. In some sense we can't see animals at all, not even if they are in the wild and we conceal ourselves, because the voice-over – on screen, but most vitally in our heads – will always be there, shaping the shards, the fleeting images of the whole life of a creature, into a complete picture of our own, based on our partial and biased knowledge and understanding. We can't know what we don't know, which is the real life of animals from the point of view of animals. Armand and Michaela creep through the forest and come across a sighting, a rhino standing still, and immediately we are told what it is the animal is doing. It is standing still. Listening. Listening out, probably, for the human footsteps, or scenting wrongness on the air, they tell us. If we tried this with people we would know how flawed our view and understanding was likely to be. But of course, we have tried this with people, and actually haven't had a clue about our flawed understanding, causing all sorts of misunderstandings and catastrophes, and it doesn't stop us from doing it, at each stage knowing a little more, but still not knowing what we don't know because like all animals we are curious, we want to look and to suppose that by looking we can see and therefore know. Perhaps, if we'd been offered still photographs, or even Dürer drawings of animals, instead of moving pictures and a narrative, we might have gazed on them and learned something without making too many assumptions about the subject of the pictures themselves, but the fact that you could have a camera and take it to faraway places and point it at rare creatures living their lives was irresistible, and impossible not to conceive of as new and better knowledge. On our behalf, Armand and Michaela stalked and Hans and Lotte swam, and brought me, a post-domestic child, as close as I could be got to the mystery of the Other living its life. Considerably closer, perhaps, than watching animals pace in concrete cages with signs warning 'Beware of Pickpockets'.

A series called *Zoo Quest* began in 1954 hosted by an achingly young David Attenborough, who had the bright televisual idea of straddling the separate strands of the BBC's nature offerings: the zoo and the wild. It was a decidedly uncomfortable position, as we would see it today. Each series centred on a filmed safari to a distant, exotic country to find and capture a particular rare animal for the London Zoo. To Sierra Leone for snakes; to Borneo to fetch a komodo dragon – of which the *Zoo Quest* camera caught the first-ever sighting on television. During the search, the camera took in and examined the local habitat, the other animals and the people living in the area, so just as the winds of change had started blowing we were presented with a wildlife programme which mimicked an imperialist habit going back centuries, where one of the locals (a non-human animal at this point in British history) from a distant land was taken out of the wild and brought, captive, to live as part of a collection for study and amusement back at home.

Each programme began in the studio, where David Attenborough, as enthusiastic as now and genuinely boyish then, in his first natural-history job, described the quest and how it was going, before returning us to the film of the adventure and speaking the voice-over. In the final episode of each series we were shown the captive animal live in the studio, in a cage or enclosure, around which a panel of experts discussed it. In retrospect, as dismal a concept of engagement of the natural world as I can imagine, but then it was exciting and morally untroubling to most people. A travelogue, a wildlife film, an adventure whose goal was always in doubt, and at last, the proof of the pudding, a living, breathing creature that we had seen being looked for, eventually spotted, filmed and captured in its natural habitat, the mysterious black-and-white jungle, now pacing and snarling in a cage, right there, live in the brightly lit television studio down the road, as it were, at Alexandra Palace, while you sat on the floor at home eating your fish-paste or Marmite sandwich.

David Attenborough, charming and knowledgeable, pretty much took charge of natural history for the future. Over the decades, the ground rules changed about the politics of interacting with natives of all species, animal and human. The equipment became increasingly refined so that it became possible to see things never seen before in ways that are less and less intrusive to those being watched. The appetite of the public for observing the lives of animals has grown so that entire channels are devoted to wildlife films, and no expense is spared to find new and startling ways of looking at non-human creatures. You watch the Attenborough blockbusters with your jaw dropping, always astonished anew by novel ways of seeing animals, seeing more of them in every way, but especially in ways we have never seen before. Now we can see everything, but there is a new sense that something is always hidden from us, and if only we are technological enough, we will reveal it. We even watch subsidiary documentaries about how the miraculous revelations are achieved by naturalists and infinitely patient, heroic cameramen, who are now the performers of prodigious feats, as the old hunters and explorers were. Perhaps they are becoming even more important than the animals they film. We have, after all, seen almost everything there is to see, by now, and it is the humans and what they are prepared to do to get the shot that is beginning to become the story. As to whether the hidden aspects of animal lives they reveal are more 'real' than what we used to see, I'm not sure. The lights and angles of the equipment present a spectacular that has less to do with nature than with our renewed capacity to look. It may not so much show us reality better as distort it more brilliantly. *Life in the Freezer*, *The Blue Planet*, *The Life of Mammals*, *Planet Earth* and others are multi-million-pound fantasias, producing a huge return on their outlay for the BBC and co-producers, beyond the wettest dreams for profit and glory of the Disney *True Life Adventure* producers.

Recently, there has been a return to a more modest yet equally popular version of nature on television. It is almost a reappearance of the black-and-white days of Armand and Michaela, though the technology and sophistication is unimaginably greater. *Springwatch* is a children's programme for adults (actually, for that guarantee of the neither-here-nor-there, the 'family') which goes out on the BBC for a month in mid-May and June each year, for an hour at 8 p.m. Monday to Thursday. A huge outside-broadcast team moves into a nature reserve and sets up webcams in whatever nests they can find: songbird, raptor, field-mouse; cameramen are positioned in hides day and night to catch local badgers and foxes – really anything that moves on more than two legs, or has wings, and is in the process of reproducing. The nation settles down to a feast of chicks and cubs doing their lovable, fighting and growing thing, being fed by exhausted and devoted or neglectful parents, being eaten, eating each other, surviving and leaving the nest to get ready to provide the substance of next year's *Springwatch*. If you want you can follow the goings-on of your favourite creatures, moment by moment, day and night, on your computer; otherwise each evening the presenters will summarise the events of the past twenty-four hours.

The human presenters are crucial. Cute babies alone aren't quite enough. Until recently, Bill Oddie, a short, spherical and very grumpy ex-comedian in his late sixties, who has an amateur passion for bird-watching, sat on a bench, or in a shed full of monitors, commenting on what was happening, alongside a modern version of Michaela and Lotte. Kate Humble is a wild-haired blond beauty to Oddie's beast. It always seemed to me as if Oddie might leave the script and say something just awful, for which she would have to apologise. It was a little like watching Hepburn and Tracey, though much less witty and well dressed. Oddie had no problem at all with anthropo-morphism. Almost a latter-day, unrepentant Johnny Morris, he would relate difficult matings to human gender battles and stereotypes, talk about birds getting 'a leg over', relate a female eagle's protection of her nest to women's obsession with the domestic and decorative, for all the world as if it were still 1954. Watching a pair of sparrows mating, he observed, 'The female is asking for it – and getting it basically. She was fluttering her wings and pretending to be a child –

that's kind of weird when you think about it. Oh, and again. She is doing that wing-fluttering thing like that as if to say "I am a baby, feed me"; she is getting quite the opposite basically. That's a wing-trembler she's just had there.'

While watching the mating habits of stag beetles, Oddie narrated: 'He crash-lands on top of a likely looking lady. There's a bit of luck. One thing is sure, this boy is horny.' After a fight between two male beetles for a female, he put on a mimsy 'female' voice and said, "Come on, big boy, come and get it."

There were complaints, but, as much as the cute chicks, Oddie's anthropomorphism was a great factor in the popularity of the programme. Partly, it was the joy of watching car-crash television; partly his anthropomorphism voiced the real responses of a large proportion of viewers. Serious zoologists are not allowed to compare animal social behaviour to human society, but everyone secretly does (doubtless even many of the serious zoologists about their own dogs and cats), and the audience rejoiced in it. But underneath the jocular misrepresentation of animals, there seemed to be a genuine bitterness, something quite disturbing, and it wasn't surprising to learn that Oddie suffers from bouts of depression. We watched as Kate, wide-eyed, ever-smiling, seemed to struggle not to let her embarrassment show on camera. Oddie left the programme in 2008, just when filming was due to start, perhaps having a bad patch. He has been replaced by another man, Chris Packham, still cheeky and chirpy, but younger and more manageable. In 2009, even without Oddie, the first programme of *Springwatch* was watched by 3.9 million viewers. A year earlier, one Monday night, 300,000 people saw the programme, while only 90,000 people tuned in to *Big Brother*, a programme that also uses webcams to observe the unscripted behaviour of animals. *Springwatch* and the Attenborough masterpieces sit side by side quite comfortably, fulfilling a variety of audience desires. But the 'serious' programmes are no less emotionally manipulative, for all their apparent scientific virtue.

In addition to *Springwatch* and the David Attenborough series, these days wild animals are followed in their own habitats throughout their lives and over generations by dedicated zoologists with cameras. Often the material they record is made available for television wildlife programmes, with the result that the boundary between scientific fieldwork and entertainment becomes blurred, as the entertainment pays for the fieldwork, and the fieldwork begins to have to take account of the needs of entertainment. A serious, ongoing, sixteen-year study of six colonies of meerkats in the South African Kalahari is run by Professor Tim Clutton-Brock, head of Cambridge University Zoology Department. In 2005 it became the subject of a television series, *Meerkat Manor*, filmed by Oxford Scientific Films, and meerkats became international stars. Here and in the United States there have been four series following Clutton-Brock's study groups. They were known by name, their matings and territorial battles were presented as soap operas, through editing away from the field and without violating the scientific nature of the study. Everyone was happy, and we now have a new adorable species to rival higher primates and penguins, the previous wildlife celebrity species. Meerkats have become toys and ornaments; they front television advertisements, increase tourism to the Kalahari and are still the subjects of a serious and conscientious whole-life study. Let's hope everyone wins. We all know much more about meerkats, and although people will flock to see them in zoos, if they can't afford to go out to see them in the wild, there is no attempt to capture meerkats to study in the laboratory, or to bring more of them into captivity for the added pleasure of their adoring public. Meerkats in the wild are what we want to see. The public and the scientists know that we can only witness how they really are (their natural cuteness or zoological and evolutionary features) if they are free to be where they are supposed to be and behaving as they would behave if no one was there at all. But what we most adore has to become an object, so the toys, keyrings and puppets will keep coming. Does this play back into the scientific study, or change how we view the actual animals? It must. It's another way in which it's impossible to look without altering what is being looked at.

People are present in the Kalahari meerkats' lives, virtually all the time. You can even, at a price, join the study, either as a graduate volunteer or as a fee-paying amateur, though you will be carefully overseen and trained. In its brochure, the organisation Earthwatch, which conjoins holidays and eco-study, offers anyone who can run well enough to keep up with their subjects a meerkat study-fortnight, and the chance to mingle with real scientists for $3,950, not including airfares. You can observe and work with

six habituated colonies of meerkats in this 25-square-kilometer reserve. You'll learn the techniques of radiotracking and focal sampling, GPS referencing, as well as how to weigh meerkats. This data will help evaluate how cooperative breeding affects the survival of both pups and helpers. You will also investigate interactions between the meerkats and a kleptoparasitic bird species, the forktailed drongo. Supplementing the meerkat studies, you'll help conduct biodiversity, invertebrates, and plant surveys and spend some time recording the size and activity of social bird colonies, like pied babblers and weavers, in response to rainfall levels. You'll also help outreach efforts to assist the local community primary school – all this against a backdrop of gemsbok, hartebeest, springbok, duiker, steenbok, bat-eared foxes, three kinds of mongooses, many birds, and the fantastic creatures of the Kalahari night.

You will be housed in your own thatched-roof rondavel with a cold-water sink, basic furnishings, electricity, and a fan. Hot showers and flush toilets will be available in a nearby building. The team will be part of ongoing research programs at the reserve and you will have a chance to interact with a variety of researchers – whether discussing their current studies or joining them in a game of volleyball! Breakfast and lunch will be self-serve and a local cook will provide wonderful evening meals, including pasta, fish, chicken, and traditional dishes. Volunteers will be invited to help with food preparation at a weekly barbecue.[2]

The Kalahari meerkats are 'habituated' to humans. This is what makes them visible to the cameras. Before the study can start, they have to be made so used to people being there with their clipboards and cameras that they no longer take any notice – any more than they would if a tree continued to be a tree, after the surprise of it suddenly growing in their territory had worn off. Researchers, paid and paying, spend their days with the families of meerkats, keeping up with their life by sitting on a rock making notes, and running after them when they make a move to find new places to forage, or to go to war with a neighbouring colony. So long as the humans do not feed them or interfere in any way in their day-to-day activities, it is assumed that the meerkats now behave completely naturally while people are around. It is the basis of zoological field studies, but I'm not sure that habituating an animal to human presence necessarily means that its behaviour remains the same as when it wasn't being watched. Just carry on, pay no mind to us, we're only looking.

Watching Elephants
Getting the chance to watch what you can't see by sitting in your room looking out at the garden is irresistible. In 2006 I was asked to

write a travel article for the *Observer* newspaper. With one eye on this distantly projected book, I decided to go on an Earthwatch expedition, not to see the meerkats of the Kalahari – I don't run fast enough – but to join an ongoing study of elephants in Kenya. I was also interested in the idea of Earthwatch.

Just giving money where it is needed has rather gone out of fashion. Almost invariably, in order to get your money for a good cause, someone has to run a race, or cycle round the world, offer you dinner with the stars, write you regular letters telling you how they're getting on, or allow you to pretend to be a scientist. Only some of these things might actually be helpful to those in need of what your money will buy. There are a variety of travel businesses which attach the now essential commercial prefix to their products and offer *eco*-tourism, but they are generally profit-making enterprises. Earthwatch is a registered charity which sets up and funds, or helps to support, peer-reviewed research projects, and offers untrained, non-academic individuals the chance, for a payment equivalent to the cost of an exotic holiday, to contribute money and assist scientists with those projects all over the world. When you sign up with Earthwatch you are not a holidaymaker or a paying customer, but a 'volunteer'; you are encouraged to feel that you've come to work and be of use to the project you choose, as well as to support it financially. You may not have a PhD in zoology but you can look, count and fill in vital data sheets – the kind of labour-intensive data collection that doesn't necessarily need to be done by highly qualified scientists.

The Earthwatch expedition guide had a question on the first page: 'Where do you want to go to make a difference?' followed by more than 130 potential answers. I could have studied Malaysian bats, Sri Lankan temple monkeys, Madagascan lemurs, Australian koala ecology, Costa Rican sea turtles, Britain's basking sharks or those meerkats in the Kalahari. There were two limiting factors: I've got a foot problem and I am indolence personified. Elephants were the answer. Not that they don't range far and move surprisingly fast, but the rules of the Tsavo Wildlife Park, and the common-sense requirement for staying alive in the bush, meant that all the surveying had to be done from a jeep.

My first sighting of elephants as I'd arrived at my destination was startling. It turned out that elephants are red. At least, they are in the spring in southern Kenya's Tsavo wildlife reserve, when they are coloured a rich terracotta from the brilliantly henna-coloured mud and dust in which they wallow. A troop of them were waiting for our group of seven volunteers when we arrived at the hotel. Just beyond the hotel veranda was the edge of the wildlife park, marked by an electric fence, and right there, no more than twenty-five feet away, as we stood looking out, was a waterhole, and around it were fifteen glowing-red elephants, drinking, showering and grazing idly. It might have been staged (there were dark rumours of bananas scattered at night by hotel employees to attract wildlife to the waterhole, and either the hotel or the waterhole didn't *just happen* to be there), but it was thrilling. None of us, from the UK, the US and Europe, was so familiar with wild animals just doing what they do right in front of us that we didn't gasp at the sight. People may not instantly identify with elephants as they do with meerkats; but they are indisputably large, and size is important in the human hierarchy of beloved animals. Very big and quite small are good; the very small (insects and bacteria) are generally excluded from the lovability list. People, of course, unless they are small children of the sort that please us, are also not very high on the adorability scale.

In order to get to the elephants we had paid to watch, we had a six-hour journey south by jeep from Nairobi along the Mombasa road to Tsavo. This was also looking. I peered out of the window as we sped towards our elephants. We passed one shanty town after another, strung out along the side of the road like rotted teeth. For 100 or 200 yards, shacks made of corrugated tin, bits of sacking and timber offcuts advertised themselves as hotels ('Invitation to Happiness'), butcheries (unnervingly, usually attached to the hotels), general stores ('Strongest, longest, most lasting barbed wire available here'), bars ('Honeymoon Pub and Restaurant', 'Lifestyle Bar', 'Ghetto Heaven Bar'), makeshift medical centres and coffin-makers ('Specialists in coffins of all sizes'). Potholes filled with fetid water after the first rains of the year were splashing-pools for small children, while the adults sat – as if exemplars of what happens after the children have used up their young energy – listlessly, chatting or staring, or lolling outside the shops that it was hard to imagine had much trade apart from the drivers of the parked trucks lining the road, spewing diesel and making the bright Kenyan daylight grey-green with fumes. There was plenty of opportunity to think about tourism, eco or otherwise, as we slowed down a little to drive past these jerry-built villages. Children waved wildly at us and we waved back in a way I wished not to be regal but had to be under the circumstances; while the adults, if they noticed us at all, just glanced up for a moment with little curiosity, and then looked away to get on with their own thoughts and conversations, knowing that we were not likely customers and had nothing to do with their lives. We were just passing through on our way to a wildlife lodge. I wasn't at all sure during that journey that paying to collect data for a scientific study saved me in any way from being a first-worlder gawping safely from my expensive vehicle at the harshest end of the real world and throwing it a few quid I could easily afford to salve my conscience: a tourist, in other words. No one suggested we stop at any of the villages. We were paying, after all, to look at elephants, not people.

Earthwatch had funded this particular elephant research project for a couple of years. It was conceived and headed by Dr Barbara McKnight, a woman in her early fifties, originally from Colorado but now firmly Kenyan. She met us and (with a degree of impatience) gave us a few moments to find and settle into our rooms before she started our training. McKnight, although blond, was much slighter and less lush than Michaela or Lotte; it was very unlikely that she had a scarlet lipstick in the pocket of her khaki shorts. She was intense, brisk and rugged in her tiny way, and had the beauty of someone with perfect bone structure and compelling blue eyes who had much better things to do than worry about how she looked. She had devoted the past sixteen years of her life to elephants. In order to do so, she was obliged to train and work with others, deal with officials from Earthwatch and the Kenyan civil service, and even put up with a stream of well-meaning amateurs who, though they had their uses (money and some degree of data-collecting), were annoyingly time-consuming. She was a little out of the way of polite small talk, but made a tremendous and nearly successful effort not to show her irritation with having to deal with another bunch of elephant-ignorant incomers.

We were a willing bunch, though, and tried to prove it by showering, changing and assembling in a classroom at the hotel within the hour to be introduced to our task. We had that afternoon and the following day to get up to speed and become useful observers. McKnight and her assistant, Patrick Kodi, who she had trained herself, gave us lessons in sexing elephants (occasionally extremely obvious – 'That elephant's got five legs . . . Oh, I see' – but not always), understanding what kind of social groupings we would be seeing, how to spot a calf under a year old, how to identify and mark down the individuals on our clipboards by the holes or raggedy and unique notches in their ears. We learned to recognise when a bull had massively (and dangerously) raised testosterone levels during his

period of *musth*, by the weeping glands on his face, the runnel of
semen seeping down his hind legs and the fact that each ear flapped
alternately instead of together as was usually the case, and when to
spot that it was time to get the hell out of his way – if he's trumpet-
ing and running at you, you've left it a bit late. In addition, we were
to count and identify any other wildlife we came across: giraffe,
hippo, zebra, buffalo, gazelle, gerenuk and, my personal favourite,
the diminutive, meticulously formed dik-dik.

Tsavo had been a trophy-hunting game park before it was a
wildlife reserve, and once the rich folk arriving to kill for fun had
stopped, local gangs poaching for ivory and bushmeat became
rife. Of the estimated minimum of 35,000 elephants in 1969, only
10,397 remained to be counted by 2005. There was also a conflict
between the human population, rural people who were growing
crops or keeping livestock, and the elephants who roamed their
traditional territories which now included the land people had
planted up in order to try and make their living. Having your year's
corn trampled by a passing elephant going the way they had always
gone en route to their different waterholes and oblivious of its
new use, caused lethal hostility. Elephants were being killed to
preserve local people's livelihoods. An important funding reason for
McKnight's research was to survey the movements of the elephants
in the area over several seasons to understand their traditional routes,
and to see how to establish safer pathways in order to protect both
the local communities from the elephants and the elephants from the
local communities.

Sixteen years of being in Tsavo, living miles from the lodge, up in
the hills in a two-roomed cabin in the bush with no electricity or
plumbing, thinking, breathing and, for all I know, dreaming elephants
had had their effect on Barbara McKnight's pronouns.

'When you're all in the jeep scanning for elephants, one person always needs to be looking in the other direction. Someone might be coming up behind.'

It took a while for us novices to understand that by 'someone' Barbara meant an elephant. It became increasingly clear that elephants peopled her world, and that people were generally what got in the way of her study of her chosen species. She was a delight. Single-minded, obsessed, passionate about elephants, but, once she had decided that we were going to be reasonably serious and useful assistants, she was in addition wry, witty, considerate and good company. I whisper that last sentence. 'What are you gonna write about me?' she snarled when, in a moment of lapsed concentration, I was chatting politics or possibly frocks with my fellow volunteers in the jeep, instead of silently, intently, monitoring the landscape.

'That you're a harridan, terrifying, a totalitarian monster who had us all cowering and weeping in the back of the jeep.'

'Good,' she beamed, entirely satisfied. 'Now stop talking and look for elephants.'

Her obsession and her purpose in making the world safer for elephants made it seem perfectly reasonable to sit all day long, from early morning until dusk, in a very slow-moving jeep, on the look-out, counting, noting GPS coordinates, and even, on some days, seeing no wildlife at all. Barbara's passion for elephants gave the point to the whole exercise and made us want to work at it seriously. (Apart, of course, from those times when Miss was distracted by her mapwork, and we became indistinguishable from a bunch of chattering schoolkids.) Our days began with a group breakfast at 6.30 a.m., and we spent up to twelve hours in the field, jeep-bound with packed lunches. Bush-breaks for a pee were allowed only when we came across an acceptably safe arrangement of shrubbery. 'Make a noise, sing or something while you're at it,' we were advised.

The difference, if there really was one, between a regular modern safari holiday purchaser and us Earthwatch volunteers who paid 'minimum contributions' to participate in our chosen project, was the nature of our looking. We sat and stood in groups of three or four at the back of two jeeps, which moved at a glacially slow pace. We stood proud of the open roof looking north, south, east and west for elephants, some of us focusing on the distance with binoculars, others looking more closely into the surrounding bush. When we saw any wildlife, we called out the species and the number of them ('five kudu, three giraffe, a partridge in a pear tree'), the person with the GPS called out the coordinates and the designated notetakers wrote the information down on the grid sheets on their clipboard. Once we spotted elephants, the driver (Patrick or Chege) stopped and we all stood and peered through our binoculars, whispered to each other, trying to assess the composition and gender of the group. This one's head was more domed, that one's flatter, so this many young males, females, juveniles and infants, we concluded, once we had stopped adoring the babies, who had the same awful and touchingly hilarious difficulty with their trunk as kittens do with their tails: unable to get it under control, it generally lagged behind them and got in a terrible tangle between their feet and sent them flying. When we pulled ourselves together, or Barbara had called us to order (Patrick and Chege were more benevolent) we described the adult elephants' ear notches and tears, broken tusks and scars for the note-taker to draw on the sheets. Then we remained perfectly still and silent, as perfectly still and silent as half a dozen people in a jeep at ninety degrees of heat could be, while we waited and watched, sometimes for half an hour or more, to see what the elephants we had come across would do. The concentration is intense. I flick a fly away from my sweaty face, and it buzzes off to the person sitting next to me. She flaps her hand and the fly tries its luck in the back of the jeep, darting with each wave of a human hand on to the next nearest dripping forehead. No one is conscious of the journey of the fly, which perhaps we might have watched with as much interest as we did every move of the elephants.

In their groups, they crossed the made-up track in front of us or behind us, with their leisurely, swaying walk, stopping some-times to let 'someone' catch up, or to investigate some interesting marker dung or possible food, and we waited for as long as it took. Sometimes they stopped to eat some grass inches away from our window, on the edge of the road, and while we watched, hushed in awe and because any sudden noise might frighten them, used as they were to Barbara's jeeps, we tried to identify any known indi-viduals by their oddities, and add new ones to the database.

If Barbara was in our jeep, she would whisper the name of an elephant, pointing out the notch at the bottom of the right ear. Or further in the distance, identify a male in *musth*. 'There's Darwin,' or 'Livingstone,' like a proud parent, awed by the beauty and energy of her boys. She knew most of the elephants and described their history, including the illnesses, accidents and human cruelty they had encountered. But she spoke in a different voice about the *musth* males; they were her special favourites. Most of the time, during the years of research, outside the tourist or 'volunteer' season, Barbara drove a jeep alone around the tracks, to sit and watch, and although the elephants weren't completely habituated as the meerkats are, they began as the years rolled on to ignore her or accept that her presence was inevitable. I wondered if they recognised her, knew her, as they knew each other. Did they know the difference between her in her jeep and the tourists? 'How can I tell?' she said, shrugging and reject-ing a hint of sentiment, not leaving any space for the question I really wanted to ask about whether she would like them to regard her as a friendly familiar. For us volunteers, we got satisfaction in identify-ing which were male or female, and increasingly noticing details of elephants' ears. I was content simply to have the opportunity to watch at such length these most extraordinary graceful, delicate creatures getting on with their lives. Completely strange, and also familiar. Like anything you look at intensely, even flies, even people. There was never any sense that we should move along, get on to the next sighting, no matter how much time our elephants chose to idle in our path. It was more of an elephant contemplation than a safari and certainly, everyone agreed, as of course we would, much more gratifying.

Tsavo is a regular wildlife park, so while we were sitting in the blasting heat or waiting for a family of elephants or a tortoise to make their way across the road in front of us to wherever they were going, other jeeps were speeding along the trail, stopping for a heartbeat to take snaps in front or behind us, before passing on excitedly to the next entertaining spectacle. The 'tourists', as we thought of them, were in a way collecting sightings and making identifications, in a thrill of expectation, but evidently without a sense that the longer you looked the more you saw. We felt tremendously virtuous and professional with our research cameras (their unnecessary clicks turned to silent not to alarm the animals), clipboards and GPS. But actually we were just concealed and more privileged holidaymakers. We had paid more to make us feel better than gawkers, to pretend to be mini-scientists, while we got a much more exclusive look at the creatures of the wild than regular tourists on a budget. The speedier tourists were collecting snaps to take home, making sure they saw the requisite kind and number of animals (the Big Six, or is it Seven?) that gave evidence of a great safari holiday. Just 'seeing' instead of 'looking' wasn't enough for us, as it was for the tourists who, after all, may only have had a day-pass to the park and wanted to get in as much as possible. In any case, the wildlife park itself was not God's natural wilderness. Many of the animals had been brought in from other areas to Tsavo over the past twenty-five years for the purpose of creating a tourist attraction. The sign outside the front gate said, troublingly but truly, that we were entering the 'Theatre of the Wild'. Waterholes had been dug to ensure the animals passed by the route of the safari jeeps. No one shoots the animals dead these days, and they are not beaten out of their shelter like pheasant and grouse are in the managed wilderness of the Scottish Highlands so that people can kill them for their pleasure. Now, rather than mounted heads or wastepaper baskets made of elephant feet, photographs and videos put up on YouTube provide the evidence that you've 'experienced' the wildlife of Africa. Nevertheless, these are zoos of a kind, which are in conflict with the local human population nearby who are farming or rearing livestock, and where animal populations are monitored and culled when they get too numerous for the convenience of the humans and their idea of how an environment should be.

Earthwatch had helped support the training of Patrick and Chege, and a young man, Benedict, aged twenty-six, who was assisting Barbara. He told me how much he loved looking at the animals and learning about their ways of life. He hoped to go to college to get his game-warden qualification. Benedict had grown up in a village outside Nairobi. It was, he said, so amazing being with Barbara and seeing the elephants just living their lives. Weren't you interested in animals when you were a boy? Oh, yes, he said, but he only knew them through books in the library and on television. 'I never saw any real wild animals.' I couldn't understand why not. Weren't they just living freely in the bush, available for any enthusiastic youngster to find and watch? He explained patiently, 'All the animals living in the bush around Nairobi had been collected and sent to the wildlife safari parks. I couldn't ever afford the entrance fees they charge the tourists.'

*

Our slow, considered watching in the wildlife park wasn't limited to the largest land mammal. We stopped to note and look at giraffe, gazelle, water buffalo, whatever happened by. I became the recognised dik-dik devotee and cried out triumphantly whenever I spotted one, minutely racing into the shadows of the bush away from us, and my fellow volunteers cheered (quietly, of course) as my dik-dik count rose.

We spent one morning simply stopped in one place near a waterhole, waiting to note what animals came by. Apart from a couple of giraffes doing the splits to drink, nothing did come, but no one was very disappointed. Waiting had become our mode. One day, as we were driving at our regulation five miles an hour, someone spotted a dung beetle staggering on the path just in front of us, with immense care and patience rolling and pushing a black ball of dung four times its own size across the road. We braked to a sudden halt and waited, watching in silent admiration for the twenty minutes it took battling with the unevenness of the track to complete its arduous journey to the relative safety of the bush on the other side and into the undergrowth with its treasure. It was as memorable as any elephant sighting.

Sometimes the elephants came so close that we could have stroked them by putting an arm out of the window. This was quite scary and very astonishing. Mostly, the group, a mother with young and often a baby, loped across the road, just like the dung beetle, on their way to a waterhole or following the low rumblings (inaudible to us) of other troops. What made this watching through a windscreen different from getting up close to an elephant in a cinema was that we had no control over them. We couldn't be sure we would see them, that they would cross our path, as was inevitable in the wildlife film, so when it happened the good fortune stopped the breath. To be ignored by animals in their own territory is an indescribable honour.

Actually so is being ignored by my cat at home, splayed out here next to me on the sofa as I write, because that is where she wants to be and if there's room, I can sit here too, it's OK by her so long as I don't annoy her. Another species paying you no attention is a most marvellous thing, and something you can't achieve by sweeping past them at twenty or even ten miles an hour, or walking by their cages in the zoo.

The elephants didn't just march in their stately manner across the road. Sometimes they stopped, or they were there before us, curling their trunks around the grass at the roadside to yank it out of the soil and then winding it in their trunk so that the two delicate fingers at the end could pop it in their mouths. If you stopped when you saw them, turned the engine off and kept the noise down, they usually paid no attention. But sometimes the younger males took an interest, as adolescents will, and moved closer and curious to the jeep. The strategy – or the hope – then was that he would lose interest if nothing happened, if we kept still and quiet. If we turned on the engine and moved suddenly we would startle the youngster and the rest of the family. Only once or twice did a young male get very close and stay very curious, and that was a bit of a worry. One got close enough for me to see the pores of its trunk as it reached out to investigate the window. The temptation to watch him get closer and closer was dangerous but irresistible, not even Patrick could tear himself away, and that time we had stayed too long. The young male stopped being curious, and slapped the window once or twice with his trunk. We held our breath. Then he began to flap his ears slowly, annoyed at our disregard for his irritation, and Patrick decided it was safer to move on than to stay still. It was the fastest we moved during the whole ten days. But most of the time, the elephants simply passed by or performed recognisable family tableaux. A very young female, just a year or so old, mercilessly teased her older brother, jostling him and charging at him, and whenever he turned to do what older brothers do to aggravating little sisters who take liberties, she raced back to her mother and stood behind her huge safe legs. The mother lifted her head and raised her trunk a little as her son approached until he stopped and went back to his patch of greenery. And out came the little one for another round.

At one waterhole a young male elephant of ten or so was having a really good time in the water, whacking it with his trunk and stomping the mud. So good a time that his two siblings aged about seven and three tried to join in. He wasn't sharing: as soon as they got to the edge of the waterhole he trumpeted threateningly at them, then got out of the waterhole and chased them away. The littlest one disappeared into the bush, and in a few moments returned (I swear, looking sneaky), walking behind its mother who marched purposefully down to the waterhole and bellowed at her oldest son. Then she stepped into the water and butted him out with her massive head, giving him a final, serious wallop with her trunk. The other two immediately jumped in and began trunk-splashing and rolling around while their mother stood guard at the edge. The ten-year-old stood behind a shrub, and with great concentration pulled up blades of grass with his trunk, for all the world like a naughty boy pretending he wasn't in disgrace and standing in the corner.

No matter how much I want to remember Wittgenstein's warning, it was impossible not to see this episode in precisely the human, familial way I have narrated it. I really tried to refocus and look at it as pure behaviour, but it seemed that there was no other way to understand the events I had just witnessed. All of us humans in the jeep, including Barbara who had no problem, for all her number-crunching, with seeing her elephants in an anthropomorphic light, could only look through our own eyes, which were connected to our own brain. And my brain refused to allow me to think that I had misinterpreted what I had seen happen in this family group. It also wouldn't allow me to think that there could have been any other way a differently socialised Martian could have seen it. But Martians are one thing, human beings in their extraordinary variety and capacity for contrariness are quite another.

6

IN THE LAB

Ants and Rats

> . . . animals are always the observed. The fact that
> they can observe us has lost all significance. They
> are the objects of our ever-extending knowledge.
> What we know about them is an index of our
> power, and thus an index of what separates us
> from them. The more we know, the further away
> they are.
>
> John Berger, *Why Look At Animals?*

People must always have watched animals, either because they
were sizing them up for dinner, or because they were there and it
happened that when you turned your gaze on them they were interesting. In addition, you need to know how animals behave if you're
planning to stalk them and your life, or at least your well-being,
depends on catching one every now and again. You might draw them
on the walls of your cave while thinking about them and putting

together what you learn. You would also watch animals because they are so unlike those who are like you that it is surprising to find that they seem to behave, at least sometimes, in ways you recognise in yourself or others in your group. And vice versa. People whose lives are quite leisurely, gathering and hunting when needed, building and taking down accommodation as required, carving canoes or tools or decorations, have plenty of time to take pleasure in watching the world around them. Now, and surely then. In 1974, on the cusp of Thatcher and Reaganite economics and the world of the Yuppie, a book called *Stone Age Economics* by Chicago anthropologist Marshall Sahlins[1], proposed, after analysing the daily life of present-day 'simple' societies closest to those Stone Age primitives we assume so much about, that they were the original (and perhaps the only) affluent society. Time to stand and stare, or more likely, sit and watch.

Stones are good to watch, clouds too, but animals are even better, since they both move and interact. Watching, over a period of time, means getting to know at least something about what you are watching, even if it wasn't your intention. But modern science requires more than staring and putting together what you see into an explanation. That is known in scientific circles as 'common sense' or 'folk psychology' (both intended as wholly derogatory terms, sometimes rightly). Scientific watching demands professionalism and agreed rules. Professionalism and agreed rules are the only ways to gain respect and acknowledgement from those fellow watchers who belong to your peer group. Science becomes Us, common sense Them, and there is no common ground. It is, as those scientists who still think like that put it, the only way to find out the objective truth. In terms of animal studies, for more than a century the question for biologists and zoologists, if not for volunteer elephant eco-tourists, has been whether observations in the field with some degree of anthropomorphism, or controlled, 'objective' laboratory experiments give the best (that is 'correct') understanding of animals; of how they behave and why they behave as they do.

The fashions of zoological procedural preferences have followed a similar path to the animal television programmes of my childhood. Those first programmes in the studio with individual zoo animals in cages or on tables, and an expert standing behind them talking about their morphology and characteristic behaviours, followed the scientific belief, which had been gathering pace since the Enlightenment, that to gain knowledge it is necessary to bring things into the laboratory under proper conditions (that is, human conditions) to observe and test. Early TV animal programmes simply tried to popularise the procedure. Some of the most Olympian scientists disapproved of those programmes, even when they treated animals most like laboratory subjects, because 'popularisation' was inimical to science, which was to be done by a small group of initiates and it didn't matter very much what the wider world knew since the knowledge in the wider world was irrelevant. The true results would gradually filter into the general population on a need-to-know basis. That sort of attitude still holds in some quarters, but, in the later years of the twentieth century, the views of a number of animal researchers began to change and a gradual, if grudging, acceptance began of the alternative on-the-spot ways of the likes of Armand and Michaela and Hans and Lotte. TV viewers, presenters, producers and even some scientists like a bit of adventure with their science, so 'the field' was ideally a faraway exotic venue, an 'africa' of some sort, where the largest, most dangerous, strangest, rarest creatures could be discovered, in situ, for everyone's delight. In the late 1950s, like the ancient division of the world into the Dionysian and Apollonian, the study of zoology seemed to be inhabited by either exoticists who stalked the white rhino and described what they saw in awed voices, or laboratorists who set rats in labyrinths and timed them learning their route to a food incentive. Let's say humanists versus behaviourists.

The history of behaviourism goes back at least as far as Descartes, but in recent times it was declared ready for the modern world by John B. Watson, who in 1910 described 'The New Science of Animal Behaviour' in an essay for the readers of *Harper's Magazine*: 'Apparatus and methods are at hand for forcing the animal to tell us about the kind of world he lives in.' In the 1930s B. F. Skinner designed the notorious 'operant conditioning chambers' which took his own name and became the template for animal behaviour experimentation. Inside these Skinner's Boxes, rats, pigeons, dogs and monkeys (even babies, it was rumoured) had to press levers to get food or avoid electric shocks, in order to prove that all behaviour could be conditioned. In effect, that all behaviour was nothing more than the result of physiological stimulus and response in a direct and simple way that could be understood by laboratory experiment. And once biochemistry was up to speed, it followed that all activity could be broken down into particular chemicals being turned off and on by other chemicals to improve the organism's position in relation to the conditions in which it found itself. The behaviourists declared whatever individual, personal sense human beings (let alone animals) had of a mind that was outside or supplementary to the stimulus and response of physical organs to be subjective, untestable and therefore deemed not to exist. Subjectivity, the sense of the self, became a fairy story, the great illusion, to the behaviourists who wanted and now believed they could get precise answers under controllable experimental conditions to their questions. It's what we all want, deep down, isn't it? Precise answers, preferably with numbers attached, to very complex questions.

Behaviourist theory escaped captivity in the 1950s and ran feral through the real world for the next three or four decades. It was implemented in the forms of new educational theory, the design of gambling slot machines and most recently the use of Cognitive Behavioural Therapy, that quick and dirty method of dealing with all manner of mental ills. It's not hard to see how behaviourist theory in its various forms could look sparkly in the second half of the twentieth century: it was so neat, so modern and promised to solve messy problems without any resort to mucky metaphysics, or the unsettleable notion that any creature on earth needed to have something as nebulous as a mind of its own.

There has always been a humanist resistance to the idea, naturally. *The Papers of Andrew Melmoth* is a strange novel by Hugh Sykes Davies, published in 1960. It tells the posthumous story of a 'young scientist, chiefly concerned with genetics and animal behaviour' who mysteriously disappears after giving increasing cause for alarm by his own unaccountable behaviour. Melmoth worked in a laboratory with rats, 'specially bred albinos, who spent their whole lives in laboratories, as their fathers and grandfathers had done before them, since about 1897'.[2] The narrator, who is trying to piece together Melmoth's disappearance, had been invited to visit the laboratory where he found Melmoth noting down the variations of the clicks on a machine which recorded the activities of the rats in the next room. In each of ten drums there was a rat running on the wire at the bottom which was turning a structure in the middle of the room, beside each drum was a much smaller cage. Melmoth was taking an interest in one particular rat. 'You've come at an interesting moment. There's a female rat in there who looks like breaking the record for distance covered in a revolving cage. Well over seven thousand miles already – not far short of the diameter of the earth.'

Melmoth tells the narrator that she's been in the cage for four years.

'Do you really mean that she has spent her entire life in that tread-mill and that minute cage?'

'Yes,' he said, still smiling, a crease of tolerant amusement under his colourless eyes. 'We have to make the living cage small, because we want them to make most of their movements on the drum, where their activity is recorded. She hasn't had a bad life, you know. Well fed, kept at a nice uniform temperature, no worries.'

Again I decided to ask the obvious question. 'How would you like to spend your entire life like that?'

He was almost childishly pleased at the predictability of my reactions . . . 'But I do spend my life just like that . . . We all do. We all have one little cage where we live and eat and sleep; and we all have some kind of drum we climb into, and run and run and run. Earning money, doing a job, even doing research like this. Sometimes we think we're getting somewhere, not just going round in circles. Perhaps that rat thinks she's getting some-where. She's seen the world, you know, in a sense; nearly the diameter of the earth. In a way she's better off than I am. I've got my two cages just like her, but I'm not at all sure I'm getting anywhere.'[3]

This is a precis of the song 'Little Boxes', written by Malvina Reynolds, and sung by Pete Seeger in 1963, which described the American sub-urban conformist mid-century world in much the same conditioned/ response terms as Melmoth, though without using the word 'rat':

> *Little boxes on the hillside,*
> *Little boxes made of ticky-tacky,*
> *Little boxes on the hillside,*
> *Little boxes all the same.*

There's a green one and a pink one
And a blue one and a yellow one,
And they're all made out of ticky-tacky
And they all look just the same.

Folk singers, anti-nuclear protesters and 'mad' scientists in novels (as well as a few not-so-mad real scientists) were seeing the stainless-steel laboratory world in a similar light. It was, perhaps, not so much the misuse of animals they were objecting to, as the equating of laboratory animals and humans in some of the social solutions of the time. High-rise housing projects, rat-tested tranquilliser drugs, the educational division of children by dubious IQ testing, were all looking particularly nifty and economic to some people in charge of planning and development. Melmoth is one of them, but working closely with rats, and having a dark trauma in his childhood, he becomes more involved with the animals than with people. Hugh Sykes Davies writes a chilling and pitiful (perhaps pitiless) description of the female rat going for the record, as watched by the novel's narrator:

I moved so that I could again see the cage and its occupant. She looked very feeble, and staggered a little from side to side as she tried to run at the bottom of the drum. It was going so slowly that the clicks, widely spaced, sounded louder and more spasmodic, like despairing gasps for breath. She stopped for a moment, swaying unsteadily from side to side on her paws; the drum ceased its revolutions, but still swayed up and down. Then she tried to run again, but failed, and fell on her side against the wire side of the cage. Her mouth was opening and shutting convulsively – I remember it was surprisingly pink inside. The clicking stopped.

She wasn't quite dead, and the narrator suggests that she looks in pain. Melmoth, the clear-eyed pain-giver answers: 'That only means that she's alive,' he said soberly. 'Pain is inseparable from life; inability to feel pain is death, in a limb or a whole body.' The rat dragged herself back to the drum and began to run again at a steady rate. Melmoth became hopeful that she might, after all, make the diameter of the earth.

> She raised her head higher, until it was painfully strained against her back, her mouth wide open, her red eyes staring up the endless slope of wire mesh which had always reared itself before her, and eternally rolled down beneath her flying feet. She no longer gave the impression of fear and feebleness, but rather of a fierce strength of purpose. The clicks were coming in such quick succession that they almost merged into one another . . . And she went faster, always faster, so fast that she was within an ace of gaining on the wire that rolled down and under her, of climbing at last a little way up that endless descending hill whose summit had been the goal of her lifelong journey . . . Suddenly, without any faltering or other warning, she fell over on her side, rocking a little with the movement of the still swaying cage, but otherwise motionless . . . She was without motion or force, her paws drawn up to her body, her furry flanks quite still. The red eyes were wide and open, but I felt sure that they saw nothing.

Before he goes in to check that she is dead, Melmoth jots some calculations on a piece of paper:

> 'Seven thousand, three hundred and fifty one point six miles,' he told us, not without a certain note of pride and even of respect. 'About six hundred miles short of the diameter. But I don't suppose she knew that.'

Melmoth the scientist is at odds with his own traumatised child-self. He gets more and more immersed in rats, and starts to pay attention to them even outside the laboratory. Soon he spends all his free time watching a colony of rats in a rubbish dump, and then he descends into the sewers. His eventual disappearance is inevitable as he becomes increasingly sucked into the underworld of wild rats.

The Papers of Andrew Melmoth is a parable or a warning, or simply the story of a damaged human and a scientist living impossibly together in one body. All those things. But the monstrous and pitifully heroic last moments of Melmoth's female rat stands at the centre of the objective observer/anthropomorphism debate that has been going on for centuries.

In parallel to behaviourism, the new discipline of ethology developed, which looked at animals in their natural environment, but equally on human terms even, and especially, with the intention of understanding human behaviour through watching animals. In 1973 Karl von Frisch won a Nobel Prize for his work on the bee dance and its meanings, sharing it with Konrad Lorenz and Nikolaas Tinbergen who studied the social behaviour of geese, jackdaws and herring gulls. They worked outside the laboratory, on whole animal behaviour, and they were happy to draw exact parallels between their animal subjects and human behaviour. Lorenz wrote entertaining books about being followed around by the geese which had imprinted on him as chicks so that he became their mother. He embraced anthropomorphism, referring to his jackdaw pair as 'Mr and Mrs Jackdaw', and applied the lessons he learned from animals to the ways humans behaved. Lorenz used the word 'family' about the reproductive behaviours both of humans and animals, and he seemed untroubled by the simplicity of seeing the biological usefulness of animal mating arrangements as an explanation for human social organisation.

It became politicised. The Dutch Nikolaas Tinbergen was imprisoned by the Nazis, while Konrad Lorenz joined the Austrian Nazi party in 1938 and took up a party-funded university chair. He wrote, 'I'm able to say that my whole scientific work is devoted to the ideas of the National Socialists.' He used his studies of the linkage of inheritance and behaviour patterns to give scientific weight and language to the eugenicist ambitions of the Nazi regime. Lorenz was eventually forgiven by some, but the usefulness of ethology to the Nazis was firmly imprinted on those who had paid attention to more than the scientific investigation. It left a taste that was recognisable when in the 1960s and 1970s ethology became the source of several massively bestselling books. Desmond Morris (*The Naked Ape*) and Robert Ardrey (*The Territorial Imperative* and *The Hunting Hypothesis*) looked at studies of primates – chimpanzees and baboons – which examined their sexual, aggressive and social behaviour and, in a popular and palatable form, made those primate behaviours ancestral to everyday human activities. Aggression and social positioning were innate and inherited parts of primate behaviour derived from their evolutionary history, so *therefore*, violence, war and greed for power in politics, business and gender relations were merely natural in humanity who are, after all, primates themselves. Morris and Ardrey explained that we humans do this or that because it is in our nature, coded, programmed. Baboons and especially chimpanzees could be studied and nicely fitted out by humans with human explanations for their behaviour (male baboons fight and manipulate each other to decide which animal becomes the boss), then the resulting elision of human-language and animal-activity was returned to human nature as insolubly innate, biological and only to be expected explanations of ourselves (male adolescents, businessmen and nations fight and manipulate their way to the top of the gang or the corporation or world because, well, it's in our deepest nature). Baboons and tycoons scramble over weaker members of the group, and society is all the stronger for it, and anyway, it's how nature intended baboon and therefore, by evolutionary extrapolation, human society to be. Those of us (humanists, socialists, women) who didn't fancy being either baboons or tycoons, raged at the reductionists. *Nature* and *the natural* came to mean quite different things according to what side you were on. What chimpanzees and baboons thought of all this, no one knows.

Edward O. Wilson is the world's leading authority on the life and behaviour of ants, but he is even better known as the man who established the modern behaviourist discipline of sociobiology as a scientific method. In *Sociobiology: The New Synthesis*[4] he suggested that his use of evolutionary principles and the tracing of genetic history in understanding the behaviours of ants should be applied to all animals, including the human kind. Evolutionary selection and gene expression, he claimed, set actual limits on the influence that culture had on human behaviour, and possibly had even more influence on us than culture.

> Scientists and humanists should consider together the suggestion that the time has come for ethics to be removed temporarily from the hands of the philosophers and biologicized . . . Only when the machinery can be torn down on paper at the level of the cell and put together again will the properties of emotion and ethical judgement come clear . . . Stress will be evaluated in terms of the neurophysiological perturbations and their relaxation times. Cognition will be translated into circuitry. Learning

and creativeness will be defined as the alteration of specific portions of the cognitive machinery regulated by input from the emotive centers.[5]

Philosophers, politicians and scientists took sides. Those who believed that 'human nature' was infinitely malleable and subservient to cultural influences and constraints, like the philosopher Mary Midgley, went into battle against Wilson and sociobiological methods. She replied that

> You cannot explain a piece of behaviour by digging into the body of the behaving person, unless your attempts to explain it in more immediate ways have reached a point where that information is called for.[6]

I imagine that for Wilson, the reductionist scientist, and Midgley, the humanist philosopher, 'more immediate ways' mean completely different things. Stephen Jay Gould, biologist and humanist, was having none of it.

> [G]enes make enzymes, and enzymes control the rates of chemical processes. Genes do not make 'novelty seeking' or any other complex and overt behaviour. Predisposition via a long chain of complex chemical reactions, mediated through a more complex series of life's circumstances, does not equal identification or even causation.[7]

This doesn't seem to have had much effect on Wilson's certainties. But those on the side of humanism (and these days, post-humanism) preferred not to think of themselves or other animals as an engine capable of being stripped down to its component parts and thereby completely known when put back together again. The old battle between physicalists and humanists, raging since Descartes and the division of the world into spirit and mechanism, continues.

Still, of all the creatures we watch, the social insects, along with the higher primates, have been irresistible to those looking to animals for an explanation of human behaviour. For millennia, human beings have peered into hives, termitaries and ant heaps and found in their seething interiors, for better or worse, reflections of themselves. The intense busyness and division of labour in insect colonies provide us with a compelling, nature-driven excuse to draw conclusions about us from them. Ants and bees have given writers and polemicists metaphor, analogy and allegory for their economic, political and moral teachings. Ants, in particular, have been used by supporters and detractors of military, socialist and fascist societies as emblematic. So strange, so many and so well organised. Like us, but stompable if things get out of hand, although they're also capable, in movies at least, of overwhelming individual humans with their sheer numbers and single-mindedness – providing a messy death for a Cold War Russki in the last *Indiana Jones* movie (ants don't take sides, being alien, other and emotion-free, but the bad guys always make the wrong decisions, which amounts to the same thing in the sticky end).

If ants tell the story of our negative potential, bees, on the other hand, usually have top billing in our affections (except, again, when paradoxically gone bad in some well-beloved bad movies like *The Swarm* and *The Killer Bees*) since they produce something that human beings can utilise and like very much. Also bees are what you might call furry. You don't see many cuddly ants in the stuffed-companion section of toy shops. Bees haven't always been benign, however. Bernard Mandeville wrote his satire *The Fable of the Bees* in 1714, claiming that their individual vices such as greed and desire for power are essential in the production of their (and our) healthy society, and that the strict division of labour within a limited monarchy was by far the most efficient way for bees to produce honey and humans to make a living. *The Fable* was written, Mandeville explained, 'in order to extol the wonderful Power of Political Wisdom, by the help of which so beautiful a Machine is rais'd from the most contemptible Branches'. Mandeville's thriving hive collapses when the bees start murmuring about instilling virtue and honesty in individuals. His warning had not been heeded by 1895 when in a pamphlet, *Liberty Lyrics*, Anarcho-Communists extolled bees, 'for their freedom from masters, money, newspapers and "property tyrants"'.[8] Ants had their admirers, too: in the Bible, for instance ('Go to the ant, thou sluggard, consider her ways and be wise.' Proverbs 6:6), while Aesop's virtuous, labouring ant rebukes the lotus-eating grasshopper who asks it for a handout, having sunned itself all summer instead of storing food. In the 1920s, metaphorical reflection on the social insects became altogether hazier, if not downright mystical. Rudolf Steiner, having broken away from the theosophists to create his very own splinter philosophy, anthroposophism, tried to answer 'certain questions on the nature of the human being and the universe' by comparing the collectivity of the beehive to the singular human brain: 'Inside the beehive things basically happen the same way, only with slight differences, as they do in the head of a human being.'[9]

Maurice Maeterlinck published *The Life of the White Ant* in 1926, though he actually stole it from the Afrikaner poet Eugène Marais, who had published *The Soul of the White Ant* in 1925 in Afrikaans. Marais had spent much of his life staring into termitaries in South Africa and built a theory about the nature of group existence:

I am trying my utmost to prove that the termitary must be looked upon, not as a heap of dead earth, but as a separate animal at a certain stage of development. You must take my word for it that all this is very important and necessary if we are to get even a faint inkling of the perfect group soul and its characteristics.[10]

If ants weren't theosophical, perfect, group souls, then they were warnings against totalitarianism. In 1921 Karel Capek's *The Insect Play* included the Ant Realm where blind obedience to state and work produces a pitiless drive to overcome the world, and a report on the Communist International deliberations on what to do about Fascism in January 1934 was headed *Communists' Aim White-Ant Fascism*. The oxymoronic, neurotic, rebellious ant and bee were late-comers to the parade. These are breakaway individualist ants for the Me generation. In 1998, egged on by love, an animated ant called Z, voiced by Woody Allen, tries to make a break with his totalitarian society in *Antz*. And in *Bee Movie* (2007, strapline: 'Honey just got funny') Barry the drone is appalled to find that he has no further job prospects after training to become a worker in the honey-making industry. He leaves his hive and explores the world. At present, individuality trumps communal endeavour or the group soul. In an interview with CNN in 2001, Edward Wilson summed up much of his work on ants: 'Karl Marx was right, socialism works, it is just that he had the wrong species.' But who knows what new deal the financial crisis of 2008–9 might bring to the everlastingly useful metaphor of the social insects?

Though Edward Wilson has stuck with ants and continues to write about them, he hasn't stopped generalising his sociobiological methods. In his most recent non-fiction book, *The Superorganism*,[11] he reiterates his position: 'All modern biology consists of a process of reduction of complex systems followed by synthesis.' Wilson's synthesis, based on his study of ants but also applicable, he believes, to human beings, states that natural selection has shaped social behaviour using the mechanism of variable reproductive success, and therefore particular behaviours can be studied and understood by reconstructing their evolutionary history. The key here is what Wilson understands by the word understanding. The big problem sociobiology had to confront was that observed instances of altruism in certain animals (such as worker ants who 'give up' their own personal reproduction for the greater needs of the ant heap) made no sense. Altruistic individuals seem to deselect themselves and therefore to defy natural selection – the fulcrum of evolutionary development. Why would female worker ants produce sterile eggs which they feed to the Queen's fertilised larvae, when it would seem to deprive them of the reproductive sine qua non demanded by evolutionary theory? Sociobiologists solved their problem, at least to their satisfaction, by concluding that *individual* altruism was an illusion (like *mind*), and developed the concept of 'inclusive fitness'. In 1964 William Hamilton provided the algebraic answer: $rb>c$, where r is the fraction of genes an altruist shares with the recipient of the altruistic behaviour; b is the increase in units of offspring produced by the recipient; and c is the cost to the altruist measured in units of offspring. The non-algebraic case was the man [*sic*] deciding whether to dive into a fathomless lake to save someone who is drowning. Shall I jump? Not a good swimmer, actually. Well, let's see: this is a tight-knit community, and that guy flailing around in that wet, dangerous water is a stranger in these parts. Chances of his sharing half of my genes? Minimal. Chances of my further offspring sharing half of my genes? Maximal. $rb>c$. Hell, let him drown.

When I was reading about this theory in the 1980s, it was very hard not to equip my mental images of rats and ants with tiny calculators for working out their genetic odds. Of course, I was younger and shallower then, but it's still difficult to shake off the arithmetical ant and rat. Wilson is much more grown up about it: because of the way in which the ant reproduces (haplo-diploidy: just trust me, or look it up for yourself) all the female offspring of a queen share 75 per cent of each other's genes, and have more genes in common with each other than with their male siblings or their potential children, so – tap, tap, tap on the calculator keys – it benefits the sisters to kill any of their brothers who fail to leave the nest to mate, and to nurture the Queen's larvae (their sisters) with their own offspring. They sacrifice their individual fertility in the cause of being genetically better represented in the group's future. It's all in the arithmetic, but since arithmetic in any form makes me cry, I would probably be as aberrant an ant as I am a sociobiologically rational human being. Wilson would point out that it's not a matter of making a conscious choice, it's *chemical*. And someone called T. D. Seeley provides some general comfort, to superorganisms if not to me and you, in the title of a paper, quoted by Wilson: 'Decision-making in superorganisms: how collective wisdom arises from the poorly informed masses.'

Edward O. Wilson knows more than anyone else has ever known about the degrees of ant sociability, how ant societies have developed and what makes them function as they do without human language, universities and pension arrangements, and he writes elegantly. *The Superorganism* is an elaboration of his earlier academic book on ants, but the new one, written with Bert Hölldobler, has a preface entitled 'Note to the General Reader'. The newer book is intended for a wider audience than just those with a purely academic interest in ant colonies. As part of that wider audience, and looking at the big picture, it strikes me that even if you replace words like spirit or soul with ideas of gene-relatedness and chemical descriptions in order to explain the apparent unity of purpose of the ant colony, so that various pheromones (rather than the desire of the Queen ant) control the will and organisation of an ant heap, the resulting concept of the superorganism doesn't seem to take us so very far from what the world-mind-ers, Marais and Steiner, were writing about. But Wilson is aware of the human, unscientific tendency to look at the big picture, and warns

> The extremes of higher level traits may at first appear to have a life of their own, one too complex or fragile to be reduced to their basic elements and processes by deductive reasoning and experiments. But such separate holism is in our opinion a delusion, the result of still insufficient knowledge about the working parts and processes.[12]

Ah, a delusion. But then, on that basis, isn't everything we believe we understand a delusion? How are we to know when we know everything? New information always supplements and corrects what we think is the final answer to our questions, even in the field of the social insects. And if we could be sure we knew everything about working parts and processes, would that mean we understood? Wilson offers far more detailed and fascinating information on ants than the earlier works of those vague metaphysicians and New Ageists in their search for communal meaning. However, to presume Wilson's version to be truer than the older versions is to suppose that intricate chemical explanations are not themselves a kind of mystification or metaphor. Being a non-biochemist, the phrase 'Thus, information about ovarian activity is encoded in the CHC profiles' actually means less to me than words like 'soul' or 'spirit', and to be told that β-Pinene is the precise chemical component of the pheromone which causes alerting and circling behaviour, or gets ants to bite, is not only something I'll have to take on trust, but it's also unclear to me what it is, once you know that, that you know exactly. β-Pinene and 2-Butyl-2-octenal make ants circle and bite: binary do/don't codes for particular built-in behaviours. Which is interesting; but still something seems to be missing about the 'life of their own' of the 'higher-level traits' that Wilson refers to, just as the cloudy poetics of Marais and Steiner leave a gaping technical hole. Which is to say that I can't quite shake off my tendency to illusory holism. Even after carefully reading five hundred pages of incredibly detailed chemical and evolutionary information about ants, something remains to be desired. Wilson and Hölldobler perhaps sense this, because in an epilogue to their book that begins by looking at the future of ant research, they end by trying to answer the question 'Finally, what is the significance of this knowledge for our species?'[13] Odd, really, that there needs to be any. Understanding about ant life doesn't seem to be enough. It turns out they believe that human society and ant society do have a great deal in common, such as our spectacular ecological success and the exclusion of non-social species that competed with us. Group selection, they say, has driven both us and the ants, and 'the residue of that evolutionary force affects us still in our irrational and destructive tribal wars'. Unlike the ants who are ruled by rigid instincts, we have intelligence and culture. Yet our intelligence has resulted in the fine mess we have got ourselves into, while 'the rigid instincts of the social insects have fitted them harmoniously into the living environment'. They conclude rather evasively that 'By coming to see who we are and how we came to be, our species might find better ways to live harmoniously, not only with one another but also with the rest of life.'[14] This sounds as waffly as Marais and Steiner, but I suppose that it is meant to suggest that our salvation is in our evolutionary history rather than the stars in our eyes, and that we need to look to our biochemical processes. I have no idea what we need to do, but I don't think Wilson and Hölldobler have gone very far towards solving the problem they pose of human venality. They do seem to have proved that ants don't behave at all, but merely respond to chemical stimuli and their own genetic history, but strangely or not, this seems to make them less rather than more interesting.

Ethology, behaviourism and sociobiology are very beguiling to the part of us that craves precise explanations to human problems: go to the animals. It reignites the idea of the animal-in-us and nails it with what looks like scientific modernity. The popularisers of behaviourism and sociobiology give simple (and bang-up-to-the minute technological-sounding) explanations and justifications for things that before had been difficult and worrying. They invited us to settle into a comfy pessimism, knowing there wasn't much we could do about ourselves, and as a bonus, there was no need to deal with complexity of thought or engage with theories of mind. Psychology paid close attention: if things were perhaps hopeless on the general front, in individuals behaviour could be altered simply on the basis of stimulus and response. There was no need for time-consuming talk therapies or philosophical wonderings. In addition, based on what they now understood about the genetic wellsprings of human behaviour, we could let them devise drugs, as well as procedures, to deal with the least useful aspects of how our genes forced us to go about our business.

In the mid-1980s I visited a hospital that specialised in treating disturbed and disturbing adolescents with behaviourist methods. I was tutoring a young man who lived in local authority care, who wasn't acceptable in regular school. When Social Services decided that he should be admitted to the unit in order to solve his intractable social and personal problems, he asked me to go and look at it. The unit followed strict behaviourist principles. The staff issued tokens with which anything beyond basic living requirements could be bought: beginning with better food, staying up later, watching TV and wearing your own clothes, and escalating to weekend passes and eventually discharge. Like Skinner's rats, the young people earned (and lost) tokens by conforming to (or disregarding) the rules, which covered everything from washing themselves to social interaction with their peers and staff. When patients went out of control they were physically subdued and put into one of the 'time-out rooms', padded cells with viewing windows in the locked doors, until they were calm enough to return to the group. Just before I visited, one girl who had been discharged had returned after attempting to kill herself. She told me how difficult she had found it living out in the world where tokens and rules were not provided (please note, would-be liberators of laboratory-bred animals). She didn't know what she was supposed to do, she said. Nobody told her; it was too hard. I imagine the system worked for some people. The local authority was certainly very excited about it and sent the most difficult adolescents there. During my visit, one of the nurses told me that every patient who was admitted was automatically put on a drug called Tegretol: an anti-epilepsy pill to prevent seizures, which effectively damps down the activity of the nerve cells in the brain. Sleepiness, dizziness and vomiting are some of the milder, most common side effects. Originally each patient was given an EEG when they were admitted, the nurse told me, but a high proportion of the young people were found to have 'frontal-lobe disturbance', so it was decided that everyone was to be put on Tegretol. After that, the token system trained their anti-social behaviour. Sociobiology began in rat boxes and ant colonies and inexorably widened out into human psychology. Whatever way we choose to look at animals will always have implications for how we look at human beings – that, finally, is what animals are for. We can't help it.

I'm not sure very many researchers of the behaviourist persuasion would, these days, go along with Edward Wilson in using words like 'delusion' and 'illusion' about those who are uncomfortable with a purely mechanistic description of the world. At least they're less likely to do so aloud. The case for a more humanistic, 'holistic' view of animal and human behaviour may not have convinced them but there is such a marked change of mood in the general public (about how our food is reared, transported and killed, for example) that there is a new degree of caution among behaviourists, or at least an attempt to synthesise – or possibly colonise – animal-centred attitudes with what they regard as the only testable, true realities of biochemistry.

I went to talk to Donald Broom, the world's first Professor of Animal Welfare at Cambridge University's Department of Veterinary Medicine. Although he's a behaviourist, he told me that he didn't discount the emotions or feelings of animals at all. Behaviourism, he said, was misunderstood by those who thought its practitioners took no account of the experiences of the animals they tested in labs. The point was that with animals being so variously different from human beings, it was difficult to assess their welfare needs unless they could be properly tested. Certainly, animals had emotions and feelings, it was quite wrong to suggest they didn't, but we can only reliably (as opposed to intuitively) know what these are by measuring their physiological effects. There was no proof anywhere that non-humans don't feel pain, he explained. But if I just thought how hard it is to put myself in the position of another individual human being, I would see how much harder it is to know what a non-human creature was feeling. He thought that dog owners could make objective observations as well as a scientist, based on their long-term knowledge of their own particular dog, but that, too, was a form of measurement. It was not identification: 'If this was happening to me, I would feel this,' but properly evidence-based: 'My dog usually looks or behaves like this, and now, when such a thing happens, she behaves or looks differently. She is not within her normal range, therefore her welfare is compromised.'

Broom was helpful and explained carefully what animal scientists do. He sent me a paper he had written on animal welfare. It began with a definition:

Welfare is a term which is used about animals, including man, but not about plants or inanimate objects. If, at some particular time, an individual animal has no problems to deal with, that individual is likely to be in a good state that would be associated with good feelings and indicated by a particular body physiology, brain state and behaviour. Another individual may face problems in life such that coping is difficult or not possible. *Coping implies having control of mental and bodily stability* and prolonged failure to cope results in failure to grow, failure to reproduce or death. Individuals are likely to show some direct signs of their potential failure to cope or difficulty in coping and they are also likely to have had bad feelings associated with their situations. *The welfare of an individual is its state as regards its attempts to cope with its environment.* The origin of the concept is how well the individual is faring or travelling through life. The term environment in the definition of welfare means, for an individual, something that could have an effect from outside that individual, or for any particular response system, something that could have an effect from outside that system. Potentially damaging challenges may come from outside the body, e.g. pathogens, causes of tissue damage, or attack by conspecifics, or from within it, e.g. anxiety, boredom or frustration, perhaps because of lack of key stimuli or lack of overall stimulation. Other impacts of the environment may be positive and lead to better welfare.

It is generally accepted by animal welfare scientists that the concept of welfare refers to the measurable state of the individual on a scale from very good to very poor. Since welfare can be poor, it is not logical to speak of preserving, ensuring or compromising welfare.

The paper concludes:

Welfare depends on extent of adaptation, a variety of coping methods and how well needs are met. Welfare encompasses health and any stress or feelings. Feelings are biological mechanisms and are part of coping methods. Like some other coping methods, feelings involve high-level brain activity as well as simpler physiological functioning. Although many aspects of welfare involve feelings, not all of welfare is about feelings. Many feelings are not easy to evaluate and there are occasions when feelings can be misleading or absent when welfare, and hence quality of life, is being assessed.

Some coping involves prediction and other complex brain abilities. Animals with better brains probably cope better. Established methods in welfare assessment, including measures of strength of preference and scientific measures of abnormal behaviour, physiological responses and clinical condition, should be used to evaluate welfare in clinical and other situations. Terminology should be used precisely in this area of science, medicine and veterinary medicine.[15]

This is an attempt at behaviourism with a caring face, or at any rate, the new terms in which behaviourism has devised well-being to comply with modern laws about animal welfare without offending its sense of itself. The need for precise terminology and universal tests is at the heart of science. And the idea that it is not stress, but the ability to cope with stress which counts, is useful to those working with animals, especially the finding that those 'with better brains' cope better. It permits a degree of stress in the very animals that we need to make stressed. After all, if we are using animals to find solutions for human ills, stress is at present very high on the human agenda. This is not to say that a behaviourist approach to welfare isn't useful. If we are going to do science, and have rules about the subjects that are used, science has to know how to deal with them in the terms it understands. It's simply that the tone of the article seems to speak beyond the needs of laboratory researchers and assistants and towards great and general truths. Science is inclined to do that. And those who look at science warily are inclined to dismiss its stated methods as blind to the obvious. In rebuttal, science regards 'the obvious' in the same light as erroneous 'common sense' and 'folk psychology'.

Parrots and Primates

> If you give cats a problem to solve or a task to perform in order to find food, they work it out pretty quickly, and the graph of their comparative intelligence shows a sharply rising line. But the older experimenters then say (although they will never publish on this subject): 'the trouble is that as soon as they figure out that the researcher or technician wants them to push the lever, they stop doing it; some of them will starve to death rather than do it'.
>
> Vicki Hearne, *Animal Happiness*

While it can't be said that behaviourism has gone away, it's certainly true that more people are investigating other ways of studying animals and are not only speaking up about it, they are increasingly insisting on their way being at least as fruitful as the behaviourists'.

The question of what constitutes science is much debated by those who work with animals and those who think about how we work with and relate to animals. Field observers and philosophers are talking to each other, and they are also listening to those previously unconsidered people who spend their time with animals – farmers, trainers, breeders and even pet owners.

An unpublished paper by Vinciane Despret, a philosopher and psychologist at the University of Liège, in Belgium, examines some of those other ways of trying to observe animals.[16] The question she poses is whether we need to know how the animals on which we experiment understand what it is they are being asked to do, and whether or not they can cooperate, or on the contrary actively impede the experiment. What scientists like to assume is that they themselves do not exist, and are not part of the experiment. The requirement for objectivity causes them to devise experiments and to behave, as if they (as well as their subjects) were machines. What objectivist rat and other laboratory-animal scientists have required of themselves is that they make no relationship with the animals they work with. To do so would invalidate the experiment. In real life, they do, of course, make relationships with the creatures with whom they spend their working day. Being humans as well as scientists, they really can't help it.

Dr Claire Bryant of the Cambridge Veterinary Medicine Department studies bacteria and disease resistance. When I visited her in her lab, she escorted me through a series of super-clean rooms, which involved us putting on freshly laundered overalls and unlocking double security doors. In the various rooms we peered into labelled Petri dishes stacked neatly on shelves or in refrigerators. I gazed at dark dots on gel, some of them lethal, others fit for lunch, none of them meaning anything to me until they were named (botulinus, salmonella) and I was given some explanation of their place in the world by Dr Bryant. There didn't seem to me to be much of anything I would call life in the lab, apart from the researchers in their white coats, poking pipettes into flasks, looking into microscopes or reading computer screens. Not much chance for anthropomorphising about her subject, I supposed.

'Oh, I chatter to them all the time,' she said, fessing up. 'I worry about them if they're not developing properly, too slowly or too fast. And I've been known to give them a good talking to, to buck them up, or try and coax the slower-growing colonies along. Not when anyone else is in the room, obviously. I have a relationship with all of them.' And, of course, how could anyone avoid it? We relate to what we are engaged with. If you show people slides of triangles, circles and squares in relation to each other, they will narrate stories about them chasing each other, running away, forming a crowd while a loner stands outside.

But even when scientists acknowledge that experiments might be influenced, they assume that only the observer is doing the influencing. Clearly, Dr Bryant felt differently about her rapidly growing and slower-developing bacteria. Despret describes an experiment where students were given rats to test, some of them having been told that they were dealing with specially bred bright rats, with generations of experience of maze work, and the others given rats that were regular undistinguished lab rats with no special breeding. The students with bright rats found their rats bright, and the students with dull rats found their rats dull. No surprise there, not even when you discover that the rats were all the same regular lab rats with no distinction about them or between them. But the fact is that the 'dull' rats were perceived as performing less well than the 'bright' rats even when the statistics sometimes showed otherwise. And even more complexly, one student felt warmly towards his dull rat, and became proud of its ability to excel at simple-mindedness. That rat was actually, according to the figures, doing better than average at its task.

Robert Rosenthal did this experiment in the 1960s. His aim was limited. He wanted to discover what were the 'little things that "affect the subjects to respond differently than they would if the experimenter were literally an automaton"'.[17] But how did the students influence the rats? Did the affection of the student enhance the 'dull' rat's performance to do better than its actual averageness? Did that rat respond to the careful, affectionate handling rather than the expectation of its handler, and therefore do well? Was it a case that the assumptions of the experimenters affected the experiment, or that the rats were responding to their handling? Despret takes us back to Jacques Derrida and his cat looking at him in the bathroom to remind us that 'animals look at us, respond to us and constantly ask for responses from us'.[18] Scientists might well influence experiments, and animals respond. Maybe if the scientists ask the right questions, the animals might even cooperate in the investigation.

Alex the Parrot is an example of a cooperating (and non-cooperating) partner in animal observation. Despret quotes the late Vicki Hearne, an animal trainer, writer and philosopher, on the subject of parrots and participation:

You go up to a parrot, and he's probably in a cage and you're not, so you feel pretty superior, maybe you even think you can feel sorry for the parrot, and you ask the parrot how he is, and he says something gnomic like, 'so's you're old man' or 'how fine and purple are the swallows of the late summer'. Then the parrot looks at you in a really interested, expectant way, to see if you're going to keep your end up [. . .] You start trying to figure out what the parrot means by it, and there you are. You haven't a prayer of reintroducing whatever topic you had in mind. That's why philosophers keep denying that parrots can talk, of course, because a philosopher really likes to keep control of a conversation.[19]

Irene Pepperberg discovered that parrots are most motivated by the presence of rivals. So instead of teaching Alex to speak, she started to teach her human assistant to speak while Alex the parrot was present. Alex, attentive and taking an attitude to being ignored, became a prolific talker.

Not only did he speak, describe, count, classify objects into abstract categories and use concepts like 'same' and 'different', but he could use speech so as to influence the behavior of others: 'Come here', 'I want to go to that place', 'No', 'I want this'. Moreover, intentionality is a characteristic that may be achieved through the device: not only by responding to the demands the parrot makes, but also by voluntarily 'misunderstanding' a new signifying sound the parrot may inadvertently produce. The researchers acted as if this sound was intentional and responded to this new act of language as if Alex had wanted to demand something or comment intentionally. The effect of the misunderstanding, of the 'as if', is that a sound produced accidentally not only becomes a word that signifies something for the parrot because it has signified something for the researcher, but makes the parrot enter into a world in which different beings intentionally respond to each other and become, through and for each other, intentional. 'Several researchers,' Pepperberg remarks, 'have shown that a child's competence often advances when adults interpret and respond to its utterance as "intentional" even before there is evidence to support such intentionality.'[20]

Consider how you train a captive bird to talk. You teach it to say 'hello' every time you come into view, and then you reward it by giving it a peanut. 'It somehow never occurred to the researcher,' Pepperberg comments, 'that the bird would consider the vocalization "hello" to be a request for the nut rather than a comment on the entrance of the trainer.'[21] So you get parroting, not language, and then you know for sure that what parrots do when they 'talk' is not language.

All of this, of course, suggests there might be some very different and interesting results if researchers were to take their subjects into account as reflexive, responsive beings. People like Pepperberg and others have been actively doing that both in the laboratory and in the field and publishing their findings with less hesitancy than they might once have felt. The most famous of these are several women who have devoted their lives to studying the higher primates in their native habitats: Jane Goodall with chimpanzees, Dian Fossey with gorillas, Birutė Galdikas with orang-utans, and Barbara Smuts with baboons.

Smuts described the advice she was given as a new field-worker. Which was to be 'like a rock, to be unavailable, so that eventually the baboons would go on about their business in nature as if data-collecting humankind were not present'. Despret quotes the philosopher Donna Haraway's reaction here:

> Scientists 'could query but not be queried': 'people could ask if baboons are or are not social subjects, or ask anything else for that matter, without any ontological risk either to themselves, except maybe being bitten by an angry baboon or contracting a dire parasitic infection, or to their culture's dominant epistemologies about what are named nature and culture ... I imagine the baboons as seeing somebody off-category, not something,'

Haraway writes, 'and asking if that being were or were not edu-
cable to the standard of a polite guest'.[22]

The idea that we can be rude to animals is galvanising. Being rude
means that you do not recognise the other's selfhood. It's not surprising that we're rude to animals. We wander around other parts of
the world, standing and snapping at artefacts, and treat the people
who live there as if they were not individuals but part of the scenery,
and as if no account is to be taken of them. We get what we want, a
photo of a building, while the local inhabitants are trying to go about
their business. We don't consider their customs, or their sensibilities
very much. Very gradually, we are beginning to see that this is no way
to behave in parts of the world where we are strangers. We have
hardly come round to admitting that about our sojourns in the worlds
of animals. The official, scientific advice is to behave as if you were
not there and 'just observe'. Barbara Smuts found that she got
nowhere with this strategy and tried another. She learned to behave in
baboon company like a baboon. 'I . . . in the process of gaining their
trust, changed almost everything about me, including the way I
walked and sat, the way I held my body and the way I used my eyes
and voice. I was learning a whole new way of being in the world – the
way of the baboons.' What resulted, she says, was an understanding
of how the baboons expressed themselves, and an ability to be understood herself.

Having a relationship with another species, that is, communicating with them on mutual terms is one of the great dreams of the
human species. Dr Dolittle aside, we see this yearning most clearly
in science fiction. Not the kind where we are invaded by warmon-
gering Martians and finally defeat them, but a more amiable kind
where other more advanced intelligences arrive from faraway parts
of the universe, and we learn to communicate. *E.T.* and *Close Encounters*

WHAT I DON'T KNOW ABOUT ANIMALS

of the Third Kind are the popular movie versions of this genre. Another example is the moment when my cat sits on my lap and moves her head and neck towards me to show exactly where she wants to be stroked, and when I oblige, she purrs her satisfaction and then settles down for a nap. Behaviourism, I suppose, is a reaction against that dream, a kind of heroic despair or craven arrogance that insists we are lonely intelligences in an unwitting universe. The anthropomorphic way of seeing being in things and creatures is dismissed as childlike, something that must be given up along with our cuddly bears. Anthropomorphism is not just about animals, it's an ancient and sticky human habit.

Small children (and adults) lie in bed in the morning and watch as the abstract patterns on their curtains become faces of angels and devils, old men and elegant women. Clouds are very like a whale. Ink blots transform into young men loving their mothers. Twilight fills with villains. We see animation where there is none, conjure up life from light and shade. The material world mutates under our gaze into what we most deeply understand: ourselves and our lives. No meaningless shape is allowed to remain meaningless. We can't help it. It is not just anthropomorphic, but anthropocentric. Anthropocentrism is, perhaps, a worse misvision of the planet than our anthropomorphic compulsion. We are, unsurprisingly, the centre of our universe. We remake the world according to our cultural perceptions. But it's not as if we could do otherwise. Go to Antarctica and stand in the way of a penguin. It won't look up at you. It won't pause on its journey. It simply makes a minimal detour around you and returns to its direct path. This obstacle – you – that can move is not a skewer endangering its life. Not food. Not anything known and therefore to be ignored, incorporated into the landscape with other things to be ignored. You are another kind of rock, probably. Who knew that rocks could move?

Never mind, get on with business. That is the only way you will fit into the penguin universe (though it might have changed now that 40,000 people a year are visiting them). The effort to think other than us-like is almost as difficult for us as it is for penguins. We think it our way.

But, unlike penguins, we are also hyper-self-conscious, and we can't help but know we do this. There's little point in berating ourselves, but we should at least try to place ourselves in a more organic planetary context. So some will make the effort to over-come the natural tendency, either on the grounds that it is unscientific (behaviourism), or that it is unjust and plain inaccurate (post-humanism). It is important to know what it is that we do without thinking about it. It's a gift and a curse we are inclined to believe we do not share with other creatures: to understand what it is we can't help but do.

Anthropomorphism always worries me. That remaking of other-ness as a replication of self – visually, morally or allegorically. The 'cuteness' that we see in animals, which has nothing to do with them but only with the onlooker, distresses me. I observe my own auto-matic humanising assumptions towards the young of other species, the 'feelings' which I suppose when I see an animal in pain or alone or dying, and try to keep it under control. I dislike and disapprove of the colonising aspect of finding easy connection with animals, while at the same time aching for it and identifying it in my relations with animals. The balance of the affect is always 'They are somewhat like me', rather than 'I am somewhat like them'. We deny dignity and selfhood, *whatever that might be to whatever creature it is*, by making sentimental assumptions about why, what or how an animal is expe-riencing. Animals are not there for us to relate to, I want to insist grimly when folk coo or laugh at their behaviour, but it's what we (and I) want to do most with animals, as well, of course, as eat them and utilise their fur and skin and other parts for our clothing, accessories, scent, cosmetic and medicines.

Some years ago, I was in Valencia with a friend for a weekend. One afternoon we were in a taxi driving along a wide busy street. Fleetingly, as we passed at twenty-five or thirty miles an hour, I saw a dog on a lead standing on the edge of the pavement, vomiting into the gutter, its owner standing behind it, waiting for it to finish. It couldn't have been for more than a second that I saw the image before we were already somewhere else. It was a flash, not an incident. My friend in the car noticed nothing, and recalls nothing (I've asked her). I remember it as if it were a slide on a light-box. A still and permanent image is filed in my brain, brightly vivid, with perfect detail and outline. The dog, no particular breed, with its neck extended to throw up, the owner, a woman, unexceptional-looking, holding the lead slackly, waiting for the upheaval to end, not especially anxious. Sometimes, when I wake in the night that picture comes to me, along with the rush of distress – quite physical, like juices flowing – that I had about it at the time, as I sat in the car, already speeding away from the event. An awful sense of pity, of doom even. A lightning knowledge of fear and confusion in the world. The pity is not that the dog is being sick, but that the dog does not know why this is happening to it. It doesn't understand *why* it's being sick. Of course, neither did I, nor, very possibly, did its owner. But we had the ability to find out. We could take the dog to the vet, or have noticed that it had eaten something vile on the street just a few moments before, and connect it to the vomiting. If it turns out the dog is ill, an underlying assumption I instantly made, it won't know why it continues to be sick and in pain (or even that it does continue). The pity I felt at the flashing moment I saw it, and the same pity that comes with every repeating memory of it (as if it were some trauma of my own, so perhaps a screen memory) is quite painful, disturbing, and is about suffering without knowledge. I feel the same way about very small children who are sick. As soon as it is possible to explain the cause of suffering, my distress changes to something more muted and practical. This is not to suggest some special sensitivity of mine, but an admission of the extent to which I identify the world that is not me as me. You could call it empathy, but that would require me to be in the place of the dog. In fact, I put the dog in my place and 'feel' accordingly. I can only be feeling the pity for myself, as if I were the dog, and was vomiting and failing to understand. And it's not, when you come to think of it, necessarily a terrible thing for the dog, because it might not have the assumption that it should understand, or even mind about vomiting. Experience does not have to come with knowledge to be bearable, if you are an other. I can't know. But I can assume up an everlasting storm. Even now, writing about the dog vomiting, I have to suppress an awful sense of panic. The tendency to anthropocentrism and being aware of it in myself makes me all the fiercer when I see crowds laughing at the antics of the chimpanzees in the zoo, or wailing at the cuteness of the suffering king penguins hatching their chicks in the Antarctic winter, although I know perfectly well what the anthropomorphisers are feeling and why. I am what you might call conflicted.

Despret and Haraway quote Barbara Smuts's fieldwork with baboons as a hopeful breakaway from the limitations of behaviourist observational models. Her attitude to living with other creatures makes radical common sense, that dangerous phrase. If you want to know about the other, you have to learn from them to be with them on their terms as well as your own. They and others describe it as a reappropriation of ordinary 'common sense', and a rejection of the sneer about 'folk psychology'. It is a methodology that was seen in the 1970s as new and breakaway. In particular it uses 'focal sampling' as the key. Interaction is what is studied, rather than the isolated animal, so many individual animals in a troop are followed for substantial, repeated and regular periods, having all their movements, interactions and everything they do noted. Then by collating the data, it is possible to see a pattern of social behaviour, to identify recurring contacts between the animals and to see how they operate as individuals and in a society.

This is not unproblematical. There are so many assumptions here. Words like 'friendship' are used, the meanings of the interactions are interpreted according to the fieldworker's understanding of them. The 'mood' of animals on their own and between each other is assessed – 'mental state attribution' it is called by Daniel Povinelli in a collection of articles on the subject of anthropomorphism, *Anthropomorphism, Anecdotes, and Animals*.[23] An article in the same collection by Duane Quiatt, Professor of Anthropology at the University of Colorado, takes an icy look at what he calls this altered perspective by fieldworkers on their subjects.[24] He examines the research methods of Barbara Smuts, along with other field researchers of similar views such as Shirley Strum, another baboon observer, and the writings of Cynthia Moss, an elephant watcher. He quotes Smuts as she describes the need to find a new method that allowed observers to focus 'on those behaviours that were most meaningful to the animals themselves'.[25] Much of the behaviour that was analysed was grooming activity and proximity to other individuals, and these Smuts uses to describe degrees of 'friendship' between certain animals in a troop. More regular grooming and being more frequently within a certain distance of a particular other animal was interpreted as a friendship between them. Smuts asks the question 'What exactly is friendship to a baboon?' and it is clear that she thinks she can get an answer of some sort.[26] Quiatt describes this and similar statements: Altman writing of rhesus monkeys in 1962: 'I left it to the monkeys to tell me what are the basic units of social behaviour'; Louis Leakey sending the untrained Jane Goodall to work at Gombe with chimpanzees, because he wanted someone unhampered by academic prejudice. He quotes Smuts again, saying that the detailed recording of their social interaction allowed her to see the baboons 'from a baboon's perspective', and Strum describing her 'journey into the world of the baboon'.[27] A moment comes when Strum, although trying to preserve her distance from the habituated baboons 'is approached by an immigrant male, Ray, who, positioning himself between Strum and two resident males, solicits her support in agonistic interaction with them. Strum refuses to cooperate. "Ray won his struggle alone," she writes, "but I shall never forget how honored I felt by the compliment paid me".[28] Even though I perfectly understand this emotion, if only because I feel exactly that sometimes when my cat deigns to sit on my lap, and, like the rest of the world, experienced an uprush of envy at David Attenborough's romp with the gorillas, the effect of those statements on Quiatt, and on me, is to question whether the nature of the language Strum uses can be related to effective science.

There is an unmistakable underlying sneer in Quiatt's paper, and I can't help notice that most of the fieldworkers he quotes are women. He also talks about Jane Goodall and Dian Fossey, who he says taught us to look at gorillas as individuals, 'albeit with an uncomfortable feeling that Fossey may have gone a bit too far in preferring gorillas to human beings'.[29] To call his tone patronising is an understatement. At Smuts's declaration: 'I made a determined effort to forget everything I knew about how baboons are supposed to behave. Instead, I tried to let the baboons themselves "tell" me what was important.' Quiatt responds 'Only a spoilsport would suggest that she is unlikely to recognise what is important in baboon behaviour until she puts it in perspective with all that she has learned'.[30]

This way of talking by Smuts and the others Quiatt declares to be a 'very literary and romantic way of describing one's professional work'; he wonders if the shift in perspective demanded and described by the fieldworkers is 'no more than a leap of the anthropomorphic imagination? Is it wholly metaphorical?'[31] Am I being over-sensitive to feel that he's really speaking of that long (and still) assumed split between the literary and imaginative (female), and the scientific and factual (male)? He does talk about Nicholas Humphrey and other men who have been involved in the new methodology, but the male/female, professional/unprofessional, science/imagination, objective/autobiographical dichotomies keep emerging in his text. Still, let's suppose there is a possibility that women might approach their science differently, and permit imagination in their work (I'd even allow that some men might be included in this behaviour). Science only precludes imagination, or even the literary, if the results are falsified by using them. It's right and proper that methodology be questioned, so let us also forget that Quiatt is a man and that his tone is superior in an unpleasantly familiar way. The fact is that I also find myself conflicted (again, always again) by those quotes of Smuts and Strum, and not just by the words pulled out by Quiatt, but by readings of other zoological researchers who take the same approach. At least a little wary, in spite of Despret's positive and delightful description of the upshot of Smuts methodology:

> She explains that, having learned the way baboons express their emotions or intentions, she could respond to them and be understood. As a result, the baboons started to give her very deliberate dirty looks, which made her move away. This signaled a profound change: Smuts was not treated like an object (to avoid), but was recognized as a subject, a reliable subject with whom baboons could communicate, who would move

away when told to do so, and with whom things could be clearly established.[32]

The idea that it is possible to 'become' or live with or befriend another species, or even 'learn the way of the baboons' is immensely beguiling, as Quiatt says (again suggesting that it's a soft option): '. . . isn't it what we all want, at some level? – to throw off the blinders of convention and habit and peer directly into the heart of behaviour?'[33]

Yes, it is. We all want to interact with the gaze of our cats, to know the other, although (or perhaps because) we do not even know ourselves very effectively. It is a fact that we do, but it is a fact that can be dismissed as 'literary' or ideological (as opposed to realistic) or emotional (as opposed to rational). For the life of me I cannot see why people should not attempt to spend quality time with other species and try and learn what it is like to be them and to live on their terms. Nor do I see why their reports should be dismissed as 'unscientific'. The Skinner Box is no more of a reality for an animal stuck in one than a human observer who hangs around in its habitat for years pretending to be one of them. How can animals-in-laboratory results be more 'scientifically' accurate? What can you learn about learning from rats in laboratory mazes, other than how rats in laboratory mazes learn? Something, but not 'the truth' about rats, let alone people.

But equally I worry about the suggestion by those using the new methodology that they have got to the heart of the matter – that they are more effective in being undeluded than the old-style lab researchers and the behaviourists. Certainly, Smuts and her admirers have picked up the twentieth-century notion of the impossibility of objectivity in a way the behaviourists haven't. But having acknowledged that we can't absent ourselves from what we are watching, can we then assume that simply by living there and looking very closely, we have overcome the limited one-way perspective? Quiatt remembers Richard Garner, who, at the turn of the twentieth century, shut himself in a cage in the rainforest and let the chimpanzees come and look at him while he played them phonograph recordings of chimp sounds. He supposed, when he recorded the chimps in the zoo, that he had come to understand some of their utterances as meaningful – though like Australians and Americans, they must have mutated from their wild forest cousins' language. He watched as the wild chimpanzees 'responded' to the calls. Quiatt suggests that, like Garner, we must always remain in our cage, which is made of '. . . our own cognitive limitations, which we hardly know how to take into account but cannot ignore when considering observer perspective'.[34] This is the crux of the matter, though Quiatt hardly comes up with a 'scientific' solution to this problem any more than Derrida, Haraway or I have. In all likelihood there is no solution – and there, along with our cognitive isolation – is a truth we can hardly bear, so we argue (and sometimes sneer) that we are right and they are wrong, in order to keep the uncertainty at bay.

Primate ethologist Frans de Waal describes an experiment that was later famously done with human beings, in which it emerged that monkeys (all or some is not clear) stopped pulling a handle to get food for themselves when they witnessed another monkey being shocked each time. In one case, a monkey refused to pull the handle for twelve days. 'These monkeys were literally *starving* themselves to avoid inflicting pain on others.'[35] That sentence, and the title of the book, *Our Inner Ape*, powerfully suggest a connection of concern for others between humans and monkeys or apes. After describing the refusal response, de Waal acknowledges that it is not likely that the explanation is actually a concern for the other's welfare, but 'distress caused by another's distress'. The suggestion then is that we too, *like the monkeys*, respond with sympathy for others because of the emotional discomfort it causes to ourselves (which a behaviourist like Donald Broom would then convert into analysable chemical changes and discuss in terms of evolutionary fitness). It can work both ways. If you're inclined to believe that we are like apes, then the latter argument is the one you take. If you fancy that apes are like us, you can go with de Waal's former statement 'literally *starving* themselves to death'. Then again, the infamous Stanford Experiment seemed to suggest that humans, at least, would overcome their distress and keep pressing the pain button if ordered to do so. In an experiment de Waal did himself, he placed two capuchin monkeys side by side and exchanged pebbles for food. Then he introduced inequity. He exchanged pebbles for food with both of them twenty-five times in a row, alternately:

> If both received cucumber, this was called equity. In this situation, the monkeys exchanged all the time, happily eating the food. But if we gave one of them grapes while keeping the other on cucumber, things took an unexpected turn. This was called inequity . . . grapes are among the best rewards. Upon noticing their partner's salary raise, monkeys who had been perfectly willing to work for cucumber suddenly went on strike. Not only did they perform reluctantly but they got agitated, hurling the pebbles and sometimes even the cucumber slices out of the test chamber.[36]

De Waal says, 'This surely was a strong reaction equivalent to what, with some pomposity, is known in people as "inequity aversion".' Here again we have a suggestion that monkeys and humans have something in common: a sense of fairness. The following sentence acknowledges: 'Admittedly, our monkeys showed an egocentric form of it. Rather than supporting the noble principle of fairness for everybody, they got upset about being short-changed.'[37] Surely, a real sense of fair play would have had the monkey with the grape offering some of it to his deprived neighbour? The experiments are set up and observed meticulously, and the inferences are carefully described, but in between de Waal's readers are allowed to make some, at the very least, woolly connections and conclusions about human nature. I imagine that in his scientific papers he would be unlikely to equate grapes with a pay rise and, as he does below, the bonuses of Wall Street bankers. Once again, humans look at animals and find ways to make them tell us something we want to hear about ourselves.

In an article for the John Templeton Foundation's website*, de Waal offers an overview in which he concludes that there is a capacity for morality and sympathy in the transactional behaviour of apes, and how it could be as effective a biologically adaptive feature as methods of mate selection. He ends with the suggestion that evolutionary biology is at the heart of our niceness as well as our more negative characteristics (perhaps to give evolution a better reputation, since he is writing for a religiously based organisation). He is readjusting the shadows in the darker assumptions about our animal selves made by the likes of Desmond Morris and Robert Ardrey in the 1960s and 1970s, and he does so by being a primatologist who takes anthropomorphism seriously. The italics in the following passage are mine.

---

*From the website, www.templeton.org: 'Most of the Foundation's grant-making supports scientific research at top universities, in such fields as theoretical physics, cosmology, evolutionary biology, cognitive science, and social science relating to love, forgiveness, creativity, purpose, and the nature and origin of religious belief. The Foundation also encourages and supports informed, open-minded dialogue between scientists and theologians as they work on the "Big Questions" in their distinctive fields of inquiry.'

Reciprocity . . . is visible when chimpanzees share food specifically with those who have recently groomed them or supported them in power struggles. Sex is often part of the mix. Wild males have been observed to take great risks raiding papaya plantations, returning to share the delicious fruit with fertile females in exchange for copulation. Chimps know how to strike a deal.

Our primate relatives also exhibit pro-social tendencies and a sense of fairness. In experiments, chimpanzees voluntarily open a door to give a companion access to food, and capuchin monkeys seek rewards for others even if they themselves gain nothing from it. *Perhaps helping others is self-rewarding in the same way that humans feel good doing good.* In other studies, primates will happily perform a task for cucumber slices until they see others being rewarded with grapes, which taste so much better. They become agitated, throw down their measly cucumbers, and go on strike. A perfectly fine vegetable has become unpalatable! *I think of their reaction whenever I hear criticism of the extravagant bonuses on Wall Street.*

These primates show *hints of a moral order*, and yet most people still prefer to view nature as 'red in tooth and claw'. We never seem to doubt that there is continuity between humans and other animals with respect to negative behavior – when humans maim and kill each other, we are quick to call them 'animals' – but we prefer to claim noble traits exclusively for ourselves. When it comes to the study of human nature, this is a losing strategy, however, because it excludes about half of our background. Short of appealing to divine intervention as an explanation, this more attractive half is also the product of evolution, a view now increasingly supported by animal research.[38]

It isn't that I think de Waal is necessarily wrong about either primates or people, it's simply that the terms of the discussion are so variable, and our interest is garnered by making it seem that so much is at stake for *us*.

It is impossible, I am sure, for us to study animals entirely on their own terms, yet if we don't, we ought to be clear that we interpret what we see according to our feeling about ourselves. Even the idea that we should be thinking in terms of cooperating with animals rather than studying them from on high, is an idea based on what kind of human beings we want to be. We call behaviourists and anthropomorphist ethologists by political names – of the right and the left, socialist and fascist. Biological and evolutionary research has always been tainted by service to the state, as it was in the case of Lorenz under the Third Reich, or Herbert Spencer's Victorian Social Darwinism, or Lysenko's attempted verification of the inheritance of acquired characteristics for Soviet Russia. We really can't talk about rats, either in literature or science, without talking about ourselves, and how much harder it is to investigate the world of primates without believing that they are us and we are them – or even that they are not us and never will be because only we can be us. Post-humanists may want to look the other way: to see animals clearly, no longer through the murky glass of us, but they will, like everyone, always be mired in millennia of cultural assumptions and our inability not to make human use of the non-human animal world.

PART FOUR

LOVE AND HATE

I am I because my little dog knows me, but perhaps he does not and if he did I would not be I.
Oh no oh no.

Identity A Poem, Gertrude Stein

7

UNDER OUR SKIN

A Perplexing Silence

Love and hate can so easily get out of hand. But our loving and hating of those who are (in our understanding) mute, like the sick dog in Valencia, like M Derrida's staring cat, is all the more potent for their lack of conversation. We are so very constituted by our language that when we come up against an absence of it as we know it, we supply the missing words, or at any rate interpret the silence as if it contained words. If we can't fill up the silence to our satisfaction, we take it as an indication of either extreme helplessness or extreme malevolence. The love and the hate we feel for animals is surely born out of their uncanny silence – for all that it may be our own surplus chattering which is the anomaly in the world.

We were all, once, wordless ourselves. That must be important when we encounter silence in the Other. We were, as a result, much loved and hated by the chatterers who stood over our cradles and coaxed us eventually into language. Even once we have start to talk, it takes many years before we let go of our infantile affinity with the mute, if we ever really do. Small children have secret alliances with all kinds of inanimate and conversationless entities. I talked to dolls and soft toys, confided in books, coloured bricks – even small pieces of fabric had the substance of personhood and the possibility of relationship to me. I had an invisible friend, not like some invisible friends, another child; mine was called 'God'. He was powerful but not omniscient. At any rate, one had to drawn his attention to things. I told him stories of what was happening and asked for practical, worldly assistance in return for certain repetitive behaviours (saying 'Please' a hundred times before going to sleep, or tying my shoelaces correctly three times in a row in the morning) which for some unfathomable reason gave him satisfaction. He never spoke to me. The ways of my God, my dolls and my coloured bricks, were mysterious, but they all understood language. They were not substitutes for real people, for friends, they were different and essential, because only they could be told what I dared tell no one else, and only they knew the real me and my life. Even if they never spoke to me, they *understood* what I said. It didn't cross my mind, as I try now to remember, that other children had their own private confidential intimates. I never discussed it with them, it didn't matter. It was irrelevant. A million individual other privacies didn't impinge on mine.

On the other hand, I knew, without having to think about it too much, that I wasn't alone in my confidences to the other world. I read books (as well as talked to them). The A. A. Milne stories were immensely reassuring from a very early age. Christopher Robin's whole life as it came to me from the books was involved with the soft animal toys that lived on the end of his bed. They were far more puzzled by the world than my confidants, but they had language and interacted with Christopher Robin. Most books for young children contained inanimate or languageless entities that lived and spoke and sometimes interacted with their child owners. Children talking to each other was rather rare in those earliest books. Most of all, for me, there was Alice, who talked to anything and everything, and was never surprised for long at the otherness of the world. Alice made and makes complete sense to me. Even the enclosing narratives, before she entered Wonderland or the Looking-glass World, confirmed what I knew.

> Alice was beginning to get very tired of sitting by her sister on the bank, and of having nothing to do: once or twice she had peeped into the book her sister was reading, but it had no pictures or conversations in it, 'and what is the use of a book,' thought Alice, 'without pictures or conversations?'

Or of a book with which you couldn't have a conversation?

Alice had a silent Other, one (not having a pet myself) that seemed to me even more satisfactory than a doll or God.

> 'Kitty, can you play chess? Now, don't smile, my dear, I'm asking it seriously. Because when we were playing just now, you watched just as if you understood it: and when I said "Check!" you purred! ... Kitty, dear, let's pretend ... Now, if only you'll attend, Kitty, and not talk so much, I'll tell you all my ideas about Looking-glass House.'

And then, after melting through the glass and having her strangely ordinary, or ordinarily strange adventures, Alice returned to the regular drawing room on the other side of the mirror, and to the kitten she was still holding in her lap.

> It is a very inconvenient habit of kittens (Alice had once made the remark) that, whatever you say to them, they always purr. 'If

they would only purr for "yes" and mew for "no", or any rule of that sort,' she had said, 'so that one could keep up a conversation! But how can you talk with a person if they always say the same thing?'

Saying the same thing is the same as saying nothing. Derrida points out, while having communication problems of his own with a pussy-cat, that the way cats communicate in the Alice books is the very essence of uncanny silence. The Cheshire Cat does speak, although of alarming things: 'We're all mad here. I'm mad. You're mad.' He comes and goes repeatedly up on the branch of his tree before he makes a final disappearance, leaving behind nothing more than a grin. 'I've often seen a cat without a grin,' thought Alice, 'But a grin without a cat!' (What is the use of a cat without words and pictures?) The Cheshire Cat is somewhat terrifying, while Kitty is exasperating but lovable. Neither of them is willing or able to give satisfactory or reassuring accounts of themselves or the world. Alice is not just waking up, but growing up. The lack of conversation in the Other must be confronted. Animals are not *us*. Animals are *not-us*. But the dream world hasn't quite departed, and it doesn't ever go entirely away. If living in a dream is being mad, then being mad is living in a dream where everything and anything that is not you might be your closest friend or deadliest foe.

Delusional Parasitosis

The sensation feels like bugs, worms, or mites that are biting, crawling over or burrowing into, under, or out of your skin. They must be there, because you can feel them and you are even pretty sure that you can see them. You may also believe that your home or furniture is infested, but you may be the only one who knows they are there.

No one seems to think they exist except you. Nothing seems to get rid
of them. So what are they?

University of California/Statewide Integrated Pest

Management Program/How to Manage Pests/Pests

of Homes, Structures, People and Pets

During my late teens, I discovered another kind of animal in my
life in addition to all the lovable cuddly toys, the nursery domestic
animals in books and cartoons and various real animals of my childhood. These didn't fit into any category of creature I'd previously
known. They were, for sure, 'insects', but though I hazarded the odd
guess, I couldn't say precisely which particular insects they were. I
knew them by another categorical description: parasites. Funguses
can be parasites, but what most immediately comes to mind when
I think of parasites are insects and crawling. The two go together.
The other thing I knew about them was that they were *my* parasites.
They lived on and possibly in me. I hosted them. Unwillingly. There
was, apart from their very insistence on inhabiting me, no communication between us.

It started just after I left school, and continued during (although
it was not the reason for) my period in various psychiatric hospitals
and later, in the mid and late sixties. The diagnosis by the hospitals
was specifically 'depression' and more generally 'borderline personality disorder'. (This latter was at the time a common diagnosis,
particularly of difficult young women. It has, I think, changed in the
way it is used, although it still seems to be broader than it is explana-
tory.) I had some reason for my secret anxiety, initially. A boyfriend
told me that he had pubic crabs and gave me a little pot of ointment
from the chemist to deal with any he had donated to me. I never
actually saw any on myself, although I looked carefully and often,
and used the pot of ointment until it was empty. This was a year or

two before my first hospitalisation in that period. I never really felt sure that I had got rid of the crabs – not, as I say, that I'd seen any in the first place, and I'd been assured they were easily visible to the human eye. I was horrified at the idea of crabs. Living things crawling on me, and so close to *inside* me. Of course, I was also upset that my boyfriend, much older than me, had them in the first place, presumably from sleeping around. An emotionally complicated situation, further complicated by my general decline into depression months later, my father dying suddenly, quitting school just before my A-level exams and then leaving my foster-mother's house for a bed-sitting room on my own. Enough to get me hospitalised without anyone knowing about my private alarm.

From then on for two years or more, in hospital and out, I was convinced that I was infested. 'Infested' was the word I thought, as well as 'contaminated'. The pubic lice multiplied to a plethora and became imaginatively licenced to inhabit my entire body. They crawled on my arms, my torso, my legs, my hair, sometimes my face and neck. They had become all-rounder lice. Not even lice, if someone had pointed out the impossible ethology I had invented for them. They were . . . I didn't know what they were, but they were. Insects, lice-like, flea-like, tic-like crawling creatures that lived on me, and indeed, in me. I thought they burrowed under my skin and emerged to wander about on the surface in the dark of night or under cover of my clothes. I felt them, itching in specific parts, arms, legs, head, everywhere, and the redness I saw when I finished scratching my skin convinced me that they were there (so easy now to write that rational sentence). I saw them, always out of the corner of my eye. I became most distressed at night. I would feel their presence and then turn on the light quickly to catch them, but of course, they had burrowed back into my skin by the time I could focus. It was a game of malevolent hide-and-seek. They had super-lice powers: they sensed me looking for them, and always dodged me. I turned on the lights often during each night. I was sure I saw them, yet I could never quite say what they looked like. I found evidence of them, even occasionally caught one and killed it as you do a flea, squeezing it between my fingers. Then I would put it in my palm and examine it carefully under a light. I saw it was something, a mote, a dot, black, white, grey, but never quite well enough to be sure exactly what. It could have been a flake of skin, a speck of dust, a tiny thread, but I knew it wasn't. In that special way you know when you *really* know, or are crazy.

It was a continuing hell. The horror of it lurked in my mind, on my body, in the back of my mind always, even when I wasn't frantically searching, and it went on for two or three years. And I kept silent about it. When I was living on my own, I repeatedly washed my bedding and clothes at the hottest possible temperature at the launderette, but it was never enough. Eventually, I put all my bedding and my clothes, except for one outfit, into a plastic bag and threw them away. I couldn't explain to people why I was wearing the same clothes all the time, or to myself what to do about the obvious fact that this last outfit must also be contaminated. But for all that, I functioned, as it were, normally. I didn't discuss my obsession with anyone who was available to help me, doctors or friends. I kept it to myself, making it impossible for anyone to know and therefore do anything to assist me. The reason was that I was ashamed to be contaminated. I thought I must be the only person in the world, that this was the worst anyone could imagine (I could imagine) about another person, and that people would be disgusted and shun me. At the same time I kept my distance from people. I was contagious. If people came close to me they risked becoming infested too. With that, I was at the same time both immensely powerful and completely powerless. There was another reason I didn't speak about it:

I sort of knew it was crazy, and that what I was convinced of was impossible, while nevertheless being sure that I was indeed infested. So I also didn't mention it because it was so mad.

Just once I told someone about it. When I was in the first hospital, in St Pancras, I was getting exhausted with my searching of myself, it became unbearable, and I said to a nurse who I liked that I thought I was infested. I suppose she told the doctor. I imagine now that she understood that I wasn't actually covered with crawling insects, but it was arranged to my relief that I go to the infestation clinic, which happened to be next door to the hospital (an awful confirmatory coincidence, it seemed to me at the time). I was escorted there and put into a disinfectant bath, went through the process of having my hair combed for nits and coating my body with whatever the lotion was that was used to get rid of body and pubic lice. They checked me all over, and said I was OK. I was content for about twenty-four hours before I knew it hadn't worked. I told the nurse, who explained that the treatment was infallible. So I didn't mention it again. But I bought stuff from chemists' and regularly anointed myself with the chemical insecticide and dosed my head with lice lotion. Very gradually, without my really noticing, I seemed to grow out of it, as children do those indefinable stomach pains they have. Every now and then I'd have a panic and go to the chemist, but those episodes became more spaced out and, eventually, I realised that the terror had gone away, even if somewhere in me there remains a small dark area that twitches anxiously from time to time.

No one used the phrase 'delusional parasitosis'. Actually, I only discovered that it was a condition with a name when I was researching and reading for this book on animals. I knew I'd been crazy during that period, but I didn't know I'd been crazy with a condition that had a name, and that although it wasn't common, was well known in psychiatric literature. Not just psychiatric literature.

Delusional parasitosis is where psychiatry meets academic entomology and pest control.

Varmint Guard in Columbus, Ohio, offers 'complete residential pest control services and our regular treatment programs are designed to keep your homes pest free. Insects, rodents, bats and all nuisance wildlife problems are effectively addressed'. It has an excellent website with a Pest Library that offers a chance to identify Pests of the Season and it also has a separate three-page essay describing delusional parasitosis. It gives full details of the symptoms and explains that Varmint Guard operatives are trained to examine a house thoroughly, leaving sticky traps and investigating the areas the customer is suspicious of. Then:

> If no candidate arthropods are found on the sticky monitors, upon examination, then the Varmint Guard staff entomologist will call or visit the customer, tactfully discuss the findings from the monitors, and compassionately express caution that an indoor treatment of the residence or workplace with insecticide is not the solution and is not recommended for safety and legal considerations. Rather, the solution may very well lie with consulting a healthcare professional or industrial/home environment hygienist. In most instances, the delusory sensations will not subside unless the sufferer is treated with certain antipsychotic drugs, which must be prescribed by an attending psychiatrist.
>
> The difficulty in helping victims of delusory parasitosis towards a lasting solution to their problem lies in the legal risks associated with suggesting an appointment with a qualified (DP-experienced) psychiatrist. A family physician is best-qualified to recommend this course of action to victims or involved family

members. Unfortunately, most physicians who become involved in such cases lend credibility to their delusory patient's reports of bites and burrowing sensations and mistakenly recommend pest management as the answer.

A website called *What's That Bug?* carries a letter from the operations manager of a pest management firm:

> Dear Bugman,
> I'm nearly at my wits-end. I work for a pest control company and I've had a gentleman calling me trying to verbally describe a bug that is 'burrowing' into his (and his wife's) skin. He's been to several Doctors, Dermatologists, and Emergency Rooms – nobody can identify the problem.

Several responses suggest that delusional parasitosis might be the answer, and finally one from Nancy C. Hinkle of the Department of Entomology at the University of Georgia suggests referring the clients there, where a study is being made of the subject. It's not uncommon for sufferers to go to entomologists on their own. The second (even the first) port of call for someone plagued by imaginary insects is to an expert who will provide a practical solution. There is among entomologists an instant diagnosis known as 'the matchbox sign'. The client will bring out a matchbox (or container) for the entomologist, containing what they insist is the problem bug which they have brought for identification. The bug expert sees a speck of skin, a hair with a follicle attached, or dandruff, and knows great tact is called for. Hinkle has written a detailed paper in the *American Entomologist* describing the condition of delusional parasitosis and her experiences with clients who came to her for help. It is distracting for someone whose work is to study cattle infestation to have to

deal with psychiatric patients, but she is not alone. Nor is she lacking in understanding. There is something about insects, as we all
know, and most kinds of madness have echoes in the 'normal' world.
Those with delusional parasitosis often spread the delusion to those
close to them, so that family members believe they can see the creatures too. Hinkle isn't surprised:

> Entomologists who deal with delusory parasitosis cases will attest
> to this. Despite finding no arthropod in any samples provided,
> there is a strong urge to take a shower following these examina-
> tions. Consciously, one realises that there is no infestation, but
> subconsciously one often feels the 'creepy-crawlies' after looking
> through the victim's scurf. In fact, the author, while reading
> through the delusory parasitosis literature in preparing this article,
> found herself absentmindedly scratching; before the manuscript
> was completed, her arms and legs bore distinct scarification.

People can be deluded about all manner of things, but the belief that
insects have invaded the body and cannot be seen or effectively dealt
with suggests a particular horror of something other – a living, deliberate other – far too close to our known selves. Think of *The Fly*. In
my recollection, there was a terrible secret I had, and it was shared
only by the creatures that had come to inhabit me. In some decidedly
unpleasant way, the insects and I colluded in a truth that other people
couldn't be party to or understand. The creatures had chosen me,
were closer to me than any person I knew. They and I were an *us*.
They say that there is never more than six feet between you and the
nearest rat, even though they remain invisible for most of the time.
Derrida was anxious about his cat looking from a bathroom's distance
at his naked body. I was host to a multitude of animate creatures who
had come very much closer. Animals trouble us at any distance.

More Cats

And then there's too much loving, if that's the right word. It is and it isn't. But that's always at least potentially true of the word 'love', in whatever context it crops up. The ambiguity of love is as manifest in what people feel for animals as it is in what people feel for people. Consider the Cat Lady. Most areas have one. Most areas (villages, we used to call them) have always had one. The Cat Lady has made a small but significant journey over the past three or four hundred years. She began as the local wise, if odd, woman, by definition on the fringes of society, with her companion cats, to whom you went if you needed a spell or a cure. She had a hard time when the Church and society began to persecute her, and, finally overwhelmed and often killed on account of her role as an outsider, she lost her status as a common resource. The useful, weird woman with a cat became the dangerous, satanic witch with her feline familiar. Gradually, she emerged as the (usually) kind-hearted if sometimes a little scary, solitary elderly lady who lives down the bottom of the road, and provides a social service for stray or unwanted cats and their reluctant owners in the area.

The contemporary Cat Lady might be quite benign: a member of the Cats Protection League, supported by the organisation, taking in strays and fostering them until they can be re-homed. She (or sometimes he) might, on the other hand, be a freelance cat lover whose own unmet inner needs cause his or her feline philanthropy to get wildly out of hand: someone with a mental illness who needs cats (or sometimes dogs) and whose life becomes overwhelmed by them. Our way in the twentieth and twenty-first centuries requires a re-description of the folk history as pathology. 'Animal hoarder' is not just a definition of what these people do, it is now a diagnosis. It's worth wondering if the naming of this newly described mental disorder isn't a contemporary version of the earlier designation of difficult and inconvenient old ladies, by society and the Church, as witches or heretics. Who knows whether we understand so much more now that we can identify and name a condition for a behaviour that has always existed (they're not wyse women or witches, they're pathological cat hoarders), or if we create named syndromes because it's our 'scientific' version of controlling those who won't live within civilised bounds of decency, and a way of reshaping our visceral disgust and fear into medicalised concern? An abstract of a paper in the *Clinical Psychology Review* defines the problem:

Animal hoarding is a poorly understood, maladaptive, destructive behavior whose etiology and pathology are only beginning to emerge. We compare and contrast animal hoarding to the compulsive hoarding of objects and proceed to draw upon attachment theory, the literature of personality disorder and trauma, and our own clinical experience to propose a developmental trajectory. Throughout life, there is a persistent struggle to form a functional attachment style and achieve positive social integration. For some people, particularly those affected by a dysfunctional primary attachment experience in childhood, a protective, comforting relationship with animals may form an indelible imprint. In adulthood, when human attachment has been chronically problematic, compulsive caregiving of animals can become the primary means of maintaining or building a sense of self. Improving assessment and treatment of animal hoarders requires attention to contributing psychosocial conditions, while taking into account the centrality of the animals to the hoarder's identity, self-esteem and sense of control. It is our hope that the information presented will provide a basis upon which clinicians can focus their own counseling style, assessment, and methods of treatment.[1]

This sounds suspiciously like teaching old witches to suck eggs. Surely, it's not very poorly understood, except by those writing of a new psychiatric disorder. Instead of a *Malleus Maleficarum* (*The Hammer for Witches* written for Inquisitors in 1486), we have a diagnosis and management plan for them. Sometimes we do little more than alter the language with which we isolate the difficult. Still, we don't strangle and burn them, we just sanitise and medicate them. Old people (often, but not always women, and there were male witches too) may be lonely, and some of them might have had unhappy emotional lives. Animals become vitally important to them as a way of getting affection, being in control, having something of their own. Animal hoarding is slipped into the taxonomy of madness as a subset of borderline personality disorder (BPD) and obsessive compulsive disorder (OCD). It doesn't get us very far in preventing the situations from getting so out of hand, but it does isolate the problem around the sufferer and thereby deal with what is especially inexplicable and distressing to many people about animal hoarding. Hoarding may be a sign of a general symptom, but people who hoard newspapers, though they might live in impossible, dangerous and unhygienic conditions, don't get quite such a bad write-up. They don't get arrested and charged, and only rarely are their houses condemned. But animal hoarders force us (with the escaping smell and the sight of too many living things in the same place) to confront our own intensely complex attitudes to non-human animals.

In October 2009, in Sacramento, Kathy and Paul Franco, an elderly couple, were arrested and their house condemned as unfit for human habitation. The police had been called because of the smell, and they found seventy-seven cats in the house which was almost ankle-deep in faeces. They were charged with animal cruelty.

In Boston in 2003, Heidi Erickson's apartment was raided. Five malnourished cats and a Great Dane were discovered, as well as sixty dead cats, most of them, though not all, frozen. She was banned from keeping cats in the city of Boston, but a month later a second apartment belonging to her was discovered in a nearby town, which contained fifty-two sick cats and a dozen dead bodies. 'They're my family,' Erickson told the police. She described herself as 'bereft' of her 'babies'. In the *Boston Phoenix*, Clea Simon explains:

> In a 1999 study, it found about 2000 cases of hoarding nationally each year. While not all cases are as extreme as Erickson's, most hoarders (76 per cent) are female and more than half live alone, as Erickson does. At 42, she's younger than the 46 per cent of hoarders who are 60 or over. But her actions do match the 80 per cent of cases in which dead or sick animals are found, and the 60 per cent in which the hoarder does not acknowledge a problem.

It starts out well enough, with one or two cats, and then escalates out of control. Local inconvenient cats are brought to the old person, known for their fondness for animals, they breed, strays wander in for the food and their numbers grow. Reality slips away, the cats get sick, or cost much more to feed than their rescuer's income. The hoarders neglect themselves as well as the cats, because they can't cope with the ever-increasing size of the problem, and they deal with their overwhelming difficulties, as many of us do, by denying that anything is wrong.

A study of the problem found

> Dead or sick animals were discovered in 80 per cent of reported cases, yet in nearly 60 per cent of cases the hoarder would not acknowledge the problem (Patronek, 1999). In 69 per cent of cases, animal faeces and urine accumulated in living areas, and over one-quarter of the

hoarders' beds were soiled with faeces or urine. Hoarders' justifications for their behavior included an intense love of animals, the
feeling that animals were surrogate children, the belief that no one
else would or could take care of them, and the fear that the animals
would be euthanized . . . a significant number of hoarders had non-
functional utilities (i.e., bathroom plumbing, cooking facilities, heat,
refrigeration and electricity).[2]

It becomes catastrophic and the evidence seeps out into the world.
When newspapers get hold of it and publish descriptions and pictures it's easy to be appalled at the suffering to the animals, but there's
also something else: disgust. It is partly to do with dirt, of which
there is plenty, but there is also a kind of panic, and I feel it rising in
myself, at the idea of too many non-human creatures living in a
human habitation. We use the words 'seethe' and 'swarm' to describe
alien things that are too many and make us feel queasy and overwhelmed as a result. Insects (like my illusory parasites and the real
things), snakes in a pit, and rats seethe and swarm; and cats, too,
when they are in a small, contained human space seethe and swarm,
and disturb us deep down by their unmanageable numbers, even if
we are cat lovers and can explain away our distress at animal hoarding as a result of our affection for the animals who are suffering. One
cat and an attractive woman (Cat and Holly Golightly in *Breakfast at
Tiffany's*) is eloquent and appealing. Seventy cats and an old lady who
can't keep up with the cleaning, feeding and sickness, is an infestation: repellent, and deeply, mysteriously disturbing. Animals in a
human context are fine when we are in control of them and when
they are healthy, amusing and obedient companions. We love them
and love ourselves loving them. But if they won't be loved, or get well
or obey, like the baby bird I found and brought home, and instead go
dying hopelessly, ungratefully and horribly behind radiators, or they

get sick and mangy, or multiply exponentially and shit all over the floor, creating filth and an intolerable stink, we hate them, really loathe them, and we want them away from our sight, as I did the baby bird, not to have to think about how everything can go so wrong so easily in an apparently ordered world without anyone intending it. And we are especially horror-struck by those who cause this to happen by needing so much that they don't notice the awfulness of too much. The needing is monstrous and fearful. And perhaps we are disturbed, too, by the way the animals, no matter what their condition, stay, colluding with, even loving, it would seem, their crazy unlovable carer. Too much love, or something that has nothing to do with love at all, but desperate need and a capacity to live with the intolerable on both sides – animals show us all that too.

However, prior to the pathological or the uncanny, there's a milder state of animal obsession that moves or amuses us. It's a very fine balancing point, but with reassurance (railings, say, or official approval) the distress at too many living creatures, at seething cats, swarming felines, can be suppressed. On my first visit to Rome a few years ago, I stayed in a hotel near the square of sunken excavation at Torre Argentina. I wandered across the road from my hotel to look down into the ruins; taking an easy minimal tourist moment. It is one of the oldest temples in Rome, built around 400–300 BC, the place where Brutus stabbed Julius Caesar in 44 BC and it's a perfect, neatly contained image of Roman ruins: you look down from the pavement at fragments of walls, stone columns of varying heights, upright and toppled, pathways interrupted by broken, scattered slabs of stone, worn steps leading to an altar. Most ruins are empty places, filled only by passing, wandering tourists, coming and going along defined routes, but Torre Argentina, though walled off from the city above it, is an inhabited ruin. All the paths, columns and slabs and creeping foliage are furniture, walkways, resting places in shade or sun, dining facilities and meeting areas for the hundreds of stray cats who live down there in their subterranean, antique feline city. After the excavation was completed in 1929, some feral and stray cats moved in to hang out in this safe, out-of-the-way place, and soon the *gattari* (the Italian for Cat Ladies) arrived to take care of them – one of them the almost mythic actress Anna Magnani, who was working at the *teatro* nearby.

I spent a contented hour or more every day while I was in Rome leaning on the railings, looking down at Cat Central. Safe and untroubled, they lead what appear to be purposeful, self-regulated lives among the ancient ruins. They loll in the sun, rest in the shade, sniff and scratch around in the greenery growing up and around the ancient stones; others idly stroll the paths or run swiftly along the tops of walls, leaping over gaps left by history to the next broken segment. They perch on fractured columns, watching those walking below them and sometimes pounce. They meet up, sniffing each other briefly and pass by unconcerned, or arch their backs and challenge each other with deadly stares or unearthly yowls. There are groups which are perfectly comfortable together in their own particular area, others are individuals exploring and testing alien territory, who belong in different parts of the ruins with their own comrades, while some of the cats look as if they only ever walk alone, as cats are supposed to do. But all of them choose to be there, as Bunty chooses to live in my house, and as Darcy eventually chose (or his cat-Alzheimer's chose) not to. It is their home. And it looks, from their untroubled existence down there, that they know it. As all cats do, they own it by being there.

It is safer down in the ruins than up on the streets dodging forests of legs, cars and motor scooters, but they are also there because of the saucers that are dotted around the landscape. There has been a continuous stream of *gattari* since 1929. Some are Italian, but there have also been ex-patriot English and German women who have taken it on themselves to care for the cats. They used their own money to feed them and set up Torre Argentina as a sanctuary. People now bring their unwanted cats, or cats they have found ailing, troubled or troubling in the streets, to the small office the *gattari* have made down the stairs under the pavement. Several thousand cats a year pass through, and they are inspected, nursed, fed and, if possible, sent on to a foster-home. Two women, Silvia and Lia, have been in charge since 1994, having taken over from a solitary woman who was feeding and caring for the cats without any kind of assistance. 'This woman's generous efforts put her on the verge of economical and emotional collapse,' writes Silvia on the Torre Argentina website. Now, teams of volunteers help to keep the cats fed, clean and overseen. Vets offer their services as charity. Almost all of the cats living in the sanctuary have feline leukaemia, but they are given treatment and taken into the office, which doubles as a hospital, to be cared for when they need it. There are around 250 cats permanently at Torre Argentina, as well as the cats people bring along, all of which are spayed and neutered before they are released into the ruins. The ones that don't find foster-homes stay in Torre Argentina and some are 'adopted at a distance' as a means of providing income for the sanctuary. Nevertheless, Silvia and Lia are still squatters in their underground office, which remains unconnected to the city sewers. They display devotion and offer Rome a service (though one that is apparently unappreciated by the city council), and no one suggests that they suffer from the pathology of cat hoarding. The differences are structural – the cats they care for are outside rather than in their own homes; they have created an organisation that helps to fund and find volunteers and medics, who offer

181

their services to deal humanely with the animals and their needs. There is no denial. It doesn't seem to threaten to get out of hand, and, of course, for the onlooker, it is a sunken separated site with substantial containing walls and railings. This alleviates any anxiety of excess. Idiotic, of course, because the cats easily slip through the railings when they want, and the *gattari* and even the public can open the gate and descend into the ruins. But it remains a contained spectacle. There is no need to do more than stand, as many do, and as I did, looking down at the lives of the animals, spectating, almost believing they are creatures in the wild, cats as we rarely see them, leading their own uninterrupted lives, as it seems, and to feel grateful to the women who are prepared to take responsibility for them. Nothing too frightening there, and much to be grateful for.

In America, Craig Grant also seems to have managed to sidestep the diagnosis of animal hoarding. His story reads remarkably like the pathology, but stays just this side of alarming for the observer. He was retired and his son left home, not taking his cat with him, or perhaps deliberately leaving him for his father who would otherwise have been alone. Grant objected; he didn't like the cat much, but gradually he and the cat saw eye to eye, and people brought one or two more cats. When he had seven, his landlord evicted him. He moved, but the cats kept coming and outgrowing the human space. Eventually, Grant spent his own retirement money (amounting, it is said, to $100,000) purchasing lots of land on a Florida tree farm. Now, he lives there, on Caboodle Ranch (think 'Kit 'n' Caboodle'), in a trailer, in thirty acres, with his five hundred cats, brought to him by the public, where, he explains, 'cats aren't treated like animals'.

Cats should be able to roam free, and at Caboodle Ranch, that's what they do. We are in the middle of 100 acres of wildlife. The cats follow me through the nature trails that I put in and maintain, they climb in tree forts that I've built and hide in underground dens I've dug for them.

All cats have been spayed or neutered, all shots are kept up to date and I keep regular visits to the vet for each of them. I travel the 250 miles round-trip many times a week to work and back again to keep a safe haven for them to live. Every one of my expenses have come out of my own pocket and I do with very little so I can give them a happy life, but it isn't always easy.

Grant's vet bills exceed $2,000 a month and the food he puts out every day, calling, 'Babies, babies, come on, babies' (there are videos on the website), costs $800 a week. Altogether the ranch costs $6,000 a month to run and survives on donations, now that his own funds have run out. People can visit the ranch, though not until after 2 p.m. each day. Before that he likes to do his rounds alone, feeding and checking on the cats. They come running to him as he nears, a trickle that grows larger as they come from all directions, and then follow him, a festival of feline Lilliputians trailing a lanky elderly gent with a grand drooping moustache that dates back to the 1970s. He calls to and welcomes the oncoming, gathering herd of animals who stream towards him, and treads warily as the cats weave invisible threads around his ankles, mewing greetings and for all one knows telling him the latest news. Grant is no Heidi Erickson; he is realistic about his situation, poignantly but practically so. In his January blog he worries that he hasn't got enough to keep the ranch going past April. He makes plans:

> I need to sell off one of my 5 acre parcels, up the back of the ranch. That property isn't needed at this point. And I'm considering selling my PT Cruiser, which was to become the Cat Taxi; hopefully I can get what I bought it for. The land line to the office

will be turned off to save money as well. You can call my cell
phone (which will be working again this weekend!), just be persistent – you will reach me.

And he is aware of the questions people might ask, the anxiety
people might feel. In the FAQ, he imagines or reiterates the question: Isn't what you're doing considered hoarding? He explains
calmly that 'Caboodle Ranch has the seal of approval from the
Tallahassee Humane Society and Tallahassee/Madison County
Animal Control. Representatives from both have been to the Ranch
and both have liked what they've found. We're happy to say that the
answer is no, Caboodle Ranch is not in violation of hoarding.' It
comes as a relief to find this FAQ.

The videos are delightful. He is a happy man, the cats are happy
cats, the ranch is funny and silly, decked out like a town with miniature courthouses, cottages and churches along the pathways.
Nevertheless, there is something about the seething carpet of cats running around him which sets off the beginnings of that feeling of
distaste. The fact that they are outside and that there is plenty of room
is reassuring, but you wonder what will happen when this elderly man
can no longer cope with his daily round of feeding and caring and the
trips to the vet. The FAQs attempt to reassure about this, too. There
is a plan for trained people to take over the ranch, apparently. Craig
Grant isn't mad, that is, no madder than any cat lover, and he takes
care to soothe our nerves about the too-much love of too many non-
human others. The son goes and five hundred cats take his place. He
copes. The authorities say it's OK. And we are thankful that it's none
of our business and that he hasn't caused us to have to watch animal
services clearing up the mess that human love can make.

*

Loving cats isn't only a pastime of the lonely or old. One of the strangest pages on the Internet is the official site of Charles Mingus, the great, the very great, jazz bass player. He was cooler than a human could possibly be, an exemplary musician and composer, and I played his records (*Mingus Ah Um*, *Tijuana Moods*, *Mingus Mingus Mingus Mingus Mingus*), along with those of Miles Davis, incessantly in my teens. On the webpage called *In His Own Words*, among articles written by him such as 'What is a Jazz Composer?' and 'Open Letter to Miles Davis', is a non-musical legacy left for the world by my musical hero: 'The Charles Mingus Cat Toilet Training Program'. It is a solemnly written step-by-step description which ends, if you follow the programme correctly, with your cat going to the bathroom and sitting on the loo, instead of using a litter tray. If you're lucky, it will also flush the lavatory when it has finished. Mingus's instructions end:

> It took me about three or four weeks to toilet train my cat, Nightlife. Most of the time is spent moving the box very gradually to the bathroom. Do it very slowly and don't confuse him. And, remember, once the box is on the toilet, leave it a week or even two. The main thing to remember is not to rush or confuse him.
>
> Good luck. Charles Mingus

This, if you have a cat, and no way of letting it come and go outside easily, is doubtless a real addition to goodness in the world. But it points up an overwhelming devotion to this one particular partly domesticated mammal that is almost an integral part of the World Wide Web. Cats seem to be particularly adored by Internet users. In the Internet's short life, cat lovers have come up with an entire language and world in which cats are the masters of the universe and we, essentially, their hand-maidens and enablers.*

Lolcat is close enough to a language, with grammar, spelling and syntax, that it is studied by academics. It is based on misspelling, typos, abbreviations and the sheer stupidity to be found all over the Internet, but it is put into the mouths of cats as captions to photographs of them taken by their owners. There is a Wiki where the Bible has been communally translated into the language of lolcat. Ceiling Cat is God, and Basement Cat is Satan. To get the full flavour of lolcat, I offer you Genesis 1 in its entirety:

> 1 Oh hai. In teh beginnin Ceiling Cat maded teh skiez An da Urfs, but he did not eated dem. 2 Da Urfs no had shapez An haded dark face, An Ceiling Cat rode invisible bike over teh waterz. 3 At start, no has lyte. An Ceiling Cat sayz, i can haz lite? An lite wuz. 4 An Ceiling Cat sawed teh lite, to seez stuffs, An splitted teh lite from dark but taht wuz ok cuz kittehs can see in teh dark An not tripz over nethin. 5 An Ceiling Cat sayed light Day An dark no Day. It were FURST!!!1 6 An Ceiling Cat sayed, im in ur waterz makin a ceiling. But he no yet make a ur. An he maded a hole in teh Ceiling. 7 An Ceiling Cat doed teh skiez with waterz down An waterz up. It happen. 8 An Ceiling Cat sayed, i can has teh firmmint wich iz funny bibel naim 4 ceiling, so wuz teh twoth day. 9 An Ceiling Cat gotted all teh waterz in ur base, An Ceiling Cat hadz dry placez cuz kittehs DO NOT WANT get wet. 10 An Ceiling Cat called no waterz urth and waters oshun. Iz good. 11 An Ceiling Cat sayed, DO WANT grass! so tehr wuz seedz An stufs, An fruitzors An

---

*http://www.icanhascheezburger.com

vegbatels. An a Corm. It happen. 12 An Ceiling Cat sawed that weedz ish good, so, letz there be weedz. 13 An so teh threeth day jazzhands. 14 An Ceiling Cat sayed, i can has lightz in the skiez for splittin day An no day. 15 It happen, lights everwear, like christmass, srsly. 16 An Ceiling Cat doeth two grate lightz, teh most big for day, teh other for no day. 17 An Ceiling Cat screw tehm on skiez, with big nails An stuff, to lite teh Urfs. 18 An tehy rulez day An night. Ceiling Cat sawed. Iz good. 19 An so teh furth day w00t. 20 An Ceiling Cat sayed, waterz bring me phishes, An burds, so kittehs can eat dem. But Ceiling Cat no eated dem. 21 An Ceiling Cat maed big fishies An see monstrs, which wuz like big cows, except they no mood, An other stuffs dat mooves, An Ceiling Cat sawed iz good. 22 An Ceiling Cat sed O hai, make bebehs kthx. An dont worry i wont watch u secksy, i not that kynd uf kitteh. 23 An so teh . . . fith day. Ceiling Cat taek a wile 2 cawnt. 24 An Ceiling Cat sayed, i can has MOAR living stuff, mooes, An creepie tings, An otehr aminals. It happen so tehre. 25 An Ceiling Cat doed moar living stuff, mooes, An creepies, An otehr animuls, An did not eated tehm. 26 An Ceiling Cat sayed, letz us do peeps like uz, becuz we ish teh qte, An let min p0wnz0r becuz tehy has can openers. 27 So Ceiling Cat created teh peeps taht waz like him, can has can openers he maed tehm, min An womin wuz maeded, but he did not eated tehm. 28 An Ceiling Cat sed them O hai maek bebehs kthx, An p0wn teh waterz, no waterz An teh firmmint, An evry stufs. 29 An Ceiling Cat sayed, Beholdt, the Urfs, I has it, An I has not eated it. 30 For evry createded stufs tehre are the fuudz, to the burdies, teh creepiez, An teh mooes, so tehre. It happen. Iz good. 31 An Ceiling Cat sayed, Beholdt, teh good enouf for releaze as version 0.8a. kthxbai.[3]

Icanhascheezburger.com has thousands of photographs of cats, cute or weird with deliberately misspelled, syntax-muddled, garbled messages appended – illiterate and childish, but always with a sense of them being or revealing that they have been all along, in control, or at least are preparing to take over.

Millions of people find this funny and satisfying, and have enough of an imaginative relationship with their cats to 'get' lolcats. Look at the icanhascheezburger site for a while and it's clear that the cats are perceived to have a mysterious life of their own, quite aside from what their owners believe their lives to be. This is one answer to Derrida. There are several million hits on the site every day. It is a mass understanding of the jokes that cat lovers make about their beloved animals: 'Dogs come when they're called; cats take a message and get back to you later.' *Everyone*, it turns out, is a little worried by the way their cat looks at them when they're standing naked in the bathroom. What, you know, are they up to?

The lolcat phenomenon is not mad or dangerous (though it can be time-sucking), but perhaps it's a jocular version of the compelling mystery of animals, and of taking animal love too far, at least a recognition that it would not be hard to do so. Lolcats don't frighten us, not the thousands of pages of them on the web, because we are really remaking them in our own image. They threaten to take over, but only because we allow them to as their devoted owners. We give them ambitions that are our own ambitions of world domination and control. So, after all, we still haven't answered Derrida's question. Or rather, haven't really discovered the question that Derrida's cat might be asking him – other than, Can I leave the room? Cats remain enigmatic and other, and their owners give them voice – wittily and desperately.

There is another kind of loving animals too much. But that's not exactly what we mean when we carelessly use the word love, either.

Classically, it was the gods, Zeus in particular, who desired human women and came to them in the form of animals – a swan, a bull – to impregnate them. This is a grand and troubling idea; paintings and poetry deal with and depict the cross-species (animal/human, god/mortal) sexual moment:

> *A sudden blow: the great wings beating still*
> *Above the staggering girl, her thighs caressed*
> *By the dark webs, her nape caught in his bill,*
> *He holds her helpless breast upon his breast.*[4]

Even the God of the monotheistic Christians came to a human woman as the Holy Spirit, later described by St Matthew as a dove, which also comes to Jesus at his baptism:

Then said Mary unto the angel, How shall this be, seeing I know not a man? And the angel answered and said unto her, the Holy Ghost shall come upon thee, and the power of the Highest shall overshadow thee: therefore also that holy thing which shall be born of thee shall be called the Son of God.

There's nothing about desire here, as there is with the ever-desiring Zeus, but in both cases, the deities embody themselves as animals rather than humans when they want to take or procreate.

However, the idea of regular humans desiring animals has never been grand. On the contrary, it is either justified as necessary to humanise the non-human (*Beauty and the Beast*, *The Frog Prince*), or it is unmentionable and then becomes the subject of jokes by the urbane about the unsophisticated. Sometimes it is used to tell ourselves about our own emotional absurdity and lack of control. Although she is magicked into it, Titania's love for Bottom the Weaver, who has taken on the form of a donkey, is low humour and high hilarity about the arbitrary nature of human desire. Before the spell is taken away, the Queen of the Fairies trills to her beloved ass-headed yokel (cross-species, cross-class):

> *Come, sit thee down upon this flowery bed,*
> *While I thy amiable cheeks do coy,*
> *And stick musk-roses in thy sleek smooth head,*
> *And kiss thy fair large ears, my gentle joy.*

This is love being blind. But there are those who use, abuse and even love (in what we might term the correct use of the word 'love') animals, with eyes wide open. Certainly, it was a real enough phenomenon for the rules laid down for proper living in Leviticus to include bestiality in the prohibitions:

Neither shalt thou lie with any beast to defile thyself therewith: neither shall any woman stand before a beast to lie down thereto: it is confusion

Confusion between one thing and another, of course, is the point of many rules in Leviticus, and what could be more confused than humans and animals – ask Derrida, ask Bunty? Just to nail the seriousness of the offence, the punishment is spelled out:

And if a man lie with a beast, he shall surely be put to death and ye shall slay the beast.

And if a woman approach unto any beast, and lie down thereto, thou shalt kill the woman, and the beast; they shall surely be put to death: their blood shall be upon them.

How to live rightly and wrongly is basic to any theology, and the writer of Leviticus knew his congregation – nomadic, sheep- and goat-herding people – and was realistic about them, just as those who joke about the prevalence of bestiality in out-of-the-way rural communities express a similar reality – though from a different frame of mind.

In his book, *Dearest Pet – On Bestiality*, Midas Dekkers explains that Kinsey – that great expresser of reality to 1950s suburban America – received answers to his questionnaires suggesting that 8 per cent of men and 3.5 per cent of women had had a sexual encounter with an animal, while the figure for men living in the countryside who had done so rose to 50 per cent. It can be a practical solution where other more usual objects of love are scarce, or servicing a need without breaking the stronger social rules of society that values virginity in young women, or risking the consequences of unwanted pregnancy. It can be unimaginably violent and abusive, where men penetrate live chickens and then decapitate them at the moment of the man's climax to cause muscular death spasms that give extra pleasure. Humans using animals for sexual purposes has always to be a disregarding of the other, since an animal cannot give knowing consent to a sex act with our species. Dekkers discusses women who train dogs to provide cunnilingus, and men finding the back end of cows sinuous and desirable. There are those who believe their chosen animal gets pleasure, even loves them, but until an animal is able to convey unequivocal consent, sex between a human and an animal must, like sex between a human and another human who has not consented, be rape. There is common ground between the imperialist power-demonstration of the human rape of humans and the act of bestiality. Both assume that the Other (human or animal) is either beneath consideration, or, where there is a delusion of consent or even seduction, that the rapist believes that he (or she) is able to think for or with their victim, and that they can know what the assaulted other really wants. The lack of (our) language in animals is taken, like silence is in law, for consent. But it's impossible, actually, to ask animals the question.

8

THE GOOD, THE BAD
AND THE HELPFUL

Babyface

The great advantage over real live creatures that my Three Bears had in common with Walt Disney's Mickey Mouse, aside from not needing to be fed or produce droppings, was *neoteny*. Mickey and my ursine family looked only glancingly like a mouse or brown bears, and much more like babies. Not even so much baby mice or baby bears, but human babies. And according to Konrad Lorenz, there are certain qualities of newborn human babies that cause human adults to respond (as a result of hormone surges, he suggests) with affection and therefore bond with them, rather than carelessly leave them lying around the house or cave. These qualities are evolutionarily necessary because, after all, babies are quite hard work.

Infants and toddlers, you will have noticed, are not just smaller than adults, but proportionally different. They have an exceptionally large head in relation to their body, and exceptionally shorter legs and smaller feet, compared to adults, who become the opposite: small heads on a sizeable torso and long legs with relatively large feet. Babies also have a rounded cranium, bulging forehead and high, prominent cheekbones above a diminishing lower face and receding chin, rather than the slanting, lower brows and longer face with jutting jaws of adults. Babies' and toddlers' eyes, which hardly grow and so, as it were, are already adult-sized, appear very large in the still expanding face. Think Mickey Mouse without the ears, or your child's favourite soft toy. Think of that terrible cooing noise people make over strange (and not especially beautiful) infants in their prams, or the fact that the vast majority of us do not shake our babies till their brains turn to butter when they cry so hard that it actually causes us pain in the solar plexus. There may be other reasons why we don't kill our babies (though, of course, some do) but simply the sight of them goes some way to quelling or at least helping us to control our helpless rage at their helpless rage.

Why human babies look like that is the result of *neoteny*: the retention of foetal characteristics after they have emerged from the womb. It was an evolutionary master-stroke. Get the babies born before they're fully developed and two good things result. First, and rather importantly, babies do get born more often, instead of stuck on their way out, and as a bonus less frequently kill their mothers whose small pelvic girdles have not kept pace with the increased brain and therefore cranium size of human primates. (There was a theory that one reason the Neanderthals died out was not their stupidity, but on the contrary their brains, bigger than those of *Homo sapiens*, which caused far more of them to fail to be born.) Second, being born too soon and retaining foetal characteristics after birth means, quite by happy chance, that human babies remain, of necessity, helpless for much longer than other animal species. They can't feed themselves or get around on their own, or communicate as the adults (or other infant non-human animals) do, for an exceptionally long time. Parents have to carry their offspring around and attend to its needs, while it watches the world and has nothing to do but eat, develop and learn. The still unsolidified skull of the human infant continues to grow long after it is born. A human brain is only about 25 per cent of its full size at birth, while a monkey is born with 70 per cent of its brain developed. For another six years the child's brain continues to grow while it lives and experiences in the outside world. What can't be passed on genetically has until puberty to be learned in the developing brain, from the surrounding culture and from the necessary closeness of one or two parents, their kin and the local community. We must suppose that a few premature infants, with their smaller head size, happened to survive, and those survivors passed on their tendency to early birth and robustness, and their prolonged neediness, which, by the wonderful happenstance that evolution is, enabled the cultural revolution that is human society. The neotenous baby face is the result of the fact that human babies really ought to be in the womb for another ten months. And something about that conformation makes them irresistible (or it signs their extreme helplessness combined with that kin-related tendency to altruism, which gets our hormonal juices going) so that we mostly want to cherish our offspring enough to put up with them for the years and years it takes them to become independent. Neonate chimpanzees are also generally cherished by their kin, but baby chimps stay babies (and cherished) for a far shorter period and progress to adulthood in both ability and appearance very much faster. Neoteny – our slowed-down development – ensures that even as adults we look more like our babies than adult chimps look like their infants. And we emphasise that when we want to influence others to care by often making big eyes and lowering our heads to make ourselves more child-like (think of that look of Princess Diana). We are creatures who are always becoming.

Who knows whether it is really innate (chemical, hard-wired), our bonding with our round-headed, big-eyed babies? Certainly, the combination of features has a virtually physical effect on our responses, but cultural and innate responses long ago mingled inextricably in our species. Whatever makes our juices flow, the process works so well that any creatures, even non-human ones, even stuffed ones, which conform to the neotenous criteria of our babies, get our automatic approval, and conversely, those that don't have a much harder time from us.

In one of his wonderful essays, the biologist Stephen Jay Gould traced Mickey Mouse's canny fifty-year reverse journey into neoteny. The original Mouse of the cartoon *Steamboat Willie* in 1928 is a very different-looking creature from the one that appeared in his final seven-minute film, *The Simple Things*, in 1953. The physical changes are tracked also by a change of character, from quite wild, and even unpleasant, 'a rambunctious, even slightly sadistic fellow', to the much blander and inoffensive creature that Christopher Finch, in his history of the Mouse, describes as '... virtually a national symbol, and as such he was expected to behave properly at all times'.[1] Mickey's physical features kept pace with his altered behaviour and he became progressively more desirably juvenile, as Gould describes:

> To give him the shorter and pudgier legs of youth, they lowered his pants line and covered his spindly legs with a baggy outfit. (His arms and legs also thickened substantially and acquired joints for a floppier appearance.) His head grew relatively larger and its features more youthful ... Mickey's eye has grown in two modes: first, by a major, discontinuous evolutionary shift as the entire eye of ancestral Mickey became the pupil of his descendants, and second, by gradual increase thereafter ... Mickey's improvement in cranial bulging followed an interesting path since his evolution has always been constrained by the unaltered convention of representing his head as a circle with appended ears and an oblong snout. The

circle's form could not be altered to provide a bulging cranium directly. Instead, Mickey's ears moved back, increasing the distance between nose and ears, and giving him a rounded, rather than a sloping forehead.

Gould explains his biologist's interest in Mickey Mouse's reverse development:

> National symbols are not altered capriciously and market researchers (for the doll industry in particular) have spent a good deal of time and practical effort learning what features appeal to people as cute and friendly. Biologists also have spent a great deal of time studying a similar subject in a wide range of animals.[2]

When we give soft, cuddly toy animals with short legs, big eyes and rounded heads to our babies, we are training them, or reinforcing a natural tendency, to feel comfort and tenderness at baby-like features, even if concealed in other forms. We give them a metonymy of themselves, showing them how lovable they are, also training them in how to find their own babies lovable, and that the whole damn thing of being here is about reproducing the species, which includes caring for what is smaller and more vulnerable than you. Of course, we put it differently to ourselves, being also the products of socialisation.

Perhaps, also, we are reinforcing our own tenderness for our babies by doubling them with soft toys. Perhaps the plush teddies and bunnies might even be more like *aides memoire* for us than for the little ones. While we melt over neotenised features, infants recognise individual characteristics in a face rather than the whole gestalt. Until they begin to focus more efficiently, two circles on the same latitude of a larger oval with a single circle beneath will do to get their attention while they are so young they hardly exist. Ducks and geese do it too, and will follow two large spots on a stick to the ends of the earth (or failing that, Konrad Lorenz). We fix on what we must follow for our survival, and evolution seems to bet that what we do fix on initially will be the form of an adult face. Nevertheless, we present newborns with simplified but still elaborate faces in soft comforting fabrics that are both human and animal. The animals invariably look more like human babies in their essence than they do their real animal models, but as a by-product of our gifts of cuddly neotenous animals to babies, the animals (as well as the humans they represent) themselves become loved. The heart-melting alien E.T. (huge eyes, round head, small legs) belongs to another planet only by convention. The whole story could have been redone using a stray puppy or a baby brother. It remains an essential lesson in human love and loss.

The unfair corollary of neoteny is that the less like an infant human an animal is, the less likely it is to be loved. It's hard to represent an insect as an infant human. It has been tried and Jiminy Cricket, the variety of movie bees and Woody Allen's *Antz* testify to some success. The problem is that the real creatures being represented have very few of the cartoons' massaged characteristics. You could, but probably wouldn't, give a plush cricket or ant to a newborn to welcome her into the world. Desmond Morris connected his 1950s TV programme *Zoo Time* with his later book, *The Naked Ape*, by giving in it the results of an animal popularity poll he had done for the TV programme. In terms of types of animals, 97.14 per cent of all children gave a mammal as their top favourite animal while birds swooped down to 1.6 per cent, reptiles 1 per cent, invertebrates 0.1 per cent and amphibians (in spite of Jeremy Fisher) 0.5 per cent. The 'top ten animal loves' were: 1. Chimpanzee; 2. Monkey; 3. Horse; 4. Bushbaby; 5. Panda; 6. Bear; 7. Elephant; 8. Lion; 9. Dog; 10. Giraffe. I assume that meerkats would these days rate very highly. But it wouldn't alter the general trend that the animals with more anthropomorphic characteristics were the most popular:

1. They all have hair, rather than feathers or scales. 2. They have rounded outlines (chimpanzee, monkey, bushbaby, panda, bear, elephant). 3. They have flat faces (chimpanzee, monkey, bushbaby, bear, panda, lion). 4. They have facial expressions (chimpanzee, monkey, horse, lion, dog). 5. They can 'manipulate' small objects (chimpanzee, monkey, bushbaby, panda, elephant). 6. Their postures are in some way or at some times, rather vertical (chimpanzee, monkey, bushbaby, panda, bear, giraffe).

The more of these points a species can score, the higher up on the top ten list it comes.[3]

The insanely popular meerkat scores on all points.

These were the preferences of all children between four and fourteen. When split by age, Morris found that smaller children prefer bigger animals and older children smaller ones, and he suggests that the younger children saw their favourite creatures as 'adult-substitutes' while the older ones chose 'child-substitutes'. The key word is *substitute*. For children, animals *stand* for something, and it seems that the more they stand for humans, the better they like it, though the horse is a horse of a different colour and is a special phase that pre-adolescent girls pass or fail to pass through.

Increasingly, as children age towards and into adulthood, some animals will be called 'cute', 'sweet', 'adorable'. All words we use about small children. Playfulness (or what appears to us to be playfulness) is an important factor in finding animals adorable. Penguins, though they aren't mammals, happen to look, to us, as if they are small, hampered versions of humans, trying very hard to maintain their dignity. When they give up their awkward-looking waddling across impossible terrain and bellyflop on to the ice to slide down an incline, we laugh, not just at the simple ergonomics of the act, but at the childlike freedom they suddenly seem to allow themselves. We admire animals that maintain what we would see as their dignity (lions, for example), but we adore animals that appear to lose their dignity (an orang-utan, so sombre, suddenly putting a handful of straw on her head), just as we adore those childlike dyspraxic comics who are always falling flat on their face but get back up again and carry on, just as we adore small children toddling recklessly about and suddenly collapsing on unready legs, but getting themselves upright again and continuing their progress. The chimpanzees' tea party, only banned from the daily schedule at the London Zoo in 1972 (while the Brooke Bond chimps were still mugging their way through TV advertisements in 2002), had everything adults and children want from animals. They literally aped human behaviour, but did it playfully, and waywardly, actually because they were doing something that had no meaning to them. The main thing for the audience was that they had enjoyed the 'cute', as in imitative, antics, and it seemed as if the chimps had fun too. Which perhaps they did, enjoying the attention, the relief from their cage in the open air on a patch of grass by the children's swings; just like home but without the bars. And what is more moving and funny than a cat who fails to make a manoeuvre, missing the table she was leaping on to, falling back to the floor, and then immediately wandering casually off, gazing out of the window, carelessly washing a back leg: me, jump? No, you misunderstood, I've been making plans to kill that bird out there, and I'm far too busy with the washing to be jumping. These days, instead of laughing, I suppress it, and quickly look away as if I hadn't seen, to save Bunty's wounded pride.

What amphibian or arachnid could compete? Well, even they have their uses, because we humans have a use for everything.

Arachnophobia

Until November 2006, every autumn loomed dark and most terribly in my life. For as long as I can remember, I began to worry around midsummer, and by late August I would be filled with dread. I never thought of my arachnophobia in the same way as I did my conviction that I was infested by insects. There were obviously some similarities, but terror and delusion are curiously different, even if neither are good to live with. My terror of spiders, on me, near me, in the same room, house, garden, planet and universe, ensured that the autumnal mating urge which causes arachnids to wander into our habitations – confused by some sudden, indefinable but compelling ache in the forefront of their small but made-up minds – in search of a nice warm dark corner to nest (I couldn't bear to think beyond that), ushered in my personal annual festival of anxiety and horror. Not that I felt secure during the other ten months of the year. My ex, having been my ex for some years and grown tired of still being called out in the middle of the night to deal with a spider, gave me a blowtorch, which I used with desperate abandon. It was a professional version of the hairspray-and-lighter technique, more or less likely to have resulted in my charred remains (and those of the daughter, the cats and the occasional lover, none of whom counted for much beside my fear) being found in the smoking ruins. But death was never a worse alternative to being in the same room as a spider. I suppose that sounds like a writer's hyperbole, but I'm writing with all the accuracy I can muster. If you are not an arachnophobe nothing will convince you of that, but I discovered in the early summer of 2006 that there are some who recognise the simple truth of what I say.

An irrational fear of spiders is common. Roughly 35 per cent of women and 18 per cent of men in the UK have it, though not all of them have it so badly that it is called clinical. Just as clinical depression is different from being a bit down, so clinical arachnophobia is different from a slight shudder of the kind you get when the spider you are cupping delicately in your hand as you take it out to the garden tickles your palm. It's only thanks to the Zoological Society of London that I can even write that sentence and even now I have to breathe calmly and regularly as I do. To anyone who isn't a member of an Iron John chapter, confronting a crippling fear when you don't absolutely have to is a violation of common sense, and in addition and speaking personally, joining anything, but particularly anything with a stupid name, goes against every grain in my body. Which is the only reason I can think of as to why I had waited and suffered (and caused those around me to suffer) until I was fifty-eight before signing up for the Friendly Spider Programme offered by the entomology department of the ZSL. The title of the programme made me (as a lifelong arachnophobe) cross: tell me, if you must, that spiders are not wholly devoted to terrorising me, but don't suggest they're *friendly* – I didn't want them around, whatever they really feel about me. Being liked was never on its own a satisfactory basis for taking a lover. I saw no reason why it should be any different with spiders.

I noticed an advertisement for the programme on the Zoo's website, when I was looking for something else, and I remembered that, actually, I already knew about it. I had read about it somewhere and paid no attention. Why, in 2006, I finally decided to check out this cutely named possibility – it cost about £150; unbelievably cheap for a life-changing event, if it turned out to have any merit – I have no idea. I suppose everything eventually has its limit. There were seventeen other people on the four-hour course at ZSL headquarters across the road from the Zoo, and none of them could say what had tipped the scales and decided them at last to try and deal with their arachnophobia. Every one of them had lived miserably with the problem for as long as they could remember. Cowardice, I suppose. We all knew, without allowing ourselves to think about it in detail, that the Friendly Spider Programme must involve *spiders*. It was enough to blank out the possibility of investigating it, until at last we, or more likely someone we were close to could stand our terror no longer.

The group was a range of ages and social classes, and from all over the country. The only obvious thing we had in common (aside from our horror of spiders and of what might be going to happen that afternoon) was that we were all women. This, we were assured by John, the psychologist in charge, was very unusual, unprecedented actually. He showed his acumen by suggesting it had something to do with it being June 2006 and therefore bang in the middle of the World Cup. It occurs to me that this might also explain why I decided to deal with my fear that summer: between another afternoon of football mania and confronting my spider phobia, the latter might just have been the lesser of two evils – chewing my own leg off was a similarly attractive option.

We sat centred in the two front rows of the ZSL lecture theatre. The woman on my immediate right was crying steadily. She'd been led gently to her seat by one of the volunteers who had come in to make tea, smile in a reassuring manner and act as support during the later part of the afternoon. Eighteen fearful people secreted enough anxiety and reluctance into the air to make breathing in feel dangerous. Dave, the Head Keeper of Invertebrates at the Zoo, and John, psychologist and hypnotherapist, spoke to us in turn about fear, theirs (the spiders', not Dave's and John's) and ours. Dave offered us spider behaviour; John dealt with human behaviour. First, however, we were to pair off and share our feelings and experiences of spiders with the person sitting on our right. Third on the list of things I really don't like, after spiders and football, is sharing. I was mortified at having been suckered into a self-help group, after the considerable trouble I have taken in my life to avoid them. Sharing does the same visceral thing to me that happens when your mother pushes you forward at a party to sing a song. Nor did I need to be told that spiders didn't want to go near me as much as I didn't want them to. If I could reason the problem away, I wouldn't be here. If being part of a suffering group was the answer to my – someone used the word – issue, then I was lost. Just fucking hypnotise me and make me feel better, was all I asked.

The urgent need to run for my life lost out – just – to the even more powerful conditioning against being rude to strangers or making a scene, which so often gets well-mannered people who don't want to make a fuss robbed, raped and murdered, as well as singing through gritted teeth at children's parties. So I shared without hope. The voice of the weeping woman next to me trembled with emotion, and gulping back her tears she told me that she actually passes out if she sees a . . . she couldn't say the word. I dug deep and shared that while watching *CSI Las Vegas* I had to close my eyes during every scene set in Grissom's office because he had a huge . . . in a glass case behind his desk. I might have mentioned the nights I'd sat bolt upright in the dead centre of the bed because an unreachable spider was in the room, or about the wellington boots I kept beside the bed (one boot upside down inside the other for obvious arachnid reasons) for night-time search-and-destroy missions. Then we shared group-wise what we had shared in pairs.

None of us would walk into a room without scanning it minutely, or having it checked by someone else, though of course trusting someone else to be as thorough as you would be was impossible, so no one ever believed any room was really spider-free. Dark cupboards and the bottom of wardrobes, under sofas, behind doors, even pools of shadow were forbidden territory. Attics and cellars, out of the question. We tried very hard only to travel to cold and inhospitable parts of the world where no arachnids could follow, our only consolation being an easy moral superiority about luxury non-eco holidays in impoverished hotspots teeming with eight-legged life. I once wrote a novel set in a rainforest (called *Rainforest*) based entirely on textbooks and three trips to the Kew Gardens tropical houses. We all saw spiders much more often than anyone else we knew, always the first to spot them because we were always alert, intensely on the lookout. It turned out not to be just my paranoid theory that I summoned up spiders through the power of thought, that the dust in the corners of rooms conglomerated into the living beasts, actually given existence by the strength of my fear and apprehension. I was working towards a grand theory that maybe God, before the creation, was possessed of a neurotic fear of the idea of people and that was how we came about. No wonder we keep getting swatted. Dust to dust. I'd spend hours and hours at night trying (as fruitlessly as any intelligent portion of me knew it must be) not to think about or visualise spiders in case I made them come to me. Which, of course, they did; and where there was one spider, I knew there was always another that I hadn't spotted, somewhere, somewhere . . . I had a special stone (as well as the blow-torch), heavy, large and flat, on the bedside table that enabled me when desperate to deal with spiders from a great height. Arachnophobia was the only sympathy I had with the columnist Bernard Levin, who devised a fine solution to the ancient problem of disposing of spiders in the washbasin: an old-fashioned soda-siphon. Taps are too close, and you have to touch them to turn them on. There has to be a critical distance between your being and the thing that disposes of the spider: preferably air, or a pressurised stream of water. Something directly connected, however long, to your hand will not do. But where can you get a working soda-siphon these days?

We also all knew that spiders are malevolent. Spiders and the awareness of malevolence inhabit an identical area of my brain. Scan it and see. Silent scuttling movement, legs rising above a dark central body (yes, we're coming to that), uncanny watchful stillness. They know me and they hate me, whatever irrelevant truths Dave might tell us about them being frightened of us. He explained that they only come towards us in order to get under the sofa we're sitting on because it's a safe, dark space away from the horror of the noisy, strobing light of the TV. Natural history versus blind terror has only one victor. The finest and truest moment of the group confessional came when a women spoke up in a clear, in no way self-mocking voice: 'What I hate about spiders is that they won't stay still and let you kill them.' It was a perfect expression of the rationality of our irrational fear.

John, the hypnotherapist, gave a brief talk about the symptoms and causes of phobia in general. Sweating, palpitations, paralysis, fainting. The evolutionary hypothesis didn't do much for me: there are those who believe it was fear of spiders that made my very own particular ancestors more fit to pass on their genes so that they could eventually produce me. Ah, yes, the days when arachnosauruses ruled the earth, and australopithecines competed with hominid-eating spiders for a food niche. Luckily my forebears, from whom I have inherited no terror at all of snakes, didn't get bitten by a cobra or crushed by a python. In my rational mind, I'm quite sure there were far greater dangers to survival than even the most poisonous spiders (it seems that no one has died from a spider-bite in Australia, that hotbed of really dangerous spiders, since 1985); and in my irrational being, a dangerous spider is no more terrifying to me than a mild-as-milk variety which, more importantly, is just as scary as the man-eaters. A young acquaintance of mine had a phobia of that well-known evolutionary threat: supermarket labels on fruit.

Psychoanalysis has a take. (So you are frightened of a black body surrounded by hairy legs coming at you? You find it a threat? What could such a thing represent? No, really? You don't mean my mother's vagina as I was coming down the birth canal? Well, thank you, I feel better now.) But I was getting on, and hadn't got the years to spare for their talking cure. And there is a practical but dull psychological theory that phobias are caught by young children from fearful mothers (them, again) or traumatic encounters. Spiders, I think, were the least of my mother's worries, and my most traumatic youthful encounters were with two-legged rather than eight-legged beings (though I admit that does rather take us back to psychoanalysis, above).

I had remarkably little interest in the nature of my phobia; I wanted only for it to go away. Just hypnotise me, John, all this talk is getting me nowhere. Finally, to my relief, he took us into another room to do the deed. We lay on the floor of a meeting room while he talked us through a relaxation sequence, a body scan no different from what you might do at the end of a yoga session. Then we were instructed to descend ten mental steps, find a nice place to be when we reached the bottom, and then to relax even more deeply. Not a problem, can do, nicely relaxed, and so? Now he was going to address our 'subconsciousnesses' directly, John told us, and did so by assuring us repeatedly: 'Spiders are safe,' throwing in for free the handy suggestion that daddy-long-legs were nothing to worry about either.

He had warned us that we might think nothing was happening. He was right. Apparently, the ability to be sceptical is not impaired by deep relaxation. Certainly, my 'subconscious' didn't let on to me that it had heard a thing. Well, it wouldn't, would it? I sneered in a relaxed manner to myself. It's a powerfully difficult task to convince a person who isn't entirely sure they have a conscious, let alone a subconscious, that you are getting through to it. And in any case, it wasn't the safety or otherwise of spiders I worried about, it was their existence. After twenty minutes he reversed the relaxation and we had a nice cup of tea. Then we were taken across the road to the Invertebrate House at the Zoo, where it turned out that the tea-making volunteers had been searching the flower-beds for the sizeable garden spiders that now waited for us in small plastic aquaria on four tables.

Well, as invited, I *did* put my hand into one of the containers and touch the back leg of a big, black spider. I followed it with my finger as it ran in the direction I pointed. I *did* put my whole hand in, palm up, and let a volunteer chase the spider across my open palm. I *did* put a clear plastic cup over the smallish black creature after it had been deliberately released from the perspex tank to scurry freely around the table, then slid a card under the cup and walked around the room holding it. And after all that, I stroked one of the incredibly soft, hairy legs of Frieda, the four-inch red tarantula, brought out specially for the occasion from her quiet life behind glass. Then I held her in my cupped hands, though her stillness suggested that she was rendered as catatonic by human contact as I usually was by a spider encounter. I held her long enough to have my photograph taken, and have the picture of us both still, me looking as surprised at what I'm doing in the photo as I do whenever I see it stuck on the noticeboard in the hall.

I did all those things not with terror, but a kind of awed amazement. Only one person of the eighteen couldn't bring herself to go anywhere near the spider containers, and it wasn't the woman who had sat next to me sobbing. The rest of us were elated and astonished by what we found ourselves capable of doing. Everyone was hesitant at first, but most people went back for more, several times, to re-experience our new remarkable freedom from fear. The woman who had sat next to me in tears walked up to me with her cupped spider. 'Look,' she said in the first flush of the new her.

Mixed feelings don't come any more entangled than when, after a lifetime of terror, someone says spiders are safe at you half a dozen times, and three months, a year, even four years later you discover yourself gazing empathetically at a handbag-sized arachnid Sisyphusing in the bath. Since that afternoon autumn has arrived annually, as it does, and I cup-and-card spiders out into the garden, stand and watch them web-weaving between the wheelie bins, and dashing across the open space in the living room between two dark corners, with intense interest, and have no sense at all that they are my enemy. I am suffused with remorse at the numbers I have caused to be killed, and I live contentedly with a spider who has taken up residence in a corner of the kitchen window. I'm not positively in love with them, but I can live with them on the same planet. And yet, although life has become altogether lighter and much less fearful, for which I am profoundly grateful, I have the strangest sense of loss. A person who is not afraid of spiders is almost a definition of someone who is not me. So it is uncanny (in a properly Freudian sense of the word) to observe myself being without that fear. Without that very particular and special relation to the most extreme Other I could imagine (apart from, and similarly to, my invisible infesting creatures). Some way in which I knew myself and perhaps was known, has vanished from my understanding of myself, from my sense of who I am. It is still slightly frightening not being frightened of spiders. And then I wonder, why not get hypnotised out of all my anxieties and nervous habits, make everything awkward and resistant go away, so that I could become . . . well, *nothing* is the alarming image I have. I can't picture what would be left after I had chipped off the difficulties. I really don't believe there is a solid nugget of the person-that-is-really-me underneath it all – the difficulties and such are fragments of the fragmented thing we choose to call the person. And what if the difficulties, as the analysts of whom I am only partly contemptuous would say, were merely the armouring, the screens, that kept the really bad stuff at bay? Now, without my arachnophobia, I worry what dark, repressed beast is about to return to consciousness and make my life really unbearable? The Beast. You know? How useful animals are to us, even if we hate and fear them.

A psychiatrist friend almost saved me from the spiral of horror I found myself about to plughole down. Over dinner, listening to my miraculous tale of new-found spider freedom and boldness, she looks distinctly unimpressed. She explained that simple (as in specific) phobias are the easiest of conditions to cure. Complex social phobias (fear of other people or going out into situations where other people will be) are of a different and far more intractable nature. The feeling I describe to her of having been given permission not to be afraid of spiders was exactly that, she said. What happened to me at the London Zoo is similar to a hysterical conversion. Phobias of spiders, snakes, flying, even labels on fruit, she says, are the closest condition that there is to normal if such a thing as normal existed. Any kind of behavioural or suggestion treatment is likely to work rapidly with a willing patient. 'In psychodynamic terms,' she explained, 'phobias are the fears that the mind can afford to express directly and therefore they don't lie deep in the unconscious.' Animals, as well as our own man-made 'others', are perfectly available for helping us fear something that isn't exactly what we really fear. Especially the small, dark, scuttling creatures, as remote as dinosaurs from our lovable furry mammalian friends. Even our unconsciousnesses have a use for animals who aren't us, to help us avoid thinking directly about ourselves.

Being an insect does not, as such, preclude being loved. There are just a few who escape our hatred and the darker, primeval side of our unconscious. It doesn't take much, however, to switch them over. Ladybirds were *the* benign insect for as long as I can remember. Though red with black spots is a natural signal warning predators of poison and danger should they try and eat the otherwise defenceless creature, ladybirds are so bright and cheerful that whole editions of children's books were named after them. There is a children's clothing firm called Ladybird. Nursery items are dotted with jolly spotted red-and-black creatures. When, as a child, I picked one up (never anything to be fearful or disgusted about ladybirds) I recited the necessary rhyme:

Ladybird, Ladybird, fly away home
Your house is on fire and your children are gone.

Certainly, it wasn't cheerful, but it was concerned and caring. They wandered about for a minute or so tickling your finger and then they opened their wing casing and flew away.

In the past year, however, my lifelong amiability towards ladybirds has evaporated. A new breed has appeared. Harlequin ladybirds, originally from Japan, arrived in Britain in 2004. America imported them as pest control, but the trouble is that once they've eaten the aphids – for which gardeners welcome old-fashioned ladybirds – they start to eat their own kind, good ladybirds, each other, actually anything. They bite animals and people in the hope of lunch. Now they've moved into our houses, where it's nice and warm in the winter for their hibernation.

'They destroy wallpaper, curtains and carpets if they're not found,' says Matt Shardlow of Buglife. 'And they poo a sticky black substance everywhere.' Majerus says their reflex blood, the gooey yellow stuff that seeps out of their joints, is the main problem. 'It smells foul, tastes foul, and stains anything.'

The journalist Annalisa Barbieri has first-hand experience of harlequins in her Suffolk home, and is frustrated that they appear impossible to get rid of. 'We have had swarms of them,' she says. 'They fly all over the house and settle in huge clusters in the corners of window frames. They also fly at you, and they bite, but you know you can't squash them because they release their orange blood everywhere.' Barbieri was quite excited when she first spotted some ladybirds, as she had been trying to hatch some in her organic garden for her young daughter to watch. By the time she realised they were harlequins there were already huge numbers of them clustering around the windows on the outside of her house, and coming in through fissures in the wooden frames. 'I actually started to get quite paranoid that someone had put a biblical curse on me,' she admits. 'It was so bad last Sunday I was thinking that I don't want to live here any more if it gets any worse. But I don't think it will, because winter is coming.'[4]

They arrived in Cambridge a few years ago and reached my study and The Poet's teaching room in his college. They 'call' to each other at a distance with pheromones they deposit on windows and gather together in orgiastic groups. If you swat them they exude an awful smell. They seem unkillable; the only way I know of getting rid of them is to gather them up in lavatory paper, carefully, so as not to squash them and make them smell, and then scrunch the paper around them and flush it while you're actually holding it in the water. If you just flush it, the ladybirds escape and can live for days swimming around in the toilet bowl. The Poet is about to buy a mini-vacuum cleaner and suck up the hundreds he finds on his ceiling, but then, what do you do with a vacuum cleaner full of live ladybirds? I get emails from him from work entitled: My Ladybird Hell, telling me how many he has battled with today. After three seasons of harlequins, there is not a shred of affection left in me for the generic ladybird. They aren't spiders, stuck inside my head, hating me, nor parasites, living in me. They are pests for whom I have no pity. A whole lifetime of loving ladybirds (and of being pleased that there was at least one insect species I was fond of) has disappeared (with difficulty) down the toilet. Yet, though we call them pests and cannibals and a plague, what are they doing but making a living in the way everything does? What they're doing is making their living by inconveniencing us. Perhaps I hate them so much because they've betrayed me. Ladybirds that bite and eat their own and cluster inside my house are not the cute little bugs I learned to love, and I'm really angry with them.

Assistants

What we like much better are animals that we can rely on to stay the way they're supposed to be. But we don't just love or hate animals for our emotional satisfaction, we also use them to benefit us in practical ways. Animals can look after us and be our carers – if we choose to make them so. Dogs, ponies, monkeys and parrots are all used by humans to assist them when there is a need. Animals are bred and trained to make up for faculties that their owners lack, not as with hunting dogs, bred to use their remarkable (to us) sense of smell to find out prey for their owners to shoot and then to fetch, but as carers, where other human beings would be too expensive or unavailable. They offer people who are hampered in their lives the chance of independence. At primary school we assiduously collected silver and gold milk-bottle tops which mysteriously were exchanged for the training of 'blind dogs'. The process was never explained, but it had a quality of the transmutation of base metals into gold. As a result of their accumulation, a Labrador or an Alsatian was trained from puppyhood to be the eyes, so they said, of someone whose was born without or who had lost their sight. It was an unambiguously good thing. It never crossed my mind to think it could be otherwise, and on children's television we were always being shown how extraordinarily caring the animals were, how they looked after their master or mistress with such devotion, and in return received and deserved the love and gratitude of not just their owners but all of us. The devoted dog, that is, devoted to humans, is a commonplace. Except for working dogs, that is what dogs are for. But not only can they love you, they can, when it is necessary, actually look after you. They'll help you cross the road and lead you safely to the shops.

They can protect you from all manner of potential harm. They are called, now, 'seeing-eye' dogs.

Many people's lives are greatly improved by animals trained to help them. One man uses a parrot to help him with his bipolar disorder. Jim Eggers carries Sadie the parrot around at all times in a backpack fitted to hold her cage. When she senses, from his manner and his voice, that her owner is on the verge of a psychotic episode, Sadie the parrot talks him down saying, 'It's OK, Jim. Calm down, Jim. You're all right, Jim. I'm here, Jim.' He used to say that to himself, and she started copying him. Eggers trained her to calm him down.

> He learned that psychiatric service animals help their owners cope with things like medication side effects. Eggers takes heavy doses of antipsychotics that leave him in a fog most of the day. So he trained Sadie to alert him with a loud ringing noise if someone calls, or to yell 'WHO'S THERE?' when anyone knocks on the door. If the fire alarm goes off, Sadie goes off. If Eggers leaves the faucet running, Sadie makes sounds like a waterfall until he turns it off.[5]

There are capuchin monkeys who help quadriplegics eat and drink, macaques that alert their epileptic owners to an upcoming seizure, even miniature horses, instead of dogs, that lead the blind and partially sighted. It is assumed that we have a perfect right to breed and train animals to assist human beings. Well, we do have the right – because we can. But unless an animal flatly refuses to be trained, which I imagine must happen sometimes but rarely, they don't have the opportunity of refusing. In America, they are known as 'service animals'. They do serve their humans. Dogs and other animals are devoted because we have made them so, by breeding for devotion and juvenile characteristics, and we use animals' sharpened senses and relative intelligence to our advantage in all sorts of ways: assistance, herding, finding and chasing other animals, racing, sending messages, guarding our houses, sniffing out and arresting drug dealers and other criminals. Humans are the great opportunists of the planet – if we see a tendency in an animals we will breed it up and train it for our use. Then we talk about devotion, a man's best friend, and companionship.

In 1968 I was in Ward 6 of the Maudsley Psychiatric Hospital with nine other people. In the bed next to me was Joan, a woman in her late twenties. She was a solidly built woman who wore home-made cardigans. She, like me, was in hospital diagnosed with 'clinical depression'. She spent most of her time sitting on the edge of her bed, her feet on the floor, her hands in her lap. She smiled and talked with you if you went up to her and joined her on the bed. Otherwise, she sat quietly unless she was shooed into the day room, where she sat in exactly the same way on a chair. When she was twelve or so, living in Wales, some boys she'd been playing with at a nearby disused quarry threw lime into her face, and she had been going blind since then. She was now almost completely sightless. She saw shadows against light, so that she could make out your shape if you stood in front of the window; she could even sometimes recognise who you were from the size and stance. It was only a matter of time before she lost that, too, and the world went completely black. Of all the people in our ward, Joan seemed to have a real reason for being depressed. One of the things about depression is that you feel you shouldn't be – that things aren't so bad and that you are in some way guilty for feeling bad. Joan on the other hand would, as she often said, have been crazy not to be depressed. It wasn't that she had given up. She had learned to read Braille, when she went out she used a white stick, and if she needed something, she called out and asked someone to help her. She lived at home with her mother in Wales, but her depression had overtaken her and she was not inclined to be very active. She wanted to go home, but the doctors wouldn't discharge her. They said that in order to prove she was not depressed she had to agree to have the seeing-eye dog that the local RNIB had available for her. The proof of her depression was not so much that she spent a lot of time sitting on her bed, not wanting to risk being a blind person in a sighted world, but that she refused the solution to the problem. Only a mentally ill person could refuse what anyone would be grateful for if they were blind: the help and companionship of a dog. It would help her get out of the house, let her be independent in the house and be a friend to her, so that she wasn't totally dependent on her mother. Joan was adamant that she wasn't going to have a dog. Her stubbornness on the matter was positively rock-solid. Craggy. She flatly refused. Obviously self-destructive.

Actually Joan was happy to explain to anyone who asked her why she didn't want a dog. She had never liked dogs, but now there was something else, as well: she didn't want one. She was blind. Wasn't that enough? Did she have to be responsible for a dog, too? It had never occurred to me that having a dog wouldn't be a wholly good thing for a blind person. It had never occurred to me that looking after a dog, feeding it, having to go out for walks, worrying if it was ill, going to the vet, the difficulty of having it sicken and die – dogs not living all that long – and then having to be trained to another dog, was a responsibility a person, blind or otherwise, might not want. Somehow, the doctors seemed to be saying that her 'illness' was her lack of gratitude in being offered something she, when you stopped to think about it, had a perfect right not to want. 'Why have I got to have a dog I don't want, just because I'm blind?' she'd say. And it was a question. She didn't want to look after an animal, however useful it might be. She also wanted the right to say no. But it was unthinkable that anyone wouldn't want the care and unconditional attention of a devoted helper animal.

PART FIVE

RESPONSIBILITIES

Blessed art Thou, O Lord our G-d, King of the
Universe, Who creates many living beings and the
things they need. For all that Thou hast created to
sustain the life of every living being, blessed be
Thou, the Life of the Universe.

Jewish Prayer before eating

Through the teeth
Past the gums
Look out stomach
Here it comes

Children's rhyme before meals

9

THE DEATH OF LUNCH

Little Lamb who made thee
Dost thou know who made thee
Gave thee life & bid thee feed.
By the stream & o'er the mead;
Gave thee clothing of delight,
Softest clothing woolly bright;
Gave thee such a tender voice,
Making all the vales rejoice:
Little Lamb who made thee
Dost thou know who made thee

'The Lamb', Wlliam Blake, 1789

Down on the Farm

When I said to the young woman in the local deli that I was off to a farm for a week to catch the lambing, she told me that her Italian boyfriend's father kept sheep and goats on a smallholding in Italy. 'The first time I went there, it was spring and I spent hours with the newborn lambs and kids – they were so cute – I was always picking them up and petting them and cooing over them. Whenever my boyfriend or his dad saw me doing it they shouted, "Stop playing with your food!"

The juxtaposition of cuteness and lunch is not necessarily an impossible contradiction. 'We'll eat you up, we love you so,' said the Wild Things to Max in *Where the Wild Things Are*. Maurice Sendak drew the animalistic Wild Things as he remembered his aunts bearing down on him. 'They would lean over you with their foul breath and squeeze you and pinch you, and their eyes are blood-stained and their teeth are big and yellow. Ahh! It was horrible, horrible.' My aunts and grandmother used to do the same thing. Pinch my cheek, as if to size up the quality of the meat, and purse their lips, like the Alien preparing to strike, and then threaten to eat me up. 'Ohh, I could eat you up!' Perhaps it's a Jewish thing – translated from the Yiddish? It was always eat you *up*, which left no doubt that they didn't have just a snack in mind and that my adorableness could only be expressed by their sucking the very marrow from every stripped bone before they were done.

Lovers, too, suck at each other, nibble and swallow, getting as near to consumption as possible without actually risking arrest. And there's always been talk in anthropological circles of tribal peoples eating the brains and hearts of ancestors and those they admire. I've never felt any shiver of disgust at the idea of cannibalising, say, an already dead fellow shipwreckee, as a rational solution to starvation. I think it would be more difficult to eat someone you disliked than a good friend. Eating the lovable doesn't worry me too much in principle.

My decision to test the truth of this on a hill farm in Somerset during lambing season was a flawed experiment from the start. In the last ten years I've lost my taste for lamb flesh. It's the only meat I could happily give up and more or less have, if I can avoid it. I detect something acrid in it, and I can't stand the smell of cold lamb that pervades the house and clings around my lips and nostrils. I should really have gone to a pig farm during farrowing: I am exceptionally partial to both the live and dead pig.

Of all non-human babies, living lambs have the highest cute-quotient and the widest cultural reach. But there has always been a certain ambiguity about them. Initially, they were sacrifices. It was a ram caught in the thicket, rather than a lamb, which transformed human sacrifice into animal sacrifice, and saved best-beloved Isaac from Abraham's knife. That ram substitution was a necessary symbolic change required by the conjunction of rams and paternity; thereafter God required pure, innocent firstborn lambs as trespass or sin offerings in Leviticus. The Paschal Lamb, whose blood was smeared on the lintels of Jewish dwellings in Egypt to indicate which firstborn should and shouldn't be killed, metamorphosed into Christ, designated the Lamb of God by the Church: the Lamb of God equated to both the pure and the sacrificed one. Jesus, on the other hand, referred to himself as the Shepherd, 'So when they had dined, Jesus saith to Simon Peter, Simon, son of Jonas, lovest thou me more than these? He saith unto him, Yea, Lord; thou knowest that I love thee. He saith unto him, Feed my lambs.'

When they dined, what did they eat? Jesus wasn't a vegetarian, as far as I know. He was a Jew, so he didn't eat pig. Fish, certainly: Simon Peter was a fisherman. Steak would have been OK. Though you don't hear much about herds of beef cattle in the Gospels, the Prodigal Son does get a fatted calf on his return. The many references to sheep and lambs in both Testaments are there precisely because of their familiarity to a people with a long nomadic, herding past. Lamb (and goat) would have been a common food in Palestine. Surely no one would be surprised to discover that Christ had dined that last evening with his disciples on the lamb he used as a trope for humanity. Jesus and his disciples were fishers of men and good shepherds – *feed my lambs*. In reality, of course, lambs ought to be able to feed themselves, suckling at the ewe's teat. But for actual sheep, nature left to its own devices is terribly wasteful of life, just as it is in the human herd as perceived by Christianity. Original sin is what structures the relationship between the Good Shepherd and his flock. It's hardly less of a struggle for the shepherd trying to rear the four-legged kind. A sheep farmer's life is a wearing business.

I'd been to the hill farm in Somerset before, and written about it, but never during the lambing season. There are around three hundred ewes on the vertiginous farm that spreads across steep hills and small, enclosed valleys. Sheep suitable for this kind of rugged farming lamb late compared to lowland breeds. By mid-March, when I arrived, about a hundred ewes out of three hundred had already lambed, giving birth to single lambs, twins and sometimes triplets. A week later, when I left, there were eighty ewes still to give birth. The fields for grazing are spread over the precipitous combes. By the farmhouse in the central valley was a row of four disused pig pens, a large open-fronted barn and a sheepfold. For the first two days or so the newborn lambs and their mothers were kept in the pig pens, or in individual gated areas within the nearby barn and in two other barns a quarter of a mile or so further down the lane. Every night, all the other ewes with older lambs, which were left to graze out on the fields, were shooed down the incline into the barns to join the new mothers and their infants. This kind of pampering doesn't happen in large lowland farms with huge flocks, the Farmer said, where, except for one or two rescued orphans who might be hand-fed, the ewes are left to lamb as best they can, usually without human assistance, and the newborn lambs remain in the fields with their mothers from birth to take their chances with the uncertain workings of the weather, maternal instinct and the very certain interest of predators. It's an economy of scale. Up to 20 per cent of lambs can die in the large lowland farms, compared with often less than a 10 per cent death rate in the hill farm. By the time I left, twenty lambs had died out of the two hundred or so that had so far been born, and none of them died for lack of the Farmer and her son trying to keep them alive. There are just the two of them working on the farm. If you're attempting to make a living on a hill farm with just three hundred sheep and a few cattle, then every single lamb matters to your balance sheet. But during the three months when between two and four lambs are being born every day (and night), two people working on their own are on relentless twenty-four-hour emergency duty. The night before I arrived, the Farmer had been up until one-thirty in the morning seeing to the birth of a set of triplets. Labour costs are not taken into account when trying to balance the books. This is intensive farming with an entirely different meaning.

I emailed the Farmer (as we'd agreed to call her in the previous book) to ask if I could rent the cottage for a week and be around while the lambing was going on.

My next book is non-fiction, about animals, anthropomorphism, people . . . and me, in some way I'll discover, I hope, as I write it. A kind of travel book but with animals instead of travel. Who knows? I'd like to come to the farm during the lambing season, since I need to think about domesticated/farmed animals, and I've no experience of them. A week, say, hanging out with a few new lambs, a birth or two if I'm allowed.

She knew me well enough from my previous visit. I'd already spent two months there on my own and proved – as well as written of – myself to be completely committed to the indoors, urban and as rugged as a snowflake. She replied:

Bring gumboots and warm old clothes if you are really putting your nose outside! There will be lambs galore. Forty ewes have given birth since the end of Feb. including 3 sets of triplets. Needless to say, it is snowing! All this deep snow when the ewes are so pregnant makes me concerned for the lambing. I hope it won't be too full of disasters. And the pens are overflowing as we hate to turn new lambs outside in bad weather. But you can view activities from the window if you prefer imagining the gory reality. I hope you know what you're letting yourself in for . . . the intensive care unit, the knackers, or tugs of war extracting monster lambs? But if it gets too much, you can lock yourself away beyond reach.

It had stopped snowing by the time I arrived. It was a miraculous, teasing week in early spring which pretends to be the start of a perfect summer. The trees and hedgerows were still all naked branches, but the sun shone in a cloudless sky and the wind, even up at the top of the combes, was no more than a refreshing breeze in what felt like a perfect June day. I arrived (with The Poet clutching many books and binoculars, having declared himself absolved from lambing, and free to walk the romantic hills and daydream as poets should) in glorious sunshine. The Farmer, coming up to her eightieth birthday, was in dark overalls and gumboots, her white hair pulled back out of the way. She greeted us cradling several large, rubber-teated bottles of milk in her arms.

'You've brought good weather with you.'

She smiled a welcome that suggested she was amused that I'd even got the weather to conform to my profound desire for a comfortable life. After weeks of battling with blizzards and freezing winds that had torn down the telephone lines and isolated the farm, while the sheep had no more sense than to drop their shivering lambs in spite of the weather, I had arrived on the first warm and sunny day of the year. The whole week stayed the same. I felt ashamed. I always feel ashamed and spoiled when confronted by people who work hard for a living. And hypocritical, because I'd been dreading snivelling in the wet and cold, and remembered the last time I'd been there and stood at the window watching the sheep in the field opposite shuddering a corona of excess water out of their thick coats, and I couldn't, no matter how hard I tried, avoid projecting myself into their saturated skin and feeling the dismay and despair that I would certainly feel, but which I had no grounds whatever for assuming they felt.

Number 71 was everyone's favourite lamb. It was born, like one of those human children destined for a life of love and success, with the capacity to demand and get your attention. Others are born with that capacity, but if they don't have a special something else that Number 71 had, they lead altogether sadder and harder lives. Lovability is the extra quality, but that doesn't explain anything. In lambs and in people, that just provides a gaping and urgent question to be answered. Or perhaps all lambs are lovable, but Number 71 knew about it.

Most of the lambs were indistinguishable, though they came in different colours, patternings and sizes. They all had, as of right, the adorableness of the baby creature. Sweet, cuddly, vulnerable and neotenous: that good start in life. Just what you'd expect. But it was generic, in the nature of all newborns (maggots and some other maligned creatures not included). Their ewes take a few moments to recover from the rigours and pain of the birth, and then begin to smell and nuzzle the wet, bloody packet they'd produced. It starts as curiosity but usually after a little while the interested sniffing turns to a nuzzle and then a lick, as they learn to distinguish their own bloody packet from all the others. The licking continues, clearing away the mucus from the newborn eyes, stripping off the remains of the torn amniotic membranes from their tiny body, cleaning up the blood on its wet wrinkled skin that so far seems nothing at all like wool. Except, of course, when they don't nuzzle and lick. There were ewes who looked, sniffed and then looked away, unmoved by the sight, smell and cries of their lamb. Or some that did exactly what they were supposed to do with the first lamb, but took no notice at all of its twin born moments later, or managed to include the twin but ignored the triplet as something quite alien. Enough, at some point for ewes, is enough. We have stereotyped expectation, social pressure and finally legislation to push human mothers and to encourage any weak maternal urges. It doesn't always work, but there are, all things and numbers considered, far fewer outright failures than there are in sheep.

'Do you know why some ewes reject their lambs?' I asked the Farmer.

'Oh, it just happens,' she said, exhausted and not much inclined to analyse the practical difficulties she was confronted with day after day. But she added. 'Well, the year-old ewes are worse than the two-year-olds. Experience helps. And the younger ones have the most difficult births.'

They are anxious creatures by nature. The previous week, Ben, the over-willing sheepdog whose only interest in life is herding sheep, which he will do at any inappropriate moment, took off on his own to round up a group of sheep being kept quiet in a nearby field almost ready to give birth. One of the ewes was actually in the process of lambing, the infant's head was showing, but she took fright and ran crazily away from the dog. She got to the top of the field and the lamb dropped. By the time the Farmer got to it, it had already been pecked at by birds and died shortly after.

One evening, when the sheep and older lambs were being herded by the Farmer and her son down from the fields into the barn for the night, I held the barn door open ready to close it fast when they were all persuaded in. The Farmer called me over to have a look at one of the pregnant ewes. The ewe had a hoof and part of a leg hanging down from her vulva. It was a back leg, a breech birth. The Farmer shooed her into an empty pen and got her to lie down while her son rolled up his sleeves. The lamb was stuck. It was going to be a difficult birth. The Farmer's son hunkered down and inserted one hand into the sheep's vulva to get a purchase on the haunches of the lamb, then with both hands he started to pull on the legs to drag it out. The Farmer, who was holding the ewe down at the head end, reminded him to take it slowly. You have to pull hard, but be careful. 'I can't manage it myself any more. I haven't got the strength. It can be quite a tug,' she told me.

I stood by and watched while time did that thing it does when something urgent is happening and the outcome isn't certain. It seemed like an age – and I remember thinking it was seeming like an age but probably wasn't – as the back end of the lamb started to appear, haunches, belly. And then nothing else happened, no matter that the Farmer's son was pulling with all his might. 'Be careful, careful,' the Farmer said, soothingly, to try and calm the ewe who must have been in terrible pain and discomfort. I held my breath as you would during any long moment of life and death, hoping for one, fearing the other. The ewe remained completely silent, lying on her side, being held down firmly by the Farmer in case she panicked and started to get up and run around. I looked away from the lamb from time to time and into the ewe's face, but there was nothing I could tell from it. Perhaps the others knew something about the expression of a sheep, but it was closed to me. Her eyes remained open, those unearthly horizontal slitted pupils offering no clue as to what she

227

might be feeling. In pain, afraid, angry, or perhaps just a sense of terrible difficulty? But then was difficulty terrible to a sheep or only another thing that happened to it? Was pain a feeling? Perhaps natural endorphins rushed in to keep her going. Did she know she was giving birth? Maybe, if she had done it before. Assuming sheep remember what happened to them the previous year, and they can relate it to what is happening now. Two imponderables. But what would knowing she was giving birth mean to a sheep? And if this was her first pregnancy, she couldn't know. She might be dying, for all she could tell. But then she wouldn't – couldn't – anticipate death, either, though she might, indeed, have been dying. Perhaps 'terrible difficulty' is as close as language can get to her wordless experience, or as close as my non-ovine, language-obsessed mind can grasp. The lamb, looking very like a skinned carcass – a large rabbit, say – from the butcher, was being held hand above hand about the legs and haunch, and wasn't budging from its position half in, half out of its mother. The Farmer's son pulled and then rested, giving both himself and the ewe a breather, but for a while, what seemed an extended and dangerous while, nothing more happened. Eventually, a very long – seemingly last hope – pull did it, and the shoulders and head came through all at once, suddenly slackening the tug-of-war tension between the Farmer's son and the sheep, setting the man back on his heels and freeing the lamb from the ewe's grip. It lay on the straw handful of bedding the Farmer had put down for it, a complete carcass now, covered in its filmy torn caul, bloody and, for all that I could see, dead. After a second to catch his breath, the Farmer's son stood up and again getting hold of the lamb by its hind legs, he began to swing it upside down, its head swaying in a wide slow arc, from side to side in front of him, as if he were preparing to hurl it across the barn. For a split second, I could easily imagine the lamb dead and the Farmer's son angry and frustrated at the pointless effort he had made. He paused and the Farmer wiped the lamb's nose with a cloth and opened its mouth, putting her fingers down its throat, clearing an airway. The son swung the newborn lamb again, back and forth, as if in slow motion, for a few moments, and then put it down carefully on a clean handful of straw I'd been sent to get, placing it right next to the ewe's face, who was lying still, paying no attention to the drama. We waited for a moment.

'It's breathing.'

It took another few minutes before the ewe moved her nose lazily towards the lamb, which still had not moved, though its belly was clearly rising and falling now in a fast pant. There was a bit of nuzzling, a little licking, but the Farmer was worried. It was still no more than vague curiosity. 'She's not showing much interest. But she must be exhausted. That was a difficult one. Best to leave them to themselves.' We climbed out of the pen, I gathered an armful of silage from the trailer in the middle of the barn to put by the ewe for her to eat, as the Farmer directed, and we made our way through the milling crowd of sheep and lambs who parted skittishly, left and right, like fussed old ladies at our approach. They had taken no notice of the drama. It wasn't theirs. That night, as all nights during lambing, the Farmer and her son took it in turns to make their regular checks, at eleven, midnight and six in the morning. Often in the night I would wake and see the light on in the nearby open barn, as the Farmer checked on a lamb or ewe she was worried about. One night I noted the time; the light went on at 11 p.m., 12 midnight, 3.30 a.m. and 6.10 a.m. The morning after the birth I witnessed, I saw her striking out with her arms full of bottles at 8 o'clock, as I looked out of my cottage window, drinking tea. I went out to greet her and the Farmer told me, sounding as relieved as I felt, that the breech lamb had lived, the ewe had accepted it and they were both going to be fine.

Part of the relief was that no extra burden was going to be put on the Farmer. They had been left alone together much of the night because, after all, they were animals, not people, but the new lamb would have been taken into care that morning if it had survived but the ewe had showed no sign of feeding it. There were plenty of rejected lambs but none of them were given up on by the Farmer. Several times, while I was there, a newborn lamb lay in a cardboard box in the lower oven of the Aga in her kitchen. On the second morning of my stay, the son brought in a tiny creature he'd found born in the middle of the night to a mother who hadn't accepted it.

'They're terribly vulnerable. They get hungry and start to chill almost immediately, and they're so small that if they can't retain their body heat they die very quickly. Look how this one's shivering.' It was more like a shudder waving through its fragile body. It was too weak to suck on a bottle; it didn't have enough strength to hold its head up. The farmer doubted it had much of a chance.

'We'll give it a stomach feed, and see.' She didn't sound very optimistic as she pulled the gently warming lamb out of the oven – the door of course was kept open, the closed upper oven was for older, successful lambs who had fulfilled their destiny – took some blue rubber tubing which she put into the lamb's mouth and cautiously threaded down its throat, pushing it in, feeling where it had got to and pulling it out a little to reposition it to make sure that it went directly into the tiny stomach. The lamb didn't resist or respond at all to the tube being inserted into its body; it remained limp. The Farmer's son and I sat at the table and watched silently. Slowly, pausing often, the farmer pushed the plunger of a large syringe filled with colostrum – the early extra-rich milk that comes after birth – into the tube, to fill the lamb's belly. Such an oddly mechanical procedure for the fragile sliver of life she held. When the syringe was empty, she pulled the tube out, and instantly the lamb lifted its head just off the towel it lay on. It had stopped shivering. An immediate improvement.

'Well, perhaps it'll be all right. We'll see.'

She was about to put the lamb back in the oven when the Farmer's daughter – visiting for a few days to help with the lambing – reminded her that the lunch was in a pot on the top of the Aga waiting to be heated. The lamb in its cardboard box was popped against the warm outside wall of the cooker and the stewpot of locally culled venison and potatoes was put in the oven to warm up.

'Poor little thing's had a preview of its destiny,' I said.

'The venison will be better,' the Farmer laughed. 'That scrap wouldn't taste of anything much.'

In all three of the barns, along with the newborns and their mothers who were kept indoors for a couple of days, there were the rejected or orphaned lambs paired and penned up each with their foster-mothers. A ewe that had plenty of milk with just a single lamb, or whose lamb had been stillborn, would have a needy stranger lamb pressed regularly to her teats by the Farmer and her son. The lambs themselves, voraciously hungry, attacked whatever milky nipple they could reach, in their own way wearing down any resistance. Each ewe with its natural and foster-lambs stayed in individual pens in the barns until it was clear that the lambs were accepted and thriving. It wasn't easy. Twice a day, the ones that weren't doing so well, or the twins who were being sidelined, needed supplementary bottle-feeding by human hand. I went sometimes to help with the morning or afternoon feed. The Farmer told me which ones needed the extra milk, and I leaned or climbed over the separating metal gates and pointed the teat of the bottle at the chosen lamb.

A new lamb is almost entirely composed of will. The will to fill its belly with milk. But a reluctant ewe is a creature of will, too. When an unwanted lamb reached for the nipple of the ewe and banged its nose against it to bring the milk on, she would walk on a few steps or turn around, snatching her teats away from the lamb. The lamb would run towards or around its foster-mother, catch up, suck and nudge again with all its tiny might, and again the ewe would walk off. The really smart ewes simply sat down; it was a less tiresome way of depriving an undeserving lamb of rights to her body, although it didn't stop them butting and pushing into her side to get at the concealed teats underneath. If ever I saw an expression on the face of a sheep – and it's very doubtful – it was a look of smug satisfaction at the fruitless high-pitched bleating of a battling orphan failing to get anything from her. Sometimes ewes who had their own offspring colluded with their lamb to deprive the interloper of food. She would move subtly around as the orphan or the unwanted twin tried to get to her teats, and the lamb would push the orphan away from the side of its mother. Grudgingly, it was sometimes allowed to feed from whatever teat it could reach by standing behind the ewe and reaching through her back legs. Arsewise was the position for plaintive orphans. So when the foster-lambs in the barn saw a bottle with a teat on the end pointing in their direction, even though not attached to the expected woolly body, they raced towards it and clamped down hard with their muscular lips on the rubber to get as much into their bellies as they could before the infuriatingly limited source of their existence was yet again taken away from them. The lamb, no matter how small and scrappy a thing, tugged and sucked on the teat with remarkable strength, drawing the milk into itself like a pump. I had to hold on tight to the bottle with both hands to keep control of it. As they sucked and pulled, they quivered as if febrile, from top to toe, with excitement. Their tiny tails, not yet docked, oscillated in a frenzy of waggling. When the bottle was half empty or when the Farmer called across to me that the lamb's belly was beginning to swell (I could never really see it), I had to pull with real power to release the vacuum created by the sucking lamb. They never stopped of their own accord, and apparently, would be prepared to suckle even when their bellies were in danger of bursting. The will to life didn't seem to have a safety valve to prevent it tipping over into life-threatening danger. It was pure will, not actually will to anything specific, just will contained in a fragile skeleton and wrapped up in wrinkled, coarse baby wool. Their immense seriousness and concentration contrasted completely and startlingly with their physical masquerade as the cuddly little innocents of our dreams.

Number 71 somehow had got the business of staying alive absolutely right. All the lambs were pretty sheepish until they caught a gleam of a rubber teat. They hid behind the ewes and ran into the corners of their pen when a human arrived, upright, gumbooted and definitely in control of doors and gates and everything that made the world available, forbidden, frightening, or satisfying. Number 71 clearly understood the way of the world, but he, however, bounded up to and pressed himself against any human leg that he caught sight of. He was fearless and galloped across the barn, defying gates (under, through, over, it didn't matter how) and bad-tempered ewes to get at the source of gratuitous food – usually destined for someone else – and do his lovable lamb thing, which invariably resulted in much more than his fair share. Number 71 was twice the size of the other orphaned lambs because, although it was thriving with its accepting foster-mother, no one, not even the Farmer's son, whose opinion of sheep was very low indeed, could resist giving it a feed as it laced around his ankles and butted his calves and maaa-ed for all its lungs were worth while looking directly and completely appealingly up into his face. 'She's quite sweet, I suppose,' muttered the no-nonsense Farmer's son, who thought his mother sometimes went too far to keep a hopeless lamb alive. But he added, 'For a sheep,' in order to maintain the shepherd's proper impatience for what most of them know to be the most annoying, nervy, accident-prone and disease-ridden of all possible ways of growing a living. Number 71 was not the only personality on the farm. As the sheep were being herded out of their field into the barn one evening, I was holding the gate calling for them to come, and Ben pushing them along at the back, Number 99, just three days old, stopped dead, turned round and bleated at the dog. Number 99 had had it with Ben. They stood nose to nose, Ben barking for the tiny lamb to go on and the lamb standing its ground on its still shaky legs and shouting back at the dog. Ben was finally silenced, quite confused at the role reversal. Then with a certain dignity, Number 99 turned and ran to catch up with its mother. The Farmer and I cheered it on, although she shook her head over Ben, one of the more charming but least authoritative of working dogs.

There is another view of the life of a lamb – what might be the lamb's view. In 1970, while he was living in Caernarfonshire, the American poet Douglas Woolf wrote a story called 'Spring of the Lamb'.[1] It's written in the voice of a lamb – in the voice of a writer being the voice of a lamb. It begins:

> It was wild the way she had turned him out of the warm and dark into the cold and grey. She had not, he could tell, tried at all to wait awhile. There were better times than this out here. He could tell that much. What about yesterday, when she had been jumping all over the sky. Has she ever paused for a moment to think of him? No, she had waited for this coldest night, then pushed him out.
>
> Welcome, honey, to a bed of slush. Have some fresh frozen snow on top. Here, I'll add my big cold nose to that. Dimly he

could make out her looming bulk amid the savage flakes. Now he could feel her slapping tongue, right in his face. Cold nose, warm tongue . . . but rough. Ah, now she relented a little bit, nuzzling his cheek with her brow or woolly upper nose. One might almost say she was being gentle with him. Perhaps she thought he was dying or dead, stillborn, was it? He tried to go limp – no st-i-f-f. He got butted in the balls for that. One could say she was mad at him. Oh well now – she had her big head under his bell now, was tossing him. She wanted him to stand up, and walk!

And six very short chapters later, it ends:

Now for the poet, he heard, and leather hands threw him into the house. Grey wool with legs was piled high in a corner. A smaller pile lay in another. The sickening air was unbreathable. The tall-ness held a long blade in his hands, high over. Stiff on the floor, he stared up at it. Was this the end of everything then? No more leaping, no more prancing, no more wagging? Maa . . . ? Wasn't there next year? Maybe, but the old girl wouldn't be climbing her mountain forever. They were getting on to her ways. Maaaa! High high high high went the head.

A sheep farm, even a tiny hill farm run by two people, light years from any intensive farming methods, is a factory for meat produc-tion. The animals are raw material that keeps replenishing itself. It's as close as humans have got to beating entropy. Even the old ewes, used up, are sold on for animal feed. How could anyone observing a season of birth among sheep not simultaneously know about their near-approaching end? Lambs are an expression of delight in life, of joy in life itself. They were for Blake, who was plentifully aware of the bleakness of the world as it is. The use value of the Little Lamb is not mentioned in this Song of Innocence. Does it lurk in the shadows? Watching a newborn lamb being licked into shape by its ewe, how could anyone not consider the fact that in six months or so, the lamb would enact the point of its existence, the point it doesn't have knowledge of, but we do, and be sent with its fellows to the nearest abattoir for slaughter to provide food for the humans who, in varying roles, cause its life and death by growing it, killing and eating it? The successful lambs, like Number 71, pay for their short leaping, prancing single season of existence, for the food and care that kept them going, for the time and attention that permitted them life, with their useful death. It is what lambs are for: to delight us and then to feed us.

For thousands of years it's what they've been for. Without their usefulness to their keepers and breeders, the ancestral sheep, the *mouflon* of Europe and Asia, would almost certainly have died out. In 2004 the UN Food and Agriculture Organisation estimated that there were 1,059.8 billion sheep in the world. Breeding programmes over the centuries have separated sheep into prodigious wool-bearing animals or fast-growing lean-meat providers. Lambs destined for the table, the male lambs, are castrated very soon after birth, fattened up during the late spring and summer months and sent to the abattoir in the autumn – though some are killed in early summer for what is known as 'light lamb', most of which is eaten in Europe. At present (in 2009) a lamb will fetch between £40 and £60, though the Farmer says that prices are very erratic. A sack of bottle-feed powder to keep alive the ailing and rejected lambs costs about £20, and the Farmer gets through two or three sacks each season. The bottle-feeding continues on twice-a-day rounds from mid-February until June on the farm in Somerset, and that's when shearing of the ewes starts. The Farmer doesn't get much of a rest until autumn.

Surely, I said, you spend more time and effort keeping lambs alive than is economic? She looked rueful, not wanting to admit it, but she said, 'I don't like to let a lamb die if I can keep it alive. It doesn't always make financial sense.' She is by no means sentimental about her animals, but if sheep farming was, for her, nothing more than a way to make a living, it would make no sense to keep feeble lambs in the oven and feed them twice a day from bottles, let alone stomach-feed the scrappy newborns. Only some survive and those that don't are sheer waste of money and energy. It isn't cost-effective caring. Nor did the two blind sheep living and fed daily in the nearby field make much financial sense – though one had become pregnant accidentally when the ram had got to her. Several other adult sheep in the same hospital field were lame. The farmer didn't want to destroy any of them, though there was one she had lost patience with. It had been limping for a long time. 'It just *won't* get better,' she said, quite crossly. At some point, the sheep who stayed lame would be sent off to the abattoir and return to the Farmer's freezer. The profit margins on a small hill farm are minute; £20 here and there for bottle feed makes a real difference. The exhaustion of caring for lambs by hand, keeping the weaker ones alive, is not compensated by large amounts of money for their intensely cared-for carcasses. Not wanting to lose a lamb was not just about not wanting to lose money. There was a tiny lamb living alone in the disused stable by the back door of the farmhouse, which was fed every few hours by hand. It was an orphan that none of the ewes would foster. It had started out in the oven and survived. The farmer continued to give it time and feed, and she would go on doing so for as long as it lived. But if the little creature did survive and grow robust enough, it would be sent with the other lambs to the abattoir in the autumn, as would Number 71, the lamb with the gift for being everyone's favourite, and bold-as-brass Number 99. They have all long since been someone's lunch.

There are no pets on the farm. Or if there are, they eventually have to serve their purpose – that is, our human purpose.

What effect has this hands-on lambing experience had on me? As I say, I don't eat lamb if I can avoid it, because I no longer like the taste very much. But I am no more unable to contemplate eating meat after a week watching lambs being born, than I was unable to be a secret smoker in the boiler-hut at school after they showed us a film of an operation for lung cancer. Did I feel bad about Number 71 and his fellow adorables? Well, yes, I felt that their whole life-cycle and that of their mothers was grim, and entirely dependent on human desire, for all that they had some period of free running life and concerned, caring keepers on that particular farm. Looking at the matter from a distance, I only intermittently see why any creature's life should be grim or even shortened in order to make human life better. Animals predate animals in nature, but that is hardly commensurate with a massive worldwide farming industry that breeds species purely for our purpose. But did it stop me wanting to eat meat? No.

The Death and Lives of Animals

There were no vegetarian Jewish mothers in my young day. The idea is baffling, although as a matter of fact the single London vegetarian restaurant in Leicester Square in the 1950s, The Vega, provided a place to eat for kosher Jews wanting to eat out in town, if they didn't go to the kosher salt beef bar in Great Windmill Street, or all the way to Bloom's in Whitechapel. For Jewish children, bread and schmaltz sprinkled with pepper was a regular snack – made from the scooped-up and treasured globules of fat from the top of chicken soup and refrigerated to become a solidified yellow paste. The lump of raw fat from the side of the neck cavity was pulled from the inside of the chicken before it went into the pot, to be fried in schmaltz until it had sizzled into a small crispy nugget and offered as my special treat (along with the unlaid eggs and gizzard boiled in the soup). We weren't kosher (bacon was an essential ingredient to the Sunday mixed-grilled breakfast), we were omnivorous Jews.

But when I was eleven, I was sent by the local authority to a boarding school – the fees being paid by the local council on account of a recommendation by the Child Psychiatry Unit at University College Hospital having deemed me maladjusted. It was in Letchworth, the first garden city, just outside the town itself, surrounded by fields, a large, rambling, liberal country space in which to put a troubled urban child. It was also entirely vegetarian. When my mother read the prospectus she was horrified. Not at the unorthodox 'progressive' nature of the school (no uniforms, we called the teachers by their first names and held council meetings that were taken somewhat seriously by the teachers), or at it being a co-educational boarding school, not even at the idea of me being sent away from her by social workers. Look, she said, passing the brochure over to me. They don't eat meat there, she told me in shocked tones as if it were a dangerous place; if not evil, then wilfully radical and, well, *peculiar*. She seemed to think that the discovery of vegetarianism would make me refuse to go. It did give me pause for thought.

At St Christopher's we were fed hunks of heavy wholemeal bread, sticky fingers of dried bananas, muesli specially formulated for the school by Dr Bircher's Institute in Switzerland, vats of grated carrots, celery sticks grown in the vegetable garden, nettle soup, stuffed marrow and nut rissoles. I loathed the vegetably healthy smell of it all (although in retrospect the food was vastly superior to the vilely cooked meat served at most schools) and hankered for fatty flesh.

Vegetarian restaurants still make my nostrils twitch with the memory of school lunch. Sometimes I smuggled in salami at the beginning of term. At weekends, some of us would go into town and furtively eat forbidden frankfurters in much the same manner as we later hung around coffee bars and then smoked dope. I completely failed an end-of-term cookery exam because when asked to describe a nourishing soup recipe I wrote about how to make chicken soup, not deliberately, but I simply didn't think of vegetables as nourishing, and soup, as far as I was concerned, *was* chicken soup.* I couldn't comprehend why anyone would voluntarily lead a life without meat and meat products. And there was very little, actually, in the propaganda for the school that had to do with the wrongness of eating animals for the animals' sake – it was, like the nature cure policy, a health choice. I agreed with my mother when, after reading the damning sentence in the brochure, she proclaimed it unnatural. And even much later on, for all the brown rice and yin or yang miso soup that kept us hippies cheaply fed and mystically virtuous, in squats and bedsitters in the late 1960s and early 1970s, it never once occurred to me to become a vegetarian. I've always hankered for meat and animal fat. I like meat. I like how it tastes when you cook it every which way, or smoke it, dry it. I'll even (along with M Derrida†) eat it raw.

Although urban post-domestic that I am, I've hardly ever been confronted with the living animals who provide my meals, yet that can't be the only or main reason for not giving up meat-eating, not just

*I realise now I could have written a recipe for borscht, but I'm sure it's inconceivable without a chicken stock.
†See below, p. 248.

because my lambing week had no effect on my carnivorous desires and habits, but because even low-intensity farmers themselves who are continually confronted by the animals they sometimes even grow fond of, nevertheless send them off to abattoirs when their size and price is right and certainly aren't driven to vegetarianism. Can there be any vegetarian sheep, pig or cattle farmers? I do recall a school rumour that the nature-cure and vegan, sandal-wearing, wool-rejecting physics teacher owned a pig farm, but it sounds in retrospect more like an urban myth. While I can look on practical cannibalism with a high degree of equanimity (in theory), a meat-refusing cattle breeder or pork butcher would shock me rigid.

Somewhere in these uncertain thoughts of mine on the subject, the idea of consistency looms. It's OK to eat meat, and it's OK to be a vegetarian if you must, but like the writer of Leviticus I have an aversion to mixing. Linen *or* wool, not both in a single cloth. I scorn to call non-meat eaters who eat fish, vegetarians. I even have my doubts about vegetarians who eat cheese, drink milk and wear leather shoes. If you're going to be a vegetarian on moral grounds (the grounds that matter, as far as I'm concerned) why are you not a vegan? Leather, wool, milk, cheese are all by-products of animals bred and kept only as long as they serve our needs. Why should the moral vegetarian stop at eating flesh? Where *does* the moral vegetarian stop? Road kill would seem acceptable to eat, the creature having died an accidental death (albeit slaughtered by human technology it failed to avoid), but is the wearing of leather shoes or eating scrambled eggs acceptable? Not really. When I stop and think about it, which is what this book is for, it seems I have a highly moralistic view of non-meat eaters. Either reject the exploitation of animals altogether, or face up to the almost universal fact of eating the flesh as well as drinking the milk or covering yourself and keeping your money in the skin of animals bred and farmed or herded for those purposes and don't disguise it with half-measures. What about those who only eat animal products that have been produced by low-tech, 'kindly' farming methods? Free-range scrambled eggs, anyone? Happy animals might make better-tasting meat and eggs, but really happy animals (human and non-human) don't end their lives in slaughterhouses. Those are only-happy-for-a-while animals. If a happy animal is one that leads a natural life, chickens and many other domesticated breeds have a problem because there is no natural life for a chicken or a pig or a cow, one which doesn't involve being for the benefit (eggs, milk, wool, skin, flesh) of human beings.

There are a few people whose lives are even more completely integrated with the animals they exploit than my friend the Farmer in Somerset. They live at the top of the world and follow the reindeer herds on their trek to find winter and summer grazing. The Sami people are neither nomads nor farmers, they are transhumants. They don't breed their animals, but have villages and cabins along the routes the vast herds naturally travel, crossing the human border-lines of Sweden, Finland, Norway and Russia. Reindeer are better than money, a Sami told me, they give you everything. The Sami follow and control the animals, kill them, eat them, wear them, get their status and wealth from the numbers of reindeer they count their own, carve both useful and decorative objects from their antlers and bones; use them alive as draught animals, and wrestle and round them up to cut their ownership patterns into the animals' ears and to prove their own macho credentials. The Sami make full use of the reindeer: their skins are sheltering tent coverings and clothes, their blood makes breakfast pancakes. Reindeer exist in Sami myth, religion and survival; in their stomachs and hearts and minds. Men and occasionally women go off alone to watch over them for days and nights in the forests and sing dreamy songs they make up of words and sounds to their animals. These days they use their reindeer to take tourists on starry night journeys in the snow on traditional sleds, to earn folding money, a new necessity in a world where they can no longer make their entire living from their reindeer. I sat in a sled in freezing Norway last year, pulled by a reindeer being led by its Sami owner along a forested mountainside in deep snow, under the moon and a multitude of stars, and it was the most beautiful (and coldest) journey I've made. Also the most pointless. We travelled around for an hour or so for my pleasure and experience, and then, having doubled back at some point or gone in a circle, arrived quite near to where we had started out, at a traditional *lavvu* (a tepee-like tent) that had been specially built for tourists, where we, and others who had been on different 'arctic experiences' (dog sleds and snowmobiles), ate reindeer stew. The customary Sami life revolved entirely around and was sustained by the necessities of reindeer life. Now both the Sami and the reindeer way of life can only continue if it revolves around the need of tourists to 'experience' a way of life they both abolish by not leaving it alone, and give money to so that it can be partly sustained as a relic, or a theme park.

Nevertheless, the Sami who stick to their old way of life both love and eat their reindeer. It is an essential relationship, they would say; a symbiosis. They kill their animals with gentleness, and great efficiency, in order to be respectful: words are spoken to the creature, explaining its needful death, and then a single stab of a knife in precisely the right place at the back of the neck kills the animal instantly. There are no vegetarian Sami apart perhaps from those who have given up their way of life and are living in what we and the traditional Sami would call the modern world. The seamless, untroubled integration of respect and exploitation which I observed when I spent a week with the Sami people was a lesson in an old human reality – and in animal reality. This was how the world worked. At its best: decent praxis. Humans dominate other forms of life and use whatever is around them to make a living. There is nothing to argue about here. It is what we did for millennia. To have sentimentalised the natural world would have been to commit species suicide. Most traditionally living humans feel they are in a relationship with those they exploit. It's why they tell stories about animals, and think of themselves as belonging to clans distinguished by totemic animals. People have always attributed to animals qualities they admire in people. Animals are magic and food, they are magic food. They move and behave as roots and shoots do not. Therefore there is a special closeness between the hunter and the hunted. I suppose that most animal predators do not have the brain power to feel or cogitate anything about their prey. Owls probably don't whisper gently to the shrews they swoop down on. Lions are unlikely to tell stories in the night to their cubs about magical antelope. I guess that Bunty isn't communing with the baby bird she bats around the carpet with her paws like a football (this is literary licence: poor Bunty has never managed to catch a living creature in her life).* But we humans, owners of brains that beat out language and concepts, have found ways to think about ourselves in relation to the creatures we kill for our benefit, even just for our fun, that seem to us to elevate us above mere predators. Culture does wonders for our view of ourselves as we both romanticise and strip the natural world for what we need.

In September 2009 a lamb called Marcus was sent to be slaughtered. Marcus had been hand-reared by the pupils on their small farm at their primary school in Kent. A TV personality, hearing about the plan to have Marcus slaughtered, offered to buy him; animal-welfare campaigners complained. The head teacher, Andrea Chapman, issued a press statement:

---

*The Poet insists here that he has seen her with a dead moth, but can't swear that it was Bunty who killed it.

When we started the farm in spring 2009, the aim was to educate the children in all aspects of farming life and everything that implies. The children have had a range of opportunities to discuss this issue, both in terms of the food cycle and the ethical aspect. There is overwhelming support for the school, locally and further afield.[2]

The school council, comprising 14 seven-to-eleven-year-olds, voted 13:1 to send Marcus to the abattoir rather than keeping him. PETA sent a letter to Ms Chapman asking for the farm programme to be stopped.

We urge you once again to spare Marcus's life – teaching the children how animals feel love, joy, fear and pain, just like us. We also ask that you shut this programme down. The children have got to know and love Marcus and it is now the perfect chance to introduce humanity, compassion, respect and understanding to the school instead of betrayal.

In fact, the school has plans to buy pigs to turn into sausages. The Sami I met would smile gently at the dilemma, as they rear their reindeer and their children together, and teach the latter to love, kill, eat, wear and decorate themselves with the former. Ms Chapman is a fine educationalist. Her children will be among the few who know where their food is coming from, and be in a position to make an informed choice about whether to eat it themselves. I can't think of a better way to introduce them to 'humanity, compassion, respect and understanding'. I imagine, too, though it isn't mentioned, that the school also introduces them to the idea of industrial farming, where animals don't lead a life anything like Marcus's.*

*Ms Chapman resigned after the fuss, but in March 2010 has returned to the school after parents and children petitioned her and the local authority to get her back.

245

Yet at the same time, in the same breath, in a precisely parallel thought to all this consideration of the complexity of humans eating the flesh of other creatures, I can only really find a single non-weasely (as if they could) argument for continuing to eat meat: I like it. I have no other justification for it. I can imagine and have indeed given up all kinds of things I like very much – drugs, cigarettes, some people, baths for showers – but, even though I managed well enough at the vegetarian school, and I have allowed myself to be aware of the suffering that is entailed in meat-eating, I have not considered giving up meat. Alongside my pleasure in eating animals, I consider the way we use them for our human purpose, and how we treat them in order to use them, overwhelmingly shameful. Alongside the horrific vision of factory farming and suffering, I eat animals without guilt as I chew and swallow, as if I have managed to make the split between *animal* and *meat* an actual reality rather than a euphemistic convenience. To say, as you will, that it's hypocritical of me therefore not to give up meat is simply accurate. I am a hypocrite. No question. I am a member of the only species on the planet capable of hypocrisy (although there have been observations of chimps dissimulating to other members of the group about food sources, it still isn't really hypocrisy), and in relation to my food choices I do it as well as any of us. The gap, of which we alone are capable, between thought and practice gives us a world of philosophy and psychology to read and write and pass the time thinking about. Those adverts for private medical insurance which tell us 'You're *amazing*' are quite correct. If the extraordinary habit of thinking one thing and doing another is hypocrisy and exclusively human, which it surely is, I'm not alone in my *amazing* capacity to be double-minded.

Derrida, in his final seminar, moves away from the cool stare of his pussy cat (though not for long) to consider the past two centuries

of human exploitation of animals. In that time traditional methods
of treating animals have become industrialised and have transformed
animals into *the animal* and therefore a type of object – raw material
to be converted as in any other industrial process. The older ways in
which we exploited animals, from sacrifice in biblical times, to hunting, fishing, domestication, training, the traditional use of animal
energy for transport, ploughing, draught animal, the use of guard
dogs, to feeding ourselves using small-scale butchery and early
experimentation on them, have all, Derrida says, been superseded
and massively elaborated by the technological developments of the
past two hundred years. He is talking about the use of factory farming and battery-farm techniques, and more:

> This has occurred by means of farming and regimentalisation at
> a demographic level unknown in the past, by means of genetic
> experimentation, the industrialisation of what can be called the
> production for consumption of animal meat, artificial insemina-
> tion on a massive scale, more and more audacious manipulations
> of the genome, the reduction of the animal not only to production
> and overactive reproduction . . . of meat for consumption, but also
> for all sorts of other end products, and all that in the service of . . .
> the putative human well-being of man.

He speaks of the '*unprecedented* proportions of this subjection of the
animal', which suggests that he considers (as many do) more traditional, less efficient methods of exploiting animal life are to be
preferred or possibly acceptable. That the degree of exploitation is
what counts rather than exploitation itself. At any rate, we do what we
do, and Derrida is somewhat of a realist, but nowadays we use
extreme forms of exploitation and he insists that 'men do all we can in
order to dissimulate this cruelty or hide it from themselves; in order to

organise on a global scale the forgetting or misunderstanding of this violence, which some would compare to the worst cases of geno- cide . . .' He continues with a crucial and much-lamented analogy:

> As if, for example, instead of throwing a people into ovens and gas chambers (let's say Nazi) doctors and geneticists had decided to organise the overproduction and overgeneration of Jews, gyp- sies and homosexuals by means of artificial insemination, so that, being continually more numerous and better fed, they could be be destined in always increasing numbers for the same hell, that of the imposition of genetic experimentation, or extermination by gas or by fire.

Derrida was not a vegetarian. Derek Attridge, Professor of English at the University of York, recalls 'a lunch with Jacques Derrida in Paris, who talks to me about carno-phallogocentrism while eating with gusto a plate of steak tartare'. I find myself becoming more and more comfortable in the imagined presence of M Derrida, for all his apparent belief that his cat is more interested in his nakedness than in being let out of the bathroom. A man who eats steak tartare and is able to describe our treatment of animals in terms of the Holocaust, is someone I can understand. On the other hand, Professor Attridge also had lunch with the novelist J. M. Coetzee who 'orders a vegetarian meal before giving his first [Tanner] lecture [at Princeton] on *The Lives of Animals*'.

The Lives of Animals predates the Derrida seminar but Coetzee (or his character, Elizabeth Costello – it's an interesting and difficult dis- tinction) uses the down-and-dirty argument for not eating and util- ising animals – the genocide word, the concentration-camp analogy, in a similarly deliberately shocking, though fictional, fashion. The South African novelist was asked to give the Tanner Lectures at

Princeton University in 1999. Over two nights, Coetzee read, not a lecture, but a narrative fiction he had specially written about an elderly Australian novelist, Elizabeth Costello, who is delivering two lectures at 'Appleton' University. The question arises, of course, as to who Elizabeth Costello's views represent – just her own, or her author's as well? The greater question is why that question needed to arise. Why would a novelist choose not to speak in his own voice, indeed, choose that of a woman novelist and a highly emotionally charged *woman* novelist speaking (it might as well be in tongues) to academics, to fulfil his remit of speaking to academics? Costello, like Coetzee, is a vegetarian. She isn't, however, a vegan, as she snaps at the President of Appleton who praises her (somewhat embarrassedly) for her moral life:

'I'm wearing leather shoes,' says [Elizabeth]. 'I'm carrying a leather purse . . .'

At which the President offers his guest an excuse.

'Surely one can draw a distinction between eating meat and wearing leather.'
   'Degrees of obscenity,' she replies.

I'm with her on this. Much easier, especially these days, to wear non-leather shoes and carry a non-leather bag than to forswear meat. Why, then, does she wear leather? It hardly seems even a lesser degree of obscenity. Why not wear trainers and carry a canvas bag? Especially when she insists her vegetarianism comes not from moral conviction but that

'It comes out of a desire to save my soul.'

She even carries a wound around with her, as the Christian martyrs often did.

> 'I am not a philosopher of mind but an animal exhibiting, yet not exhibiting, to a gathering of scholars, a wound, which I cover up under my clothes but touch on in every word I speak.'

Moral or ethical conviction isn't enough, because Costello's views are an act of imagination, not principle. She suggests that like poets and writers (apparently) do, everyone should use their imaginative faculty to put themselves into the lives of animals: '. . . open your heart and listen to what your heart says'. There are those, she says, who do just that, those who can't (she calls them psychopaths), and those who won't. Once the imaginative effort is made, it becomes impossible to eat flesh because, I suppose, they are no longer *other*. We become merely clothed versions of animals – their open wounds when we kill them for our benefit become wounds we carry about on our own flesh. Empathy is what she means, I think, though she speaks rather of sympathy. Of course, you might say that animals are therefore especially *other* since as far as anyone knows, imagina-tion is a particularly human ability, but that's not the point. You might also say that actively imagining the lot of an exploited animal could have the effect in some people of increasing the distance between us and them, thankful that we are not in that position, deciding that we are dominant because animals are incapable of running an efficient (capitalist or, I suppose, socialist) world them-selves. There are those who can look and see how things are without pangs of conscience. There is, for example, meat-eating me, my eyes pretty much open, and not quite, I think, a psychopath. Costello is physically horrified by her act of imagining the lives of animals; she is actually suffering, and uses more emotive language than Derrida to make much the same deliberately out-of-order point:

> 'Let me say it openly: we are surrounded by an enterprise of degradation, cruelty and killing which rivals anything that the Third Reich was capable of, indeed dwarfs it, in that ours is an enterprise without end, self-regenerating, bringing rabbits, rats, poultry, livestock ceaselessly into the world for the purpose of killing them.'

When I discussed Coetzee's Costello in correspondence with a philosopher (and a vegetarian), he said that though he didn't very much like her or the novel, he agreed with every word Elizabeth Costello says. The odd thing is that I do too. I can't fault what she says: that we ought to use our imagination to its fullest extent to comprehend the power we wield over animals, the suffering we cause, to acknowledge the extent of it, really confront it, in spite of the scholastic distaste for the 'emotional'. When I do confront it, I am appalled – aghast, as she is. But I also can't abide Costello, and every righteous word she says makes me want to start preparing a feast of animal flesh, ache to share a plate of steak tartare with the shade of M Derrida. I am an involuntary contrarian, that has to be admitted: I put off giving up smoking for years, mostly because I loved it, but also because I hated the idea that I might become one of those self-righteous 'ex-smokers' I still find obnoxious, who hunt down every wisp of smoke and demand their right to clean air. It is Costello's moral superiority that I can't stand, even when she so moralistically undercuts it ('I'm wearing leather shoes . . .'). My dislike of Costello's self-righteousness actually overcomes my acknowledgement of the truth of her argument, both rational and emotional. Which is outrageous, quite unjustifiable, and should, possibly, disqualify me even from writing this book. Coetzee's President Garrard of Appleton College provides me with my only excuse, as he seeks (for reasons of public politeness, Costello having embarrassed her audience with her emotional arguments) to justify Costello's leather-wearing confession:

'Consistency,' murmurs Garrard. 'Consistency is the hobgoblin of small minds.'

I can take no more comfort from that than she does. Whenever I seriously consider the factory farms, the abattoirs, the haulage of animals, the breeding of them for qualities that make their meat or skin more to our liking and cheaper to produce, but their bodies less and less like themselves, I wholly agree with Costello that we are participants in 'a crime of stupefying proportions'. To play the emotional game (is there any other way to get there?), you have only to turn the idea around and imagine – *Planet of the Apes* – the animals utilising humans in the same fashion. It is stupefying. It is, Derrida says, as if for centuries we had been at war with the animals and having won, they are now our subject race. Or simply – worse or not? – all animals are merely available raw material like any other in our industrial and economic processes. Except that unlike plant material, metals or chemicals, they have what we must call *being*, as pig iron doesn't. I know that we could spend from now to eternity discussing what we mean by *being*, but whatever it is, we clearly share it to some degree with sentient animals, which is why when my cat or Derrida's pussy look at us it's so disturbing. My animus towards the human Costello's (or possibly Coetzee's) manner of expressing the problem can't, if I make the effort to think (and I must), really can't negate the enormity of what she (or possibly he), and others, have to say. She is not demanding that animals, having *being*, are therefore entitled to rights, as philosophers such as Peter Singer and Tom Regan claim. It is not a matter of *how* sentient (how similar to us) the animal is – Singer draws the rights line well before he gets to single-celled animals. She is saying unambiguously that we must not do violence to any living creature because we are able to imagine their lived creatureness (not their varying capacity to suffer) as we can imagine the creatureness of the stranger walking down the road, and would not therefore imprison and kill him (though that hardly holds universally true). It is inconvenient, but a necessity that we need to recognise, or, as Derrida puts it 'awaken to our responsibilities and obligations vis-à-vis the living in general'. The war, as he sees it, is 'being waged between, on the one hand, those who violate not only animal life but even and also this sentiment of compassion, and, on the other hand, those who appeal for an irrefutable testimony to this pity.'

How can I disagree with that? I can't; it seems to me to state the situation accurately. How, then, can I continue to eat meat? Actually, because I like it. The fact that I know my becoming a vegetarian won't alter anything in the commerce of food production isn't a good moral argument against my being vegetarian, but it is true that Costello, proselytising for vegetarianism, doesn't explain what would happen, if the world were to go her way, to the millions of food animals on the planet, let alone the livelihoods of those who are employed in the industry, nor what her soul being saved has to do with their survival or otherwise.

In the novel, written up and published after Coetzee's lecture at Princeton, the character of Elizabeth Costello has a difficult relationship with her academic son, and an even more difficult relationship with his wife, who, to their grandmother's disgust unapologetically feeds her children meat. Costello seems almost too weary and too morally superior (or self-involved) to care much about her antipathetic human relationships, but she is passionate about the lives of animals. Her passion is not for life, but for animal life. She may have a cat at home, but she speaks passionately not of any particular animal in her actual life, but of animal-in-general. Do I, like Elizabeth Costello, care more about animals-in-general than people-in-general? It's an interesting and somewhat alarming question, because I think of myself as – I can't think of a perfect word, but humanitarian is close. That is: leftist, anti-authoritarian, against the creation of suffering of people in the cause of land, nationhood or oil. I have always found it impossible to understand how we (including me) can do little more than mouth platitudes while millions of people are malnourished or actually starving. I watch the wars being waged in the Middle East and elsewhere in a state of helpless rage about the crimes committed by politicians against blameless human beings. But I don't do much about it, nothing you could call useful; similarly I continue to eat meat, knowing quite well how sentient beings suffer for it. Perhaps it's not so much that I like animals more than people, but that I am more moved by helplessness in human and non-human animals than I am by those who either dismiss the problem as unimportant or an unfortunate necessity, or people (like me) who, being quite aware of the awfulness going on, metaphorically wring our hands and continue just like everyone else. Much as I dislike Costello, I find myself, like her, easily, instantaneously responsive to the plight of animals, whereas I feel more ambivalent about the emotional demands of human relations. Remember the dog in Valencia? I see human beings vomiting in the street occasionally and on the whole I'm more inclined to suppose them drunk than ill, and have no immediate onrush of compassion at their helplessness. Animals get such a response from me because I suppose them entirely innocent, or blameless in a way that people are possibly not. Actually, this is choosing to respond to, and the creation of, the idea of 'victims', an idea I don't like at all.

Elizabeth Costello carries an animal-hide handbag; I do too, and I eat animal flesh, and I think it's very unlikely that I'm going to stop doing either of those things. The Sami people I met in Sweden and Norway would be baffled by this sorry liberal dilemma, and explain that there are those who do not have a choice because they do not live (if they can help it) in a world where making a living is so far removed from the essentials of eating and keeping warm. I say: but Christ, it's cold in the *lavvu* you (and I, once) spend your nights in watching over the reindeer herds at temperatures of twenty-five degrees below freezing and more. And I do not want to kill my own animals for food and clothing. Much happier keeping my hands clean and stomach unturned by letting other people in abattoirs process the raw materials. (I don't even know where my nearest abattoir is.) This is the time and place I was born into. Post-domestic, urban. A world evolved by methods of exchange to function by the division of labour, that allows some people never to need to know where their milk, meat and clothing come from, nor, if they can manage it, to worry too much about the lives of those who provide us with milk, meat and hides – animals and humans. If I abhor the industrial use of animals what am I to do about it? I don't want, as I say, to stop eating meat, but suppose I change the habit of a lifetime and nevertheless do what I don't want to do. I become a vegetarian – and so what? Elizabeth Costello's wish to save her soul and PETA's desire only to permit general loving kindness, may not be the best way to make people think about what they eat and what difference it would make to the world if we all chose not to eat meat.

Or we can have our lunch and eat it without moral dyspepsia. Costello is an emotional (if not practical) absolutist, but most human beings, even those with consciences, find a middle way to make themselves feel better about the inescapable fact of being the masters of the planet.

The standard argument against vegetarianism/veganism can't simply be dismissed, if only on practical grounds: we cannot undo what humans have done, unbreed the bred, wild the tame, uneat the eaten. There it is, millennia of exploitation, and you can and do feel all the remorse in the world, when you stop to think about it, but what if everyone gave up meat? One billion sheep, 1.3 billion domestic cattle, 850 million pigs and 24 billion chickens would be killed worldwide because they are only bred, fed and looked after in order to produce food and by-products. They couldn't be turned out into the wild. What wild? As it is we have to cull or safari-park wild animals who threaten to destroy what we think of as the natural environment, or overrun the farms of local people. And how would the genuinely but few wild animals survive with billions of ex-domestic creatures trying to make a living in their territory? Though the predators could feast for a while, the ecological balance would go haywire very quickly. In any case, how could they look after themselves, the sheep, pigs, cows and chickens, since we have long since bred that ability out of them? They are helpless. Maybe the fish in the sea, so depleted by our ravenous appetites, would do all right and eventually return to a balance where they could kill and be killed in appropriate numbers by each other. But what about the fish in the fish farms? If the banks were too big to be allowed to fail in the economic crisis of 2008–9, what about the massive unemployment of people involved in shutting down the meat industry – farmers, vets, feed providers, hauliers, abattoir workers, butchers, canners, freezers, pet-food manufacturers, deli workers – and the political and social consequences? What we might call the human consequences? The result of mass vegetarianism is that the animals which vegetarians seek to protect would be exterminated. Perhaps we would keep the rare and old-fashioned breeds that a few farmers have kept alive for historical and genetic purposes. But likely they would soon be scavenged by a few diehard carnivores.

So, the argument goes, it may be a shame, what we have done to animals – many things we have done on this planet are a shame – but going universally vegetarian, in the vanishingly small likelihood that such a thing could happen, would now do even more damage to those with whom we have already interfered and harmed. What can be done is to realise that the situation as it is, *is* as it is and improve it. We must, say anti-vegetarians who are not all in receipt of vast profits from the meat industry, go on eating animal flesh (for the reasons stated above), but we must ensure that we produce and provide the meat responsibly, undertaking to do it with the least suffering possible to the animals we use. Much better to eat a creature that lived, in our judgement (and what other judgement is there?), a contented life; not only does it taste better, but it gives us lunch without a bad conscience. An argument that does not go away by calling it self-interested, given the practical difficulty of dismantling our food industry. And animals in the wild also have shortened lives – very few die of old age. What, in any case, is so good about old age? An ageing human population is putting enormous strains on the economy and in return for a longer life, we seem often to be putting up with sometimes unbearable interventions or unremitting pain or confusion. Surely, a short happy life is not so terrible a prospect to aim for if we are trying to improve the lives of animals?

Dr Temple Grandin teaches at Colorado State University, and consults in the field of livestock behaviour in farms and abattoirs. She approaches the problems that the owners of these facilities bring to her in precisely the way that Elizabeth Costello suggests we all should. She thinks about animals as if they were her, or as if she were them. When she noticed that cattle were strangely uncomplaining while they waited for their vaccinations, tightly held in place in a chute, she reasoned in her own manner that the *squeezing*, as she calls it, had the effect of allaying their anxiety. She too suffers from fear and anxiety; she is autistic and finds negotiating the social world extremely difficult, nor does she like being touched by other people. So she extrapolated from her observation, and thinking in pictures rather than words (like animals?) let the pictures in her head come up with a design, and made a 'squeeze machine' for herself at home, into which she climbs whenever she feels the need for reassurance. She invented the hug from first principles.

She can work the other way, too, and fast-food corporations, burger and fried-chicken providers to the masses, looking for a more virtuous footprint in an increasingly guilt-making world, employ her to monitor and improve the welfare of animals on the factory farms and in slaughterhouses which grow and process their meat supplies. As the world's wealthier populations get more touchy-feely about their planet and their food, the burger and chicken outlets, along with other businesses, have to try and keep up, demonstrating their new green and loving credentials. Temple Grandin helps them, because she wants to help their raw materials. When cows baulk at walking into slaughterhouses and need to be prodded along with electric barbs, Temple Grandin goes down on all fours and follows their route to discover what it is that alarms the animals – assuming that they do not have the forward-thinking, logical capacity to comprehend the prospect of imminent death to worry them. Often, she discovers, it is simply a badly placed shadow which a redesign of the equipment would solve, or a carelessly left something that the naturally nervy cows think shouldn't be there and refuse to risk walking past in case it jumps out at them: a jacket flung by a worker on a fence that upsets the cow's view of how the world should be. She thinks like a cow, or pig or sheep or chicken on behalf of those animals, and devises systems that get them through their life and their premature deaths with as little stress as possible. She is undoubtedly a practical improver of the lives of animals, given the way the lives of animals are.

In a recent book, *Making Animals Happy*,[3] she describes a broad-brush theoretical underpinning, a method for even non-expert animal keepers to follow, based on Dr Jaak Panksepp's theory of four core emotions: *seeking, rage, fear* and *panic*. Assuming you're happy with the neuroscientist's elementary analysis of animal being, which is not an easy assumption for me, all you have to do with a wild animal or your pet pooch is enhance its *seeking* behaviour and reduce whatever might make it feel *rage, fear,* or *panic*. The method is pretty much the same for all animals: get their environment right according to their basic characteristic – whether they're predator or flighty prey types – and then use mostly positive and a little negative reinforcement to encourage the behaviour you want. (Though forget about using negative reinforcement on cats because, as we know and Grandin admits, they just won't have anything to do with it.) Practically speaking, which is how Grandin always speaks and writes, this means providing chickens with enclosed dark places in which to lay their eggs, as their instinct to avoid predators demands. Force them to lay in open cages for the convenience of battery systems, and they will start viciously pecking at each other and themselves in fear and panic. Understand that dogs are essentially children to their owners and are *not* part of a dominance hierarchy. They are bred to be neotenous, their juvenile characteristics having been selected for centuries. They want to make their humans happy, and be praised and cuddled when they're good: be parentally kind and firm, not ruthlessly dominant. She approves of the use of clicker training. You 'charge' a clicker with the implication of a treat (first give treats and click the clickers, then all you have to do is click – remember Pavlov?) and use clicks to reward the behaviour you want, without punishing what you don't like. In Grandin's slaughterhouses animals go peacefully, and she believes unknowingly, to their deaths by using her methods and her specifically designed systems, which ensure that the environment accords with their perceptions of a safe world. It's a sort of con trick, because we are eventually, or even imminently, going to kill them, which all animals are instinctively against when it comes to it, but it's a kind and thoughtful, as well as economically efficient, con trick.

She adds, though, that the new systems she sets up require continual outside auditing because the human handlers easily slip back into brute force (an interesting choice of adjectives, I now see) to manage the animals, and need a lot of positive reinforcement themselves not to reach for the electric prod, rather than take the slow and calm way of herding or moving creatures. She explains to the CEOs that it's more cost-effective not to frighten animals: they lay more eggs, the meat grows faster, less man-power is required to control them, which goes down well with the owners. But it takes something more than encouragement and reason to deal with the workers, who do not share in the profits, on badly run poultry farms, some of whom she has observed, for example, stamping on live chickens as a joke, and throwing living, worn-out egg-layers into garbage dumpsters.

The keeping and killing of animals as if they were raw material doesn't only brutalise the animals. The big question is, would I be prepared to kill my own animals, not just in a Sami sort of respectful one-to-one way, but in industrial quantities, day after day, as the living conveyor belt stops in front of me for long enough for me to turn life into meat? Or you? How long would it take us to become 'brutes'? What would we be like if we did that for a living? So should we at least have that experience, if we are going to eat the meat that results? Even if you won't devote your life to taking that degree of responsibility for your choice to eat meat, are you even prepared to spend a little time in an abattoir watching it happen? Have I, for example, spent a week, a day, an hour in a local abattoir watching the transformation take place? As I say, I don't even know where it is. It's not because I'm lazy that I've failed to do that particular piece of research. I really don't want to be there and watch even the most humane kind of industrial killing. But would a visit to a slaughter-house turn me into a vegetarian? I've read descriptions by people who have worked in abattoirs, and seen vivid documentary films. But what about the *being there* – the experience which is considered so important that young people write lists of what they must experience before they die. The experience of the noise, the stink of blood and fear, the mechanical methods of control that allow the workers (who are for the most part no different from me, only inured – how many people really want to work in abattoirs?) to kill living creatures all day long? We tend to revere 'experience' over thought these days, but like Costello, I don't think it's hard to imagine the slaughterhouse, and I do. Still, I might be shocked by the sensual reality of the slaughterhouse into vegetarianism. Or horrified to be confronted with the visual truth that my lunch requires other people to earn their living in such conditions. Nevertheless, I haven't visited my local abattoir, you should know, and I'm not entirely convinced by my own arguments. Perhaps, like Costello, it's another version of carrying a leather handbag. But a large part of me insists that the world can be known (in as much as it can be known) by thought, especially given the vast quantities of information we have access to. Nevertheless, a visit to an abattoir is not an experience that I want to have before I die.

Temple Grandin, on the other hand, has witnessed it all, animals and humans at their worst, and her response is to try and improve the situation for the animals through her gift of practical imagination. She is not utterly discouraged and disgusted by what she discovers about human beings in the process of doing her job, as I confess I would be, which is perhaps why I and most of us avoid looking. Her inclination to believe in and seek out practical solutions based on behaviourist research allows her to think up systems for dealing with the unspeakable – not by trying to change the darker 'brute' tendencies of human nature that we all know seem to be implacable, but by good design and strict auditing of the humans, using a scoring system for minimal poor behaviour (of abattoir workers), and keeping a watchful eye on the caregivers and life-takers of captive animals. 'Farms and slaughter plants should have glass walls.' Glass and webcams are 'wonderful technology you can use to improve animal welfare', she tells executives. You don't or can't change the people you've charged with the unspeakable; you watch them. Design helps the animals, and oversight (Bentham's old Panopticon prison) ameliorates the frequent human failure to see animals as more than mere objects.

Grandin does get round in the end to confronting the frequent questions she is asked about why she works in the meat industry. While she works practically to better the lives of animals, animal rights campaigners are dismayed by her devices for keeping animals fooled. Making animals less frightened and more manageable might make them 'happier' in some definition, but it only addresses a small area of our moral problem with how we treat the other creatures on the planet, and essentially makes life easier for humans. Her answer is simple and confident: she can improve animals' lives. Everything dies, she says logically, best make the deaths orderly and unfrightening. Becoming an individual vegetarian can't begin to solve cruelty to animals, and misunderstood dogs, left alone all day in the house, have a much worse quality of life than her cattle, she believes. She is doing something for animals, not, like Elizabeth Costello, symbolically refusing to eat them in order to save her soul. Soul is not Grandin's area of expertise. But that business of soul – we've called it *being* – is a vital question here. It doesn't disappear because someone has made the practice of herding and killing animals better than it was for humans and animals. Grandin's particular mode of practical reasoning relies on that super-simple theory of four core emotions. Her autism makes this a more comfortable way to understand the social interaction that she admits she finds baffling. Most of us, however, would feel that emotions and behaviour (what we might call our and others' *selves*) are immensely more complicated than four core emotions, and some wonder if this might not be true too of animals. The subtitle of her recent book is *How to Create the Best Life for Pets and Other Animals*. Though Dr Grandin's admirable and extraordinary work certainly makes life better for animals, her pragmatic approach to improving their conditions never questions the ability of us human animals to judge what is the best life for the non-human sort. And some would say that our assumed right to use all the other creatures for our own benefit, by definition precludes us from knowing what is the best life for any creature but ourselves. Even our relatively new interest in conservation and ecology is self-interested. And for all that, we mostly don't get it right. Yet, if we do admit that we can't know what is best for animals, what, if we are aware of the suffering and of our responsibility, can we do about doing the best we can for them?

The 'post-humanist' radical philosopher Donna Haraway considers the problem of how we share the planet with animals in a different manner from Temple Grandin, but her conclusion is not so dissimilar. Haraway also concurs, up to a point, with Derrida, but is more explicit than either of them:

I suggest that it is a misstep to separate the world's beings into those who may be killed and those who may not and a misstep to pretend to live outside killing. The same kind of mistake saw freedom only in the absence of labor and necessity, that is, the mistake of forgetting the ecologies of all mortal beings, who live in and through the use of one another's bodies. This is not saying that nature is red in tooth and claw and so anything goes . . . I think what my people and I need to let go of if we are to learn to stop exterminism and genocide, through either direct participation or indirect benefit and acquiescence, is the command 'Thou shalt not kill'. The problem is not figuring out to whom such a command applies so that 'other' killing can go on as usual and reach unprecedented historical proportions. The problem is to learn to live responsibly within the multiplicitous necessity and labor of killing . . . Try as we might to distance ourselves, there is no way of living that is not also a way of someone, not just something, else dying differentially. Vegans come as close as anyone, and their work to avoid eating or wearing any animal products would consign most domestic animals to the status of curated heritage collections or to just plain extermination as kinds and as individuals.[4]

A better life while they have it, a consciousness and real responsibility on the part of those who take lives by demanding animal products, better management of facilities: all are admirable and, though there have been improvements, are still to be fought for by those who care. When all that is put into practice, though, will we feel entirely at ease in our relations with non-human animals? Many do already, some no matter what the conditions, but will those of us who worry no longer be concerned about the condition of our souls? And before the arrival of animal utopia, will I, with all my awareness of and dismay at the suffering of animals, ever stop eating meat?

10

WHO'S IN CHARGE?

Riding

It's not just that I am post-domestic, I'm also completely lacking in the experience which even many contemporary urban women have had with animals – an adolescent love affair with horses. Once, when I was about eleven, I stayed with a school friend during the holidays on her farm and actually got on a pony (smaller? different breed? I don't know). I didn't like it very much up there. I'd previously only ridden people down on all fours pretending to be horses, neighing improbably, and the odd depressed donkey on the sands: this real version was far too high off the ground, and did not necessarily have my interests at heart or someone leading it around. When it did what it always did in the riding field with someone of my sort of size on its back and jumped over the tiniest jump imaginable, I decided there and then that I had no interest in this life in putting on a show of bravery to save face, and wailed to be let off. I was never going to be a horsewoman. I didn't want to be a horsewoman, any more than I want to be a Sami.

In my late teens I was staying in a cottage on Dartmoor and did a pony trek across the moor. It was wonderful – visually: the mist mingling with the horses' breath, Victorian-romantic, dark rolling moor, fast-running streams and bracken, rock-scattered tors and wind-twisted trees. I got the point of riding through the countryside seeing everything from the perfect height and speed. When there was speed. My pony, chosen for a complete novice, knew the kind of incompetent that was on its back, and stopped (sometimes on heart-arresting inclines) to munch at something tasty, or perhaps not, perhaps he just stopped – to show me who was in charge. So I began to suspect, as we dawdled humiliatingly behind. I had not the slight-est interest in arguing. But I needed to keep up, not knowing how to ride or my way around the moor, and I suspected that a horse or whatever it was called that stopped at will, might also trot or god-helpme gallop at will, so I tried to do what they told me with the reins and my knees, clicking and clucking encouragement, but if ever a horse laughed it was this one. I didn't care much. It was very pretty, and I had no desire to keep up with the adepts, aside from ensuring my safety. Eventually, having got quite a lot behind, the beast decided itself to catch up and started to run – trot, gallop, canter, whatever it did. I held on tight with every part of my body and knew that I was going to die. I didn't, but that was it for the rela-tionship between horses and me. Since then I have never done more than watch them graze contentedly in fields as I pass by sitting in a car or on the train.

However, as much as I have been unwilling to accept – very well, talked myself out of – the necessity for visiting an abattoir through-out the planning and writing of this book, I began to think that I really ought (ought? Rules and duties lurk in even the most contrar-ian of minds) to have a little more one-to-one experience of dealing with animals than just my life with cats, or a week down on the farm for lambing. Not in principle: I prefer to take as my writing model the traveller and surrealist, Raymond Roussel,* whose book *Impressions of Africa* was informed by his journey across the continent in a specially constructed motorised caravan in which he remained throughout with the shutters closed. I like the idea of thinking rather than doing, and I'm not entirely sure that doing doesn't sometimes substitute for thinking. Still, and even so, an inconvenient nudge started to work in me, which I recognised, albeit unwillingly, because it's true that, Roussel notwithstanding, I do occasionally find myself going out into the garden or a field in order to write, though not always, I suspect, with more success than if I'd stayed home with the blinds down. The nudge turned into a thought and it struck me in a way I had no desire to be struck that, even at sixty-one, it might be possible to get on a horse, and, as I unthinkingly thought of it, learn to ride.

I explained myself on the phone to Michael, the owner of the local riding school. I was a writer doing a book about animals and thought I'd better sit on a horse and see what happened when a person learned to ride. Although since I was over sixty and not at all fit or experienced in the ways of horses, I'd quite understand if he said I was an unsuitable novice rider.

'Oh no, our oldest rider is in her seventies.'

So no way out.

At the first lesson, I was given a hard hat and introduced to Alex, to whom I said hello politely from somewhere behind his left ear.

'Don't approach him from behind, stand in front of him so he can see you and put your hand out for him to get your scent.'

I withdrew it hastily as the lips curled back and he seemed about to take a nibble. I am afraid of animals (and some people) who are

*1877–1933.

267

much larger than me and with whom I can't have a reassuring conversation. I am horribly committed to language. Once I'd pulled back my hand, Alex showed no further interest in me in any way that I could fathom, not even when I hauled up on his back. I felt, under the eyes of a professional horseman, that the horse lost interest in me since I'd shown no great willingness to relate to him. He was held on a leash at all times by Michael, who as far as I was concerned was the priest who mediated between me and the unknown being I was risking my life on. I spoke to the human, as he led the horse at a very slow walk to the indoor practice arena. Alex was a very calm horse, excellent for novices, and no, he wasn't very big actually as horses go. I asked about how Michael got into horses and started the stables, which had some forty animals, most of them his and some liveried for their local owners. I was aware that I was trying not to notice that I was on top of a horse. We chatted as if we were wandering up the lane and I was conducting an interview. I was also aware of feeling somewhat ill mannered towards Alex, sitting on him and ignoring him, more as if he were a bicycle than a living creature. Not that I was actually ignoring him. The natural sway of his body from side to side as he walked transferred upwards to me through my legs and torso, and I felt the swing as if I were in a force-nine gale on top deck. A bicycle – for all the decades I haven't ridden one – would have made me much happier. If this was slowly walking under control, did I really want to learn to ride? Which meant, I understood, going faster and less sedately than we were presently proceeding. It was much more in my nature to walk along and talk about animals, or sit and read about them, than actually to interact with them, let alone entrust my life to one. So I didn't, as far as it was possible; I tried to keep my balance and chatted to Michael, as if I were sitting on a bus and he was the conductor. You can't really be rude to a bus, but I think it was rude of me to blank Alex as I did.

The first lesson did not challenge me with anything more than walking and trying to get my posture right. Straight, strong core, legs bent at right angles, heels under the knees, elbows lifted slightly, reins wound just so between the fingers. All fine. Just like getting a dance or Pilates posture right. Concentrating on making the right shapes of my body. I managed entirely to ignore the beast beneath my legs, for all that I was still very disconcerted by what I thought of as its wobbling, which Michael told me enabled me to judge his movement and pace. Slightly tense one rein to turn right, the other to turn left, lift a little to stop, squeeze Alex's sides very gently with my knees when I wanted him to move off. Try and sense the animal's response, look at his ears and the way he holds his head. Just like learning to drive, I thought. Steering wheel, accelerator and gauges. At any rate, I survived the first lesson and Michael led us back towards the stables while I asked him questions about his own riding. It was why he had the stables, which only had public lessons in the afternoon, he told me, so that he could fund his riding and keep horses. Every morning he worked his own horse, sometimes with an Austrian-trained dressage teacher. He had lived in London as a child but near some stables and, not able to afford lessons himself, he used to hang over the fence and watch young girls riding. He became besotted with horses, working at the stables in return for the chance to ride and eventually found a way to make horses his living.

As we talked, we were following another rider who was a few metres in front, also returning to the stables after her lesson. The woman was a little younger than me, in her fifties, her horse being led by one of the young women instructors. The woman on the horse ahead had only recently started to learn, Michael said in a reassuring way. To our right was a field where a couple of loose horses watched our stately, clopping progress. One of them, greeting or teasing, suddenly shook its head and whinnied loudly at us, and several things instantly resulted. The horse in front jerked sharply in response, the rider on it toppled off sideways; my horse, Alex, jumped sideways in surprise at the horse jumping, while the horse ahead of us abruptly took off at full speed, not quite riderless, because the woman had caught her heel in the stirrup, and was being dragged on her back along the cobbles as her horse bolted for the stables. I didn't fall off Alex partly because I was already so tense at merely being on him that I was clinging on tight anyway, and also because Michael saw what was happening very fast and got Alex under control immediately. Michael held Alex still and I watched horrified while the young woman in charge of the galloping horse in front tried to catch the reins and halt it, and the rider bounced behind on the ground, helplessly attached, like a scene in a Western but much more disturbing because it was real and unstoppable. It took a long moment before the instructor had the horse by the bridle and brought it to a halt. We waited for a second to see what condition the woman was in. It took a moment because she wasn't sure herself, and was presumably in shock. Michael, trying to contain the drama to just the one fallen rider, kept hold of Alex. The instructor, having somewhat calmed the horse, reached around to release the woman from the stirrup, and she sat up, very white and in pain somewhere around her upper back. She was, it seemed, only bruised, though nastily so, I imagine. She sat on a bench and was clearly distressed, but also embarrassed, as you would be, trying to make less of it than she felt. Michael asked some pertinent questions about mobility and after helping me to dismount, got an accident form for her to fill in. She need to go home, shaken and not wanting to be seen to be too upset. Michael spoke to her kindly, but his manner suggested, given his experience of people falling of horses, he was sure there was no real damage apart from her confidence: he said that she should see an osteopath but come back as soon as possible to ride again, otherwise she might find it difficult. She still looked upset and said she would, though I doubted that she'd be back.

When we got into the stable to take Alex's saddle off, the horse involved in the drama had been tied to a wall and was being groomed by the young woman who had been in charge of the ride.

'Poor Henry,' she said to Michael, with a slight smile. 'He's feeling very sorry for himself.'

'Poor old thing, look at you,' said Michael, much more sympathetically to Henry than he had been when comforting Henry's rider.

I asked questions. Why was Henry sorry for himself when he'd just tossed his rider? And how did they know that was what Henry was feeling? He looked to me just like a quiet, large, horse being groomed.

Michael explained that Henry had been confused by the rider falling off him just because he jumped slightly at the horse in the field whinnying, and that was why he bolted.

'You mean it was her fault?'

'Well, yes, really,' he said. Henry, like any trained horse, expected riders who weren't complete novices to be able to ride and not fall off with so slight a reason. He was startled by his rider having so little control. It gave him an awful fright, and that was why he bolted: to get to the safety and security of his stall, and then her getting her foot stuck in the stirrup when he ran upset him even more. Now, he was feeling upset and embarrassed about the whole incident and needed reassurance. He was a lovely horse, good temperament, no trouble at all. And the woman, I wondered, what of her fright? Well, she'd had enough lessons to be expected to keep her seat. She was all right, not badly hurt, and falling off is something that happens when you learn to ride. It seemed a little harsh to me, but then I was a novice rider, and Michael and the other instructor were seeing it as they could, apparently, and I couldn't, from the horse's point of view. It hadn't really struck me, before that moment, that horses had a point of view. Certainly not in the matter of people falling off. Maybe, Michael said, looking a little worried, that wasn't the best thing for you to see on your first lesson. But it was, of course.

Even more interestingly, how could they tell that Henry was upset and in particular 'sorry for himself'? Did they mean it, or was it just a way horsey people talk to each other?

'Absolutely not. Look at him. Can't you see he's upset? And he's got that shamefaced look.'

I gazed hard at Henry, although unsure which bit of him I should be looking at. He was a white horse, much bigger than Alex, quite handsome, and standing quietly with his head towards the wall where he was tied, munching on some hay and being brushed by the young woman. He looked like a horse. He wasn't sweating or shivering.

'Look at his face.'

It was a horse's face, that is to say without any expression that I could make out. Huge protuberant eyes, thick eyelashes, large nostrils, mouth closed. One of the things that makes cats so enigmatic (or annoying) is that they have no expression on their faces, they don't have the facial muscles to show their emotions with their eyes or mouth. Unlike primates, which use their features to show their fellows what they are feeling, cats, and, as far as I could tell, horses, always look the same. You need to look at a cat's body, arched, fur up, tail still or going like a windscreen wiper, or listen to the purring or yowling or mewing. Look into a cat's face and you might as well wonder what a rock is thinking or feeling. Even the eyes, those windows, apparently, on the soul, only tell you what you think you see in them.

'He looks like a horse. What's upset about his face?'

There were clearly signals that I hadn't learned. The ears are up or down to varying degrees, the head is held differently, but they were also looking at his eyes, at his expression, though I couldn't see it, and he was deemed to be 'feeling sorry for himself'. Like a child who has been confused by something he assumed and didn't understand about the world. People (grown-ups) who sat on your back were expected to be competent to do so. He was let down, like watching a father lose at the school sack race. Henry would never have reacted to the whinny of the horse in the field if he'd had a complete novice – like me – on him, or a child, or one of the disabled children I'd seen riding in a circle in a small field when I first arrived. All this could be read by looking at his expression.

'The animals know when they need to be calm. The disabled kids come once a week and some of them make sudden movements, or shout and scream all the time, but the horses never react because they know the kids are vulnerable and they have to take care of them. They have a sense of responsibility.'

'But Alex jumped, too,' I said. 'And I've never ridden before.'

'Well, he knew I was in control.'

'Are you serious about all this?'

'More or less.'

Michael was neither naive nor sentimental. He was *involved* with horses in a way I could only imagine, and more emotionally involved with them than with his human pupils whom he knew far less well. He and the others working at the stable had a language for what they did, and a way of characterising the mechanics of the relationship between themselves as humans and the horses they worked with. The language he was using to me was about trust. He trained the horses and then trusted them. They, having been trained by Michael and his co-workers, trusted them, and by analogy they trusted others who rode them. When people like me, or the disabled kids, merely sat on them, rather than rode them, the horses transferred their trust to the person leading them. But sometimes, at some midway stage between being a novice and a real rider the horses just plain took advantage if they could. They gave you a chance, but if they decided you were hopeless, you'd had it. They took over. It was a form of contempt, Michael suggested.

At my second lesson, nothing more dramatic happened than that the left flank of my horse shuddered under my knee after I gently pressed against her side to get her moving (Maddy, this time, a little smaller to my relief: my vertigo kicks in even up on a horse, the ground seems alarmingly far away if I'm not actually standing on it). I didn't notice, or rather, when Michael asked me if I'd noticed that shudder on her left flank, I realised I had felt the slight ripple against my leg, but had paid no attention. It was a living animal, it had slightly shuddered, in much the same way that it raised it head or snorted from time to time. What of it? But the shudder was important, Michael said. It meant that Maddy was telling me I had squeezed too hard when I instructed her to move forward. Not very hard, but harder than necessary to get her to understand what was wanted of her. We were supposed to have a relationship. Maddy knew this and was explaining it to me: I am not a machine that you knee as if you were putting me into gear, I am a responsive creature that you have a dialogue with. The pressing of the knee is the language you use. I was, it seems, raising my voice unnecessarily.

It could have been a turning point. It was a new idea, one of those moments when you suddenly 'get it'. *That's* what you're doing. It was, after all, the reason why I had reluctantly decided to have riding lessons. And at that point I might have decided to learn to become a rider, which is to say, learn how to be in a relationship with a horse, how to speak and listen to it so that I could work together with the immensely powerful creature who might be persuaded to accept instruction from me. This, though, was the big problem. I had no desire at all to give this or any animal instructions. I didn't want to be in charge of a horse, to dominate it, even in the most benign way. If the horse needs to know it can trust you to be in control, to be a senior partner in its life, I am not the right person to be a rider. I had no taste for being a 'master'. It was why I have never had a dog. My cat and I lead parallel lives, although clearly I am in charge – I take her to the vet when she needs it, whether she likes it or not (she doesn't), and put flea stuff on her. I am in control of what she eats (healthy dried food, not delicious dubious meaty chunks from a tin), and I get decidedly cross when she considers it too wet to go outside and pees delicately on the coir doormat. It's obviously an 'as if' game Bunty and I play. Equals up to a point. Nevertheless, having a cat is an expression of wanting a more equal relationship than with another kind of animal that can and wants to be trained by its owner. I was troubled by the idea of training a horse to do what I wanted, whether it was to trot or to perform the intricate exercises of dressage. Why should it? Spending even a little time at the stables, it was clear that the horses lived the lives their human owners devised for them for their own, human purposes. They get fed and kept warmish, but they are essentially slaves. On my first visit, Michael had taken me to a stall in which lived a regally tall and incredibly beautiful pure white stallion. It was a Lipizzaner, he told me, a horse like those the Austrians trained for dressage. He was being liveried there for a woman who had bought him, having fallen in love with him. His mane was plaited, and he stood with his head held high, looking very superior, allowing me, it seemed, to feast my eyes on him. The funny thing was, Michael said, she doesn't ride him much, but she often comes and just stands and looks at him. Michael rode him when he had time. The Lipizzaner was like a handsome prince locked up in his small stall, without even a flowing mane to let down to allow a princess to climb up and rescue him. A love object that got not enough exercise.

'Would you like to be a horse?' I asked Michael.

'Certainly not,' he said unhesitatingly. 'It would be a terrible life being told what to do all the time.'

'What kind of life would most please a horse, do you think?'

'They want to be loose in the field all day, grazing and being with their pals. They're perfectly happy like that.'

I remembered the wild ponies in the Quantocks that lived in groups on the common land until rounded up from time to time by the local farmers. Unlike, say, cows or sheep, horses, even though selectively bred, could probably get on very well without human masters. I confessed that I didn't think I was interested in getting a horse to do what I wanted it to do. I could see it was a skill, but not one I wanted. I was uneasy about such a relationship with an animal. I was happy to drive an inanimate car, but not inveigle a horse into trusting me. Michael was more understanding of the temperamental divide between us than I expected.

'I had a friend at university who rode all the time,' he told me, nodding. 'She loved riding, being on a horse, with a horse, and she was brilliant at it, but she gave it up eventually because she couldn't reconcile herself to the need to dominate the horse. She knew that she had to, and she could but she thought it just wasn't right to control animals for her pleasure. There's a clear choice, either you are in charge or you don't ride. She made the choice not to ride and never did again, as far as I know.'

Of course, we're in control of all animals really, but you can choose not to increase the underlying control by riding or farming or eating meat or whatever. Michael didn't have a problem with it. Except, as he said, if he'd been the horse. But then horses have been bred up to a point to want to be dominated, or to accept it. And they seem, some of them, to like being ridden. Then again, who wouldn't, standing in a stall all day?

I'd learned about the stables from Patrick, who is my hairdresser. He's been riding for three years and is keen enough to be thinking about getting his own horse and keeping it at Michael's stables. His friends are puzzled that he still talks about going to riding lessons. Surely you've learned to ride by now, they began to say after a year or so. What he has learned is that riding is learning all the time. It's not a limited subject where you can get qualifications and then consider yourself an expert. The better he gets, the more he discovers he has to learn (this is also true for most things worth learning). One day he told me that he'd had a bad session the previous week. Patrick was learning some dressage moves. He realised later that he was tense and being erratic in the handling of his horse, his mind not on the animal, really. His horse, he said, lost patience with him and went out of control, refusing to follow his instructions, firmly heading off in the wrong direction and jumping about all over the place. He stopped paying attention to his rider just as his rider had stopped paying attention to him. As soon as Michael got on the horse he was calm and obedient. Patrick is hooked on the idea of riding as one might be on learning to meditate. Instead of grappling with a wilful mind with a mind of its own, he is learning to make another kind of animal (also with a mind of its own) understand and work with him. He's watched videos of great riders doing dressage and tells me how you can't see that the rider doing anything at all, just sitting there, straight, and yet the horse obeys some minute adjustment of tension or posture and does exactly what is required. The relationship and movements between human and animal can become so subtle as to be invisible to the onlooker. To be in control of a horse, it's necessary to be able to communicate with it, and to enable it to communicate with you. I can see the fascination of that, but I still don't want to be in control.

I also don't want to be out of control. On the third lesson,

Michael suggested I get the horse to trot. I clicked and gently pressed against its sides. It trotted. I'd rather have ridden a whirlwind. Just trotting, and I had not the slightest sense of control, nor wanted any. I've been on a ship in a storm through the Bay of Biscay and felt more in control. I only wanted it to stop. 'I hate this,' I wailed at Michael, while I held on for dear life and completely failed to rise and fall or do anything else in the prescribed manner. 'I don't ever want to do that again.' I had also discovered that being bounced up and down was incredibly bad for my spondylitis, a condition of my neck vertebrae for which I take anti-inflammatories. The jarring of my spine just sitting on a walking horse caused me enough pain the next day to have to double the medication. Trotting was far too painful – doubtless because I was doing it wrong. So with great relief (probably not only mine) after four sessions I had an excellent excuse to stop riding, well before my instructor suggested that a bit of a canter might be a good idea. I'm not sure that Michael believed me, but I was perfectly happy to be a failure at riding, and I've never minded people knowing that I'm a coward or that I'm not one for physical pursuits. I had discovered something at least of what I wanted to know: that Henry could feel sorry for himself, that those who worked with him could know how he felt, and that in order to have a working relationship with animals you had to be prepared not just to learn to communicate with them, but also to dominate them and overcome their resistance to their loss of independence by imposing your authority.

But I wonder why I didn't empathise with Henry as I had with that anonymous dog vomiting at the side of the road in Valencia. Of course, I was not *involved* with the dog – it's so much easier to feel strongly about something you are just passing by. And linked to that, I think perhaps I judged that horses had in some way accepted the deal with humans that they should be dominated by those who showed a willingness and aptness to do so. In a probably idiotic way, I felt horses were less innocent than the anonymous dog, who was so much more neotenised and bred by and for humans. If horses were so clever and subtle, why did they put up with their condition? Just because they don't have opposable thumbs and walk on their hind legs? A similar train of thought might have gone through Jonathan Swift's mind when he wrote about Lemuel Gulliver's visit to the Houyhnhnms. Were I less innately negative, I should perhaps on the contrary have appreciated their grace and generosity at permitting coarse human beings to exercise control over them.

Welfare

What actually precipitated the decision to find a local riding school was a book called *Adam's Task*[1] by Vicki Hearne, the animal trainer, philosopher and poet who I've mentioned earlier. I read her book with increasingly mixed feelings. There seems to be very little I think or read about animals that doesn't cause my feelings to be mixed, but Hearne's book was positively alarming, for all that her work is admired by philosophers I admire such as Stanley Cavell. She was* an animal trainer first and a philosopher contingent on that, as well as a poet self-consciously in the line of Thoreau and the Transcendentals – all her concerns were primarily on the subject of animal being and its relation with human being. Her view was that of someone with a special, privileged relationship, who *knew* animals in a way that pet owners and other animal keepers rarely did. This was why I, as someone with no relationship very much with animals, was interested in reading her in the first place. She liked animals more than she liked most people, as I do, but probably for quite different reasons, and she would have found my moral equivocation

*She died of lung cancer in 2001, at the age of fifty-five.

(and my sentimental response to the dog in Valencia) as loathsome as I find her moral conviction. She trained horses and dogs, and wrote in particular about the ones she retrained after they had been driven 'psychotic' by the contemptible, well-meaning (not a term of approval) kindness and lack of comprehension of their owners. Well-meaning kindness ruined the good, innate character of animals as sugar eats away the structure of teeth. She successfully trained the most incorrigible dogs and horses using her version of the Koehler Method, which, when the animal displays an inclination to do something other than what is required of it, necessitates 'correction' – a purposefully painful pinching of the ear or a sharp knee in the groin, a swift hard jerk on the training leash that momentarily strangles and topples the trainee to a halt. This is the only proper method for making an animal understand its place in and responsibility to the world, according to Hearne. If the animal tries to go the wrong way, it encounters pain, if it goes the right way, life is good. According to Hearne and others, an animal discovers in this way that it wants to do what its master wants it to do, and then a mutually respectful and somewhat reciprocal relationship can emerge. The animal becomes itself by being firmly trained to be its true self, by humans who know that that is better than the unruly puppy or the over-indulged adult animal. She despises the friendliness and kindness of those who offer their animals rewards for doing what they are told, or who give them treats and pander to them. It belittles them (the animals – she has no concern for the owners), and denies them their full rights as beings-as-they-are. She knows the various breeds of dogs and what characteristics they have had built into them over the generations. One of her delinquent dogs, Belle, a pit bull (a breed of dogs she defends as cruelly misunderstood – bad owners not bad dogs) has what she calls 'gameness', which would fit her to be an (illegal) fighting dog of the kind that fights to the death. She says that she isn't ready to put Belle in such a situation because it would make her a dog that would fight rather than mate with any other dog Hearne owned, but she's not sure that dog fighting, with 'game' dogs is really cruel:

> The emblem . . . of two dogs who would rather fight than mate, is . . . not so clearly an emblem of something *exceptionally* out of order. We do live east of Eden where such an emblem may even be a noble one of caring for what is sacred, what matters, in the way the emblem of two ballet dancers enduring deprivation and pain in order to dance . . . is an emblem of something that keeps mattering to human beings.
>
> For fighting-dog people, at least some of them, especially the old-timers, the combination of traits called deep gameness, which leads to the possibility of dogs who would choose fighting over mating, is in fact emblematic of glory, nobility, discipline in the old sense. In their vision, gameness includes the capacity to choose, and to choose knowingly, nobility and triumph over mere survival – death before dishonour. For me the question, then, is complicated by the fact that there is reason to honour this – it is philosophically much more accurate than the notion of these dogs as mere fighting machines.[2]

To me, everything is wrong with this. In the first place the repeated use of the word *emblem*. She is talking about dogs that are bred and trained by humans, but chooses to call their resulting characteristics and behaviour mythic and emblematic. Pit dogs fighting to the death are not emblems, they are flesh-and-blood realities, bred for aggression. You can use an emblem to persuade people into bloody realities (waving a flag on the battlefield), but it is not a straightforward description of what they will be doing. The 'nobility and triumph over survival' is a Nietzschean wonderland, emblematic in America of a species of macho survivalism in the face of a society believed to have gone soft (no discipline, state interference). But the idea that a dog bred for aggression, set to fight in a pit against a similar dog, has the 'capacity to choose knowingly' simply fails to be intellectually honest. Ballet dancers and fighting dogs are not comparable and have no relation to each other. While the 'east of Eden' reference suggests an acceptance that we are fallen (says who? from what?) and therefore must engage with death and violence to achieve nobility. We do indeed engage with death and violence, but there is no necessary nobility in it. There is no question that Hearne knew how to train animals and was immensely successful, but the slide into philosophy from 'what works', and the assumption that 'what works' is therefore the right and only way to proceed, disturbs me greatly.

I'm not alone in my alarmed response to her book. *Adam's Task* was reviewed in the *New York Times Book Review*, when it came out, by Yi-Fu Tuan, a Chinese-American geographer, writer on pet keeping and fellow of the American Association for the Advancement of Science. He wrote that Hearne went 'out of her way to test her reader's credulity' and quoted her describing Belle as being 'capable of sizing people up "not as bite prospects, but as problems in moral philosophy and metaphysics"'. He continued:

> I, a person who seldom can size up another metaphysically, begin to feel so inferior that I find myself retaliating by refusing to grant even the management of a 'happy grin' (as distinct from a happy smile?) to a puppy.

And Stephen Jay Gould, reviewing *Adam's Task*, responds to her thoughts much as I did. He refers to a passage she writes about fighting pit bulls and then takes issue:

So it is possible for me to contemplate the possibility that allowing the right pit bulls, in the hands of the right people, to fight can be called kind because it answers to some energy essential to the creature, and I think of energy, when I think of certain horses, as the need for heroism.

How can anyone defend such misplaced Platonism more than a hundred years after Darwin? How can we speak of an essence so deep, so pure, so inexorable, so special, so immutably part of the creature's definition that we must follow it whatever the consequences – even to death in agony? How can we defend such a general idea in a world of change and variety, where we can only define a species by its range of momentary variability, not by any permanent essential nature? And how can we dare to suggest, in this particular case, that a drive to fight to the death defines a *Ding-an-sich*, before which we can only bow in ultimate respect – when it is we humans who have bred this trait into pit bulls for our own cruel delectation? Essential nature, fiddlesticks.[3]

Clearly, Hearne did have a special way with animals, but she extrapolates too far and far too sentimentally in my opinion, although sentiment is what she would accuse me of. Still, I can understand how a fine trainer committed to animals could get to this point. It follows on from the, possibly or sometimes, imagined cross-species special relationship we often feel we have. Sometimes even I have the feeling I know what an animal is thinking, that it and I have a momentary understanding. I used to stand in front of the female orang-utan's cage in the London Zoo (before they were sent away to France, and I wrote a novel with an orang-utan heroine called Jenny) and gaze at her gazing steadily back at me with those empty but utterly meaningful eyes, and I'd find myself nodding at something she wasn't saying but I was hearing and seeing about the human/ orang condition. Or else the opposite: our mutual gaze was completely devoid of meaning and represented only my awareness of the impossibility of communicating with another species, however much I seemed to read intent (or despair) into the blank but orangutan-not-human eyes. Blankness can mean everything or nothing, after all. She was inside, behind glass, I was outside and at liberty to move on, look at something else, go home and talk to others about what I'd seen, write about it. There was a world (a language) of difference between her and me that could never really be breached except by my dominating her enough to train her to my wishes. If sometimes I feel a kind of romantic despair about not being able to reach out to another species, and want it so much more than I want to communicate with other people, it is only the reverse of Vicki Hearne's conviction that she understood the nature of the other species, and admired it so much more for its apparent purity of being than she did her fellow fallen human beings.

In an article for *Harper's Magazine*,[4] Hearne wrote about the animal rights movement. She rejects the idea that animal rights should be defined by their capacity to suffer. From Jeremy Bentham's utilitarian 'can they suffer?' to Australian philosopher Peter Singer's twentieth-century version, this has been the core argument for demanding animal rights. There is, of course, a problem. Who decides what suffering means? Who measures it and how much of it is to be allowed? And do all animals actually suffer? Singer acknowledges a scale of suffering – based on consciousness, in turn based on brain capacity, so that degrees of consciousness and fitness for rights equate to nearness to the human capacity to suffer. Another chain of being. Primates suffer nearly as much as we do, while ants and amoeba really don't suffer at all. Who else can define suffering but humans? It's our word, and if we want to justify fishing we can decide that fish really don't suffer as we do. Which is to say, they don't suffer. We feel more warmly towards big-brained koala bears. Size, furriness and brain development often go together, found on those we call mammals, and closer to us than insects or fish. Is it pain that a fish or a koala bear feels? Pain as we know it? Which is the only kind of pain we really know, and even then defining the quality of human pain is one of the hardest things to do medically. How long must you feel pain for? When does it become suffering? A flash of pain might not constitute much suffering, and if we assume very little short-term memory, none at all once forgotten. Don't we even speak ourselves of how we forget the pain of childbirth, or else we'd never do it again? We say of people who die suddenly that they didn't suffer. Nevertheless, let's assume we can define pain, and where it is that an animal might process the experience, or be unable to. The capacity to suffer can't really be the arbiter of rights. There are brain-damaged people, babies with massive congenital disorders of the central nervous system, who perhaps can't be said to experience pain in the way that 'normal' people do. They are nonetheless accorded full human rights. We give human rights to all humans (or at least we do in international law, if not always in fact) *because* they are human, not because they do or don't suffer or feel pain or distress. And there are all sorts of equivocation when we stop and think about various 'interests': many people are prepared to consider that the giving of pain to other human beings by torture might be justified in a 'greater' cause. We have trouble allowing people who would choose to die rather than suffer intense distress to have assistance in fulfilling their wishes, no matter how close 'natural' death might be. The right to choose death over suffering remains a difficult legal and ethical problem for use.

This confusion between *rights* and *welfare* is handy for those who want to continue to benefit financially and in other ways from controlling and exploiting animals. This brings us back to Professor

Broom and his work on welfare at Cambridge University, which, he claims, unlike an entitlement to rights, is something scientists have discovered they can measure. If Professor Broom is right, that animals with the least developed brains may suffer more from inappropriate treatments because they are less able to adapt and cope, then ants and fishes ought perhaps to be higher on our caring agenda than those chimps and orangs who seem to be so much more like us, since they can behaviourally and physiologically assess their condition and either come to terms with it or find ways of improving it. This must certainly give those who use suffering as a basis for allocating rights something to stop and think about. The point of Broom's work is to be able to measure the welfare of animals, rather than to look at a sheep and suppose it must be miserable because if it were you, it would be. Quality of life is a standard that scientists claim they can now assess with accuracy – at least in animals. Broom rejects the idea that we can judge how content an animal is simply by putting ourselves in its place.

The work in Cambridge is being done in order to assess the welfare requirements of domestic farm animals such as sheep and cattle. There has to be a balance, Professor Broom explains, between cost-benefit and ethical approaches. There will be no animal welfare in the field if the sheep are so expensive to keep content that no farmer can afford to keep them at all. Welfare is a very practical study, and has nothing very much to do with rights, except possibly to find a biochemical response to those animal rights activists who want to disrupt the exploitation of animals on the grounds of cruelty. Professor Broom states again that people who deplore the use of animals always have to explain what will happen to the millions of domesticated beasts that we kill for our own benefit, which nevertheless depend on human attention for what life they have and could not be sustained on a vegan, animal-liberated planet, at least not one that is anything like our present world. If humans had to compete for resources with sheep and cattle, it is unlikely the animals would win. Is it better to kill them all rather than have them our slaves? Is some life (with good-enough welfare) better than no life at all? Or is the pain of the kind that Elizabeth Costello feels at her knowledge of the existence of the hidden slaughterhouses and her 'emotional' assumption of the concealed suffering of millions, more important than the mere existence of animals? If you sit inside Elizabeth Costello's head for any length of time (no matter how unpleasantly self-righteous you might find her) the world does begin to feel intolerably cruel, in spite of improvements in welfare measurements. But what then? For some, improving the conditions of animals that we are going to eat or wear, because it is better for them or for our souls, just isn't the issue: perhaps we have no right to use animals at all.

Bundles of Yellow Fluff

In the spring of 2009 I went to visit Professor Steven Rose in his laboratory. He is a friend of mine. Steven is an old lefty, and will have no objection to my describing him in that way, any more than I would object to such a description. We have a humanist, more-than-liberal view of the world in common, and rage happily together when we meet at the destruction wrought by New Labour on the back of the devastation left by Thatcher. He used to be heard regularly on Radio 4's *The Moral Maze*, doing battle against reactionary responses to human dilemmas. Apart from many scientific papers, he has written extensively for general readers about the nature of memory and against the behaviourist and materialist tendency in science, arguing from his own researches for the limitations of pure biochemistry and determinism, and the vital role of experience and culture in understanding and improving the lives of human beings. I like and admire him, and I knew that for decades he has been working intensively on the biochemistry of memory, and that he has reason to hope his research will culminate in a remedy for the intractable and shocking problem of Alzheimer's disease. He is on the side of life in a dry and humorous way.

In 1993 Steven Rose wrote a book called *The Making of Memory*, in which he described not only his research and the nature of memory but integrated himself into the narrative. He works with day-old chicks, from eggs which are bought in, hatched in his laboratory and then trained and tested the following day. Early on in the book, he described what happens after he has trained them. 'I have to look inside my chicks' heads,' he writes. 'Be warned, this bit is not for the squeamish.' I issue the warning, too, for the faint-stomached, before I continue the quote.

An hour after I have tested them, I am back with the chicks again. Reza [his colleague in the lab] joins me once more. On the bench in front of us is a tray of ice. Mounted above it is a dissecting microscope – fitted with two eyepieces and looking more like a pair of binoculars. To the side, a row of 48 tiny plastic tubes in a rack. I pick up the first bird in my left hand, body in the palm, head between my fingers, and with a large pair of scissors quickly cut head from body, which I drop into a small plastic bucket. If I do it fast enough, there will be virtually no blood.[5]

This is my humane and very honest friend, Steven. He goes on to describe in detail how he exposes and opens the skull, lifts out the brain and then dissects it, finding, preparing and freezing the relevant regions for analysis the following day. By writing this as baldly as he does, Rose is not just confronting the reader with the realities of animal research, he is also facing full-on the nature of what he is doing.

This killing business though. It is not easy or pleasant to reduce a bundle of yellow fluff to brain and body . . . I have destroyed life.[6]

He considers the arguments against the absolutist animal rights position: the eggs he has ordered and hatched would otherwise have gone to a farm, very likely a battery-chicken factory and after twelve weeks of dreadful life have been killed for human consumption; in the lab he abides by stringent British Home Office laws in providing decent conditions and as painless and fearless a death as possible for the chicks. At one point he said to me that, after all, animals kill each other constantly and with much more suffering than he inflicts. 'Oh, come on, Steven,' I said. 'With much less choice, too.' 'Yes, OK,' he said, withdrawing the point. As I said, an honest man. But he recognises that these arguments are not the point, and I would agree, as he supposes an animal-rights person would argue, that 'two offences – science rather than profit – against animals don't cancel out'. With all the humanity I know him to have, and as a result of that humanity, Steven Rose justifies his act of snipping the heads off his chicks:

> If I – we – society – use any pronoun you choose – want this sort of knowledge, there is no other way at present of obtaining it than to work on animals . . . I strongly oppose many things that are done to animals in farming, in hunting, in rearing animals as pets, and indeed in some forms of animal experimentation – nor would I ever accept the Cartesian view that non-human animals can be regarded as pain-free machines, so that one can do what one likes with them without it mattering. If they were, my research would probably be meaningless.[7]

He believes that the discussion of rights has to begin with *human* rights. Humans, he says, certainly have duties towards animals, but when it is a question of alleviating human suffering (and even animal suffering) and the choice is between experimenting with animals or not finding solutions, then Steven is clear that it is *necessary* to experiment on animals. Unless, of course, we are going to say that we can only experiment on humans. Not something society is likely to want to sanction. We can accord animals equal rights to ourselves and never find a cure for AIDS, Parkinson's or Alzheimer's disease, or we use animals as decently as possible (though not necessarily without pain and suffering) to explore mechanisms and find solutions to the pain and suffering humans (and indeed animals) experience. There is no way of testing what he is testing without using animals. Steven Rose is absolutely clear that all 'duties to non-human animals are limited by an overriding duty to other humans'.[8] He is a humanist.

So, in the spring of 2009, I went to visit Steven in his laboratory. I have already mentioned my failure to visit an abattoir for this book, along with maggot farms, battery farms and other abyssal hot spots. It might be said that I started out braver in my attempt to watch Steven work with his chicks. My first email, asking if I could visit, I find says:

> About your chicks . . . are you still snipping their heads off? Do you remember that we discussed me coming to watch you at work with them (live and dead). Are you still doing it? Is it possible to come and visit?

When he asked what exactly I wanted to see, I replied:

> The way the chicks are trained, killed, used.

I could claim that I intended to see the whole process, including the killing of the chicks. When I arrived on the date and time agreed (the visit having been put off once because I was ill), Steven explained what he was doing and I observed him training and testing the chicks, but it so happened, he said, that he wasn't killing them that day. Now, Steven is a gentleman, and I suspected he was giving me a way out of what he knew I didn't much want to see. However, even if that were the case, nothing prevented me from asking him if I could come another day when he was cutting the heads off his chicks, and I'm sure if I had made it clear that it was important to my project he would have allowed me to watch. I didn't ask to go again to see the chicks being killed, of course. Certainly, because I don't have the slightest desire to watch bundles of yellow fluff being reduced to body and brain, but also because I really do wonder whether or not one should watch, in the sense of witness at a safe distance, instead of either imagining and insisting on knowing without the element of voyeurism, or being prepared to perform the act yourself. Looking away is not a good thing. But perhaps looking away is not the same as not looking on. I'm inclined to turn my head away from road accidents when I pass them, not only for squeamishness, but for privacy of those involved – what is more private than death? If I really want to confront the death of animals, shouldn't I kill them myself? Just watching Steven, or someone earning a living in an abattoir is what journalists do, but even journalists have a choice to stand and watch, or to participate.

Whatever my ethical reservations, it was also at least equally my faint-heartedness that didn't ask if I could return to watch the chicks being killed. As a result, one of the things I don't know about animals is how they die in the service of human needs because I've chosen not actually to be in that place and look, or to do it myself. Apart from having my cats die in and haunt my arms, and although I think about it far too much of the time, I am not any good at all at confronting death in anything other than my head.[*]

The chicks were in pairs in ten open-fronted aluminium boxes each with a red light above, lined up on a workbench. They had hatched twenty-four hours earlier from the incubator full of eggs, some of which were beginning to crack open, in another room. Their first day of life was spent in a brooder, and then they were taken to the testing room. Steven explained what he was going to do and why. He wanted to understand the biochemical activity that resulted from learning in the chicks. He offered the new chicks two beads on a stick. Chicks innately peck at anything in front of them to see if it's good to eat, just as children instinctively put things into their mouths to find out what they are. One bead is bright and has a bitter substance on it and is offered to the experimental chick. The other is offered to the control chick and is flavoured with simple water. The experimental chicks taste the bitter bead and don't like it. When tested again, the chicks who have learned don't peck at a bright bead when offered, though they do peck at a regular coloured bead. When the chicks are killed and their brains analysed, a change is found in a particular chemical which, it can be assumed, is involved in the formation of memory. This can then be tested in a separate experiment with other chicks by blocking that chemical with an injection and then testing the chicks to discover whether the learning is undone and they will peck at the bright bead a second time. If the injection is delayed for an hour after learning, the chick remembers not to peck at the bitter substance. By discovering how short-term

[*]On reading this, Steven writes to tell me he is no gentleman, and killing the chicks just wasn't scheduled for that day.

memory is turned off and on in chicks, it is possible to understand something about the biochemistry of short-term memory loss in humans. Other experiments have used rats and mice, but Steven uses chicks now because they have a particularly quick learning response.

In the testing room the chicks stood, as yellow and fluffy as Easter, in their bare boxes. Some of the pairs huddled for extra warmth or comfort, but mostly they just stood, and some cheeped a little. First there was pre-training, checking that they would peck at a neutral stick, before presenting them with the beads. Steven moved from box to box, offering the chicks the sticks, waggling them to get their attention and murmuring at the sleepier, less interested ones, 'Come on, Gorgeous, pay attention.' I watched as they were pre-trained, trained and then tested. What I recollect most clearly was Steven's cooing at the chicks to get them interested, and their unbearably sweet, infantile, neotenous, wide-eyed cuteness in their barren tin boxes. They were tiny newborn living creatures recast as experimental subjects, and Steven spoke to them as we all speak to babies and pets, though we know they don't understand the words we say. It might be partly intentional, to create a calming sound, but it is also an irresistibly human act to speak softly and encouragingly to small living creatures, even if you are going to cut their heads off the following day. While he interacted with them Steven included them in his world as conscious beings, not as mechanical objects. I tried a bit of stick-waggling, but found myself much more reluctant to personalise them. Steven treated them gently and caused them to fear as little as possible what was happening, but none of the chicks experienced a normal first-and-last day of life, and all of them were evolutionarily programmed infants, intent on finding comfort, food and interest in order to develop and live adult chicken lives. That would have been vital for their natural existence, and it was what made them good for the experiment. Though there are very few places where they might have led a natural chicken existence. Those who did not peck at the bead during the pre-training, who had weaker curiosity than the others, were put aside, not suitable to be experimented on.

'Why don't you let those ones live?' I asked.

Steven told me that the assistants used to take them home to grow on for eggs or the pot, something quite like a decent existence, but that was stopped by the authorities. It wasn't permitted, on safety grounds, for any living non-human creature to be taken out of the laboratory. As it was, in order to enter the actual laboratories we all had not only to put on clean white coats, but also to pass through a two-minute air shower, like an air lock in a space ship, which blasted air fiercely at you much more powerfully than a regular shower rains down water. We had to go through the same procedure when we left and deposit our lab coats in the bin for laundering.

The results of these experiments may well matter enormously to all of us as humans with a chance of developing Alzheimer's disease. Even if that wasn't the case, research into memory is still in a relatively early stage, and the knowledge of what happens to the chicks' brains enhances our understanding of how we work and how things go wrong. But that, in the context of this book, isn't entirely the point. The fact was that I watched the chicks being tested, and offered them beads to peck at, knowing their fate, as they didn't. Indeed, they didn't know anything, not even if the life they were temporarily leading (not that they knew anything temporal) was normal for beings of their kind, or, I suppose, what their kind of being was. Again, there was no possibility of understanding what I was seeing from their point of view, only from my own, big-brained, language-owning point of view. And to me it seemed grim. For them, and that we were doing it for our benefit. Anthropomorphically (as how can I not be?), I was deceiving these creatures, who would have chosen, I'd be inclined to believe, to grow up and be chickens, or whatever they thought they were. At any rate, not chosen to live for just two days and then die in order that we might find a cure for Alzheimer's. When PETA talked about betrayal in their letter to the sheep-farming primary school, I thought it was sentimental and essentially dishonest, but now, faced with the chicks, I was quite gripped by the awfulness of their existence-for-us.

But at the same time, and without it seeming any less grim, I wouldn't have legislated against it had I the power because I could imagine, not just the chicks, as innocent as a dog in Valencia, having their heads and brief lives cut off, but also the devastation of a human being having Alzheimer's: the devastation both medical and social, for the sufferers, their families and friends. And I recalled my old cat, Darcy, and what I was told was his cat version of Alzheimer's disease, and the awful confusion, his yowling, wanting to come in to the house but not knowing why, wanting to approach to be stroked but being too fearful of me, remembered and not remembered as I was. Chickens don't live long enough (even if they are left to lead a normal life) to get Alzheimer's disease, so it is unreasonable, if looked at from something like their point of view, that they should live such distorted, brief lives (can you really call it a life?) in the service of humans and cats. But in none of this can I do anything more than imagine myself into the experiences of others, humans, cats, chicks or experimenters. Being none of them, when the imagining is done, when the watching is over, I have no more certainty about how humans should use non-human animals than I had before. Which in this case was with respect, without cruelty and as little fear as possible.

Steven Rose might be accused of arguing as a scientist who simply wants to get on with what he is set on doing. Donna Haraway, though, is not an experimental scientist, but a dog owner and philosopher. She writes

> . . . I will defend animal killing for reasons and in detailed material-semiotic conditions that I judge tolerable because of a greater good calculation. And no, that is never enough. I refuse the choice of 'inviolable animal rights' versus 'human good is more important'. Both of these proceed as if calculation solved the dilemma, and all I or we have to do is choose . . . The practice of holding nonhuman animals at the center of attention is necessary but not sufficient, not just because other moral and ontological goods compete in that kind of cost-benefit frame, but more important because companion-species worldliness works otherwise.[9]

The discussion of animal rights and welfare needs, she says, to be situated in the real world, not in order to reduce the force of the question, but to locate it 'on earth, in real places, where judgement and action are at stake'.[10] This can't answer someone who want to abolish all experiments on animals, and the killing of them for our food and comfort, but nothing can, precisely, answer that in the real world. Exploitation is how the real world goes about its business. This might be an unbearable truth, but I haven't come across any successful alternative in practice. Then again, the real-world argument is always put forward to prevent what people call 'dangerous idealism' from being taken seriously, and I feel increasingly strongly that sometimes the dangerous idealism is not dangerous, but an essential position to keep alive, that needs to be stated and restated even if it is never achieved because it speaks of a moral consideration to be taken into account by moral beings. The point which Haraway makes, along with anyone else concerned with animals, rather than sadistic or greedy mistreaters of animals, is that the use, our use of animals (is there another kind?), or the killing of animals should never be comfortable or clear-cut, never straightforward. Our existence on this planet is a problem, but it isn't a problem to be solved.

For many people, I suppose, it is when the heads come off the day-old chicks that they take a stand and commit themselves to a radical position. They declare that they will never eat meat again, that they'll fight against any use of animals in medical and scientific research, work to liberate animals from all forms of captivity and accept that all animals are their moral equals and should be accorded the same legal rights that humans given themselves. I couldn't get there. In fact, it was at that point that I decided to call the book I was writing about animals, *What I Don't Know About Animals*.

Epilogue

THE FRUIT STARE

In the wild ... orangs have not provided ethologists with the glamorous behaviours that, say, Jane Goodall's chimps have given her. I found no reports of orangs doing anything like the equivalent of fashioning special sticks to fish for termites, for instance. Orang observers instead report such exciting phenomena as the 'fruit stare' which some people say is a function of the difficulty orang-utans have foraging for food in the wild. Orang-utans need to develop the fruit stare because trees can be coy about when, where, and how much they fruit, and the fruit is often hidden in the canopy of leaves. The fruit stare is an expression of reverie, but it is a reverie directed outward rather than inward – 'like thinking with your eyes,' naturalist Sy Montgomery has said. 'That's why they are so spaced-out.'

Vicki Hearne, 'Can an Ape Tell a Joke?'[*]

[*]'There is one population of orangs who live on the far side of the Slough of Despond, who associate and learn from each other, and who use tools to pry open the ferociously defended cemengang fruit.' Alison Jolly, primatologist. Personal communication.

Suddenly, he grabs two thick vines, swings down until he hangs only a metre above her head and stares into her eyes, so close that her nostrils tingle from the stale odour of his sweat. In 34 years of jungle observations, Galdikas has had only a handful of such close encounters, so rare are orang-utans' meetings with humans or even with each other. But this fellow's message is clear: 'Leave me alone.'

Birutė Galdikas has learned more than any other human being about what it means to be an orang-utan, and what she has found out is that orang-utans like to be left alone.

http://www.science.ca/scientists/
scientistprofile.php?pID=7

Bunty is not an orang-utan. Though she does have some moments when I can identify 'reverie' in her gaze –inward, rather than searching – mostly she stares, intently and directly, at the world and the people in it, and she never, so far as I can tell, wants to be alone. She watches me, I watch her. Here's a funny thing: Derrida doesn't look back at himself and wonder what his own gaze means.

There is a large part of me that wishes I could have been Jane Goodall or Birutė Galdikas, and spent my life in the forest watching primates. If only, I've often thought, I'd studied zoology or got a job in the zoo. I know that I'm better suited by temperament to be a writer, though there's considerable similarity: the sitting, staring, wondering what's going on. But the writer – if she's me – doesn't have to organise academic funding, travel to difficult and intensely uncomfortable places and risk terrible (until recently) encounters with rainforest spiders as well as primates. I'm too lazy to be Goodall or

Galdikas. I could perhaps be Edward O. Wilson, and often have been, in the sense of time spent watching ants going about their business (or birds in a non-bird-watching sort of way, or people when I was much younger in Paris) while I sat in the garden not going about mine. In some way, writing is about not going about my business. To an extent so is being an animal observer. At any rate, it's focusing on someone (elephant-lady usage) else's business, but then there are all those conferences to go to and papers to write, people to persuade, theories to uphold. Best, after all, with my poor temperament, to sit here and think about people who think about animals.

It was Iris Murdoch, I believe, who advised writers to write about what they 'deeply know'. That is not the same thing as saying only write about your own experience. I suppose I deeply know how it is here with Bunty – in the sense that it simply occurs, and though I find myself perplexed and wondering about why and what she's on about, we nevertheless rub along well enough. Much like bringing up a child or living with someone you are happy living with. There are different levels of doing all three, and knowing what you're doing and why you're doing it. So in the end, with my paltry experience of animals, my reading on the subject of animals and humans, and my lack of professional expertise in animal/human psychology and biochemistry, I'm left with my knowledge of the relationship I have with Bunty. As this book insists, it's very little. Lots of relationship, little knowledge, about my own very particular, individual, unlike quite any other, pussy cat.

As I was writing about the battle of the study door which Bunty and I engage in daily, a solution came to me. What if I put a cat flap in my study door and, while I was at it, in the door connecting my study and bathroom-cum-clothes closet where once or twice Bunty has got herself trapped for the night, sneaking in and concealing herself at the back of a shelf (cosy cashmere sweaters), and thoughtfully peed, or peed thoughtfully, on my beloved green handbag in lieu of a flower-bed.

The astounding good sense of this lit my universe, as obvious ideas that have sat waiting to be noticed do once, eventually, they see the light of day. The cat can come and go as she pleases, and I can sit on the sofa working uninterrupted. I bought two cat flaps and called in a man with a hacksaw. Bunty was astounded, when she returned to the house (loud carpentry not to her liking). She sat in front of the new cat flap in apparent wonder. In fact, she seemed to be wondering what it was. Some science-fiction book I read long ago begins with a rainy day, and a cat leading its master around the house to open every possible door and window, on the premise that outside one of them it wouldn't be raining. Maybe a cat flap in a door that didn't have a cat flap before, or a door that doesn't lead to the outside world was an entirely different and new sort of thing to Bunty. I showed her how it worked. I pushed her through. I pushed her back the other way. I showed her how independence worked, though down in the kitchen she knew exactly how it worked. Now that she could get on with her life as she wished, would she leave me alone to get on with mine? I thought, if nothing else, writing this book will have achieved that.

You will be thinking about that quote from the animal experimenter warning never to work with cats – how once they get that you want them to do something, they would rather starve than comply. Why I didn't think of that must be accounted for by the split that exists between the writer and the person who lives in the same body. Bunty now sits in front of the cat flap and turns to stare at me on the sofa, waiting for me to open the door. When I open the door to leave the room, she races to get through it in the regular human way.

Eventually, if I hold out against her baleful stare, though it might be an hour, she will laboriously go through the flap. In some way, it has worked. But the sight of a cat that comes and goes with no problem through the garden cat flap sitting, determinedly, in front of the one in my study drives me crazy.

'Go! Go on!' I cry. And she looks at me.

As far as I know she has never used the flap between the study and my clothes closet and bathroom, although when I go into them and leave the door open she invariably gets up and sits on the threshold (always just on the study side of the opening), looking at me, as Derrida's particular pussy looked at him. If I'm in the bath, on the loo, getting dressed, undressed, changed, she sits and watches. When I'm finished and back on the sofa, she comes and sits beside me, very close, always touching so that one of my forearms is constricted while I type.

I am very proud of the catness of Bunty. Honoured at her insistent presence. Sometimes I glance at her and she seems to glow, as Blake's Tyger must have to Blake's inner eye, or with the peculiar glaring *reality* that I recall from the days when I took LSD. She is so Other and so here. So here and so Other. It may be she has no questions about me. Why I am here, why I do what I do, or how, or what kind of consciousness I inhabit. Perhaps she just watches, noting without wondering. I wonder about her all the time. There is the difference between us.

Unless, I'm wrong, and she too wonders. Sometimes when I look at her she stares at me so intently that I really do expect her to say finally what she has to say. Or she is saying it, and has been all along, and simply looks at me thinking, 'How stupid is this human who can't speak my language? It's hopeless trying to communicate with it.'

NOTES

CHAPTER 2: DREAM ANIMALS

1 A. A. Milne, *Winnie-the-Pooh*, Methuen, 1926, p. 3.
2 'Can an ape tell a joke? Learning from a Las Vegas orang-utan act' by Vicki Hearne, *Harper's Magazine*, November 1993, pp. 58–67.
3 Sam Savage, *Firmin*, Weidenfeld and Nicolson, 2008.
4 http://www.wildlife.alaska.gov/

CHAPTER 3: DIVISIONS

1 *An Intellectual History of Cannibalism*, Cătălin Avramescu, trans. Alistair Ian Blyth, Princeton University Press, 2009, p. 224.

CHAPTER 4: OTHERNESS

1 Dante, *Divine Comedy*, Canto XXVI, lines 118–20.
2 Jacques Derrida, *The Animal That Therefore I Am*, trans. David Wills, Fordham University Press, 2008, p. 5.
3 Ibid.
4 Spinoza, Ethics, Part IV, proposition 37, note 1. Quoted in Midgley, *Animals and Why They Matter*, Penguin 1983.

5 *Thinking with Animals*, eds Lorraine Daston and Greg Mitman, Columbia University Press, 2005, pp. 62–3.

6 Jeremy Bentham, *An Introduction to the Principles of Morals and Legislation*, 1781. Quoted in Matthew Calarco, *Zoographies: The Question of the Animal from Heidegger to Derrida*, Columbia University Press, 2008, p. 113.

7 Immanuel Kant, *Lectures on Ethics*. Quoted in Midgley, *Animals and Why They Matter*, Penguin, 1983, p. 46.

8 T. H. Huxley, *Man's Place in Nature*, 1863, Dover Books, 2003. Quoted in G. Radick, *The Simian Tongue*, University of Chicago Press, 2007.

9 Martin Heidegger, *The Fundamental Concepts of Metaphysics: World, Finitude, Solitude*, trans. William McNeill and Nicholas Walker, Indiana University Press, 1995, p. 185.

10 Jacques Derrida, op. cit., p. 45.

11 Martin Heidegger, op. cit., p. 198.

12 Jacques Derrida, op. cit., p. 143.

13 *The Paradox of Morality: An Interview with Emmanuel Levinas*, trans. Andrew Benjamin and Tamra Wright, in *The Provocation of Levinas: Rethinking the Other*, eds Robert Bernasconi and David Wood, Routledge, 1988, p. 169.

14 Thomas Nagel, 'What is it like to be a bat?' *Philosophical Review*, 1974, pp. 435–50.

15 Jacques Derrida, op. cit., p. 30.

16 Friedrich Nietzsche, *The Gay Science*, trans. Walter Kaufmann and R. J. Hollingdale, Vintage, 1974, p. 374.

17 Jacques Derrida, op. cit., p. 13.

CHAPTER 5: GETTING NEARER NATURE

1 http://www.wildfilmhistory.org/film/259/Filming+Wild+Animals. html

2 http://www.earthwatch.org/exped/cluttonbrock_research.html

CHAPTER 6: IN THE LAB

1 Marshall Sahlins, *Stone Age Economics*, Tavistock Publications, 1974.

2 Hugh Sykes Davies, *The Papers of Andrew Melmoth*, Methuen, 1960, pp. 33–4.

3 Ibid., p. 29.

4 Edward O. Wilson, *Sociobiology: The New Synthesis*, Harvard University Press, 1975.

5 Ibid. Quoted in Mary Midgley, *Beast and Man*, Methuen, 1980, pp. 562–75.

6 Ibid., *Beast and Man*, p. 170.

7 Stephen Jay Gould, *The Lying Stones of Marrakech*, Vintage, 2001, p. 282.

8 Claire Preston, *Bee*, Reaktion Books, 2006, p. 17.

9 Rudolf Steiner, *Bees*, Lecture One, Anthroposophic Press, 1998, p. 16.

10 Eugène Nielen Marais, *The Soul of the White Ant*, Penguin, 1973.

11 Bert Hölldobler and E. O. Wilson, *The Superorganism*, Norton, 2009.

12 Ibid., p. 60.

13 Ibid., p. 502.

14 Ibid., p. 502.

15 Donald Broom, 'Welfare Assessment and Relevant Ethical Decisions', *Annual Review of Biomedical Sciences*, Vol. 10, 2008.

16 Vinciane Despret, *From Ethology between Empathy, Standpoint and Perspectivism: the Case of the Arabian Babblers*, 2008.

17 Ibid.

18 Ibid.

19 Vicki Hearne, *Animal Happiness*, Harper Collins, 1994, p.5. Quoted in Vinciane Despret, ibid.

20 Vinciane Despret, ibid.

21 Ibid.

22 Ibid. Quoting Donna J. Haraway, *When Species Meet*, University of Minnesota Press, 2008.

23 'Anthropomorphism and Mental State Attribution', Daniel J. Povinelli, in *Anthropomorphism, Anecdotes, and Animals*, eds Robert W. Mitchell, Nicholas S. Thompson and H. Lyn Miles, SUNY Press, 1997, p. 96.

24 'Silent Partners? Observations on Some Systematic Relations

among Observer Perspective, Theory, and Behaviour', Duane Quiatt, in ibid, p. 220.

25 Ibid., p. 223.

26 Ibid., p. 223.

27 Ibid., p. 224.

28 Ibid., p. 225.

29 Ibid., p. 234.

30 Ibid., p. 224.

31 Ibid., p. 225.

32 Vinciane Despret, op. cit.

33 Duane Quiatt, op. cit., p. 224.

34 Ibid., p. 226.

35 Frans de Waal, *Our Inner Ape*, Riverhead Books, 2005, p. 178.

36 Ibid., p207.

37 Ibid., p208.

38 'Does evolution explain human nature? Obviously says the monkey', the John Templeton Foundaiton, www.templeton.org/evolution.

CHAPTER 7: UNDER OUR SKIN

1 'A Theoretical Assessment to Inform Assessment and Treatment Strategies for Animal Hoarders', Gary J. Patronek and Jane N. Nathanson, *Clinical Psychology Review*, 2009, 29: 274f.

2 *Psychiatric Times*, Vol. 17, No. 4, 'People Who Hoard Animals', The Hoarding of Animals Research Consortium, Randy Frost, PhD.

3 LOLcat Bible Translation Project. Portions from LOLCat Bible Translation Project are under the GFDL. Latest text can be found at www.lolcatbible.com.

4 'Leda and the Swan', W. B. Yeats, 1923.

CHAPTER 8: THE GOOD, THE BAD AND THE HELPFUL

1 Christopher Finch, *The Art of Walt Disney*, H. N. Abrams, New York, 1975.

2 Stephen Jay Gould, 'A Biological Homage to Mickey Mouse', *The Panda's Thumb*, Penguin, 1980, p. 81.
3 Desmond Morris, *The Naked Ape*, Corgi, 1972, p. 197.
4 Sophie Morris, the *Independent*, October 2007.
5 Rebecca Skloot, *New Times Magazine*, January 2009.

CHAPTER 9: THE DEATH OF LUNCH

1 Douglas Woolf, 'Spring of the Lamb', Jargon Society, 1972.
2 BBC *News*, 14 September 2009.
3 *Making Animals Happy: How to Create the Best Life for Pets and Other Animals*, Temple Grandin and Catherine Johnson, Bloomsbury, 2009.
4 Donna J. Haraway, *When Species Meet*, University of Minnesota Press, 2008, p. 79.

CHAPTER 10: WHO'S IN CHARGE?

1 Vicki Hearne, *Adam's Task: Calling Animals by Name*, Skyhorse Publishing, NY, 2007.
2 Ibid., p. 222.
3 'Animals and Us', Stephen Jay Gould in *New York Review of Books*, Vol. 34, No. 11, 25 June 1987.
4 'What's Wrong with Animal Rights?', Vicki Hearne, *Harper's Magazine*, September 1991.
5 Steven Rose, *The Making of Memory*, Bantam Press, 1993, p. 25.
6 Ibid., p. 27.
7 Ibid., pp. 27–8.
8 Ibid., p. 30.
9 Donna J. Haraway, op. cit., p. 87–8.
10 Ibid., p. 88.

BIBLIOGRAPHY

Ardrey, Robert, *The Territorial Imperative*, Atheneum, NY, 1969

Atterton, P. and Calarco, M. (eds), *Animal Philosophy*, Continuum, London, 2004

Bekoff, Marc, 'Cognitive ethology: the comparative study of animal minds'. In: *Blackwell Companion to Cognitive Science*, William Bechtel and George Graham (eds), Blackwell Publishers, Oxford, 1995

Berger, John *Why Look At Animals?*, Penguin Books, London, 2009

Bernasconi, R. and Wood, D. (eds), *The Provocation of Levinas: Rethinking the Other*, Routledge, London, 1988

Broom, D. M., 'Quality of life means welfare: how is it related to other concepts and assessed?', *Animal Welfare*, 2007:16

— 'Welfare assessment and relevant ethical decisions: key concepts', *RBS Annual Review Biomedical Science* 2008:10

Bulliet, R. W., *Hunters, Herders, and Hamburgers*, Columbia University Press, NY, 2005

Burt, J., *Animals in Film*, Reaktion Books, London, 2002

Calarco, M., *Zoographies*, Columbia University Press, NY, 2008

Carroll, Lewis, *Alice's Adventures in Wonderland* and *Through the Looking-glass*, Penguin Classics, London, 2003

Cavell, S., Diamond, C., McDowell, J., Hacking, I. and Wolfe, C.,

Philosophy & Animal Life, Columbia University Press, NY, 2008

Cheeta, *Me Cheeta: The Autobiography*, Fourth Estate, London, 2008

Coetzee, J. M., *The Lives of Animals*, Princeton Paperbacks, NJ, 2001

Connor, S., *Fly*, Reaktion Books, London, 2006

Darwin, Charles, *The Origin of Species*, Penguin, London, 1985

Daston, L. and Mitman G., *Thinking with Animals*, Columbia University Press, NY, 2005

Dekkers, M., *Dearest Pet* (trans. P. Vincent), Verso, London, 1994

Derrida, Jacques, *The Animal That Therefore I Am* (trans. David Wills), Fordham University Press, 2008

Despret, Vinciane, 'Animal subjects under observation', unpublished paper given at 'Observing Animals' Conference, Cambridge, 2008, to be published 2011; http://vincianedespret.blogspot.com

Douglas, M., *Purity and Danger*, Routledge and Kegan Paul, London, 1980

von Frisch, K., *Bees*, Jonathan Cape, London, 1983

Goodall, Jane, *In the Shadow of Man*, Collins, London, 1971

— *My Life with the Chimpanzees*, Pocket Books, NY, 1996

Gould, Stephen Jay, *The Panda's Thumb*, Penguin Books, London, 1990

— *The Lying Stones of Marrakech*, Vintage, London, 2001

Grandin, Temple, *Making Animals Happy*, Bloomsbury, London, 2009

Grandin, Temple, and Johnson, C., *Animals in Translation*, Bloomsbury, London, 2006

Guthrie, S., *Faces in the Clouds*, Oxford University Press, US, 1995

Haraway, D. J., *The Companion Species Manifesto*, Prickly Paradigm Press, Chicago, 2003

— *When Species Meet* University of Minnesota Press, 2008

Hearne, Vicki, *Animal Happiness*, Skyhorse Publishing, NY, 1994

— *Adam's Task*, Skyhorse Publishing, NY, 2007

Heidegger, M., *The Fundamental Concepts of Metaphysics: World, Finitude, Solitude* (trans. William McNeill and Nicholas Walker), Indiana University Press, 1995

Huxley, T. H., *Man's Place in Nature*, Dover, NY, 2003

Kalof, L., *A Cultural History of Animals in Antiquity*, Berg, Oxford, 2007

— *Looking at Animals in Human History*, Reaktion Books, London, 2007

Kipling, Rudyard, *The Just So Stories*, Macmillan, London, 1984

Lorenz, K. Z., *King Solomon's Ring*, Methuen, London, 1953

McHugh, S., *Dog*, Reaktion Books, London, 2004

Mandeville, B. and Kaye, F. B., *The Fable of the Bees*, Liberty Classics, Indianapolis, 1988

Marais, E. N., *The Soul of the White Ant*, Penguin, London, 1973

Midgley, Mary, *Beast and Man*, Methuen, London, 1979

— *Animals and Why They Matter*, Penguin, London, 1983

Milne, A. A., *Winnie-the-Pooh*, Methuen, London, 1988

Mitchell, R. W., Thompson, N. S. and Miles, H. L. (eds) *Anthropomorphism, Anecdotes, and Animals*, SUNY Press, NY, 1997

Morris, Desmond, *The Naked Ape*, Corgi, London, 1972

Nagel, T., *Mortal Questions*, Canto, Cambridge, 1991

Pearce, J. M., *An Introduction to Animal Cognition*, Lawrence Erlbaum Associates, NJ, 1991

Pinker, Steven, *The Blank Slate*, Penguin, London, 2002

Preston, C., *Bee*, Reaktion Books, London, 2006

Radick, G., *The Simian Tongue*, University of Chicago Press, 2007

Rogers, K. M., *Cat*, Reaktion Books, London, 2006

Rose, Steven, *The Chemistry of Life*, Penguin, London, 1991

— *The Making of Memory*, Bantam, London, 1992

Sahlins, Marshall, *Stone Age Economics*, Tavistock Publications, London, 1974

Singer, P., *Animal Liberation*, OUP, Oxford, 1984

Steiner, R., *Bees*, Anthroposophic Press, Great Barrington, MA, 1998

Sykes Davis, H., *The Papers of Andrew Melmoth*, Methuen, London, 1960

de Waal, F., *Chimpanzee Politics*, The Johns Hopkins University Press, Baltimore, MD, 1989

— *Our Inner Ape*, Riverhead Books, NY, 2005

de Waal, F. et al., *Primates and Philosophers*, Princeton University Press, Princeton, 2007

Watson, Burton, trans., *The Complete Works of Chuang Tzu*, Columbia University Press, New York, 1968

Wilson, E. O. and Hölldobler, B., *The Superorganism*, W. W. Norton, London, 2009

Wolfe, C. (ed.), *Zoontologies*, University of Minnesota Press, 2003

Woolf, D., *Spring of the Lamb*, Jargon Society, Winston-Salem, NC, 1972

Wylie, D., *Elephant*, Reaktion Books, London, 2008

ACKNOWLEDGEMENTS

I would like to thank everyone who has helped me in thinking about this book. Among them are Patrick Ashman, Professor Donald Broom, Dr Clare Bryant, Dr Vinciane Despret, Professor John Forrester, Barbara McKnight and the Earthwatch Organisation, 'Michael' at the Riding School, Professor Steven Rose, Dr James Russell and Professor Justin E. H. Smith. My everlasting and especially autumnal thanks to the Friendly Spider Programme of the Zoological Society at the London Zoo for making spiders seem like animals and not enemy aliens. The *London Review of Books* published the results of this experience and part of the chapter on delusional parasitosis. Assignments for the Travel section of the *Observer* and the *Guardian* enabled me to visit elephants and reindeer, and the English students of Newnham College, Cambridge, have indulged me for the last couple of years while I threw all sorts of animalish thoughts at them to discuss. My thanks also to everyone who sent me snippets about animals (they can stop now). To Ian Patterson, for everything. And obviously to Bunty, who couldn't care less, one way or the other.